Praise for *Beyond Balancing the Books*

"Full of insight and wisdom, this book offers a clear and practical path towards personal and professional well-being."

—Steve Taylor PhD
Author of *The Leap: The Psychology of Spiritual Awakening*

"*Beyond Balancing the Books* clearly articulates mindfulness in a way we can all move toward actualizing. I found the book to be highly readable and well-prepared with research, footnotes, clear indexing, and specific and simple exercises to put the techniques into action. As a former practicing CPA and lifelong devotee to the profession, I was engaged by the references and stories connected to CPAs and the world of business. At the same time, it was fully clear that what Marino is articulating applies to everyone."

—Robert Fligel
President, RF Resources LLC

"*Beyond Balancing the Books* gives you practical advice you can use every day in your professional work and personal life. The book is full of useful information, insights, and exercises that can help you live with more meaning and purpose. Author George Marino draws on his experience as both a CPA and mindfulness coach to help readers deal with the obstacles of the external world as well as our internal worlds. Each chapter covers a specific topic with examples from science, poetry, nature, etc. all approached with an open mind. The result is a journey to live a more fulfilling and meaningful life. I highly recommend this book to anyone no matter what your profession."

—Daria Bushueva
Audit Associate, Real Estate Service at Mazars USA

"This is a must-read for professionals who value their life as much as their work. George Marino eloquently applies ancient wisdom to today's common challenges and goals, resulting in a practical guidebook for anyone no matter their profession looking for a step-by-step path to positive ROI in every area of their life."

—Sean Fargo
Founder, Mindfulness Exercises

"For the working professional, this book is a great collection of tips and techniques to become more mindful and ultimately healthier in mind, body, and soul. Though the examples are given through the author's experience as an accountant, the material could easily be applied to just about any profession. George Marino has harnessed the essential teachings of history's great teacher-philosophers and incorporates them into this guide to a more satisfying and self-aware life. The author draws from the wisdom of the world's spiritual and artistic traditions, which validate the evolution of conscious mind. It is as though Mr. Marino is guiding you on a life-changing meditation. *Beyond Balancing the Books* is a personal and informative read that can help any working professional to indeed bring balance to the entirety of their life."

—Susan T. Dicosola
MS, CMPE, Chief Operating Officer Practice Queens Medical Associates

"*Beyond Balancing the Books* engages the reader in a path to self-discovery. George Marino guides us to develop a relationship with the most important person in our lives—ourselves—by being present and living in the moment. He does a great job in explaining many complex concepts for people who are not familiar with topics like mindfulness, emotional intelligence, and awareness. The reader will develop skills such as being aware, being present, listening attentively, and having compassion that will ultimately help us balance the books and balance our lives."

—Janneth Gaona
CPA

"I started my career in public accounting in June of 1979 in Houston, Texas. Without a doubt, I wish I had this kind of empowering book to read then as well as now. This is not your typical book for professionals—it is a book with easy to understand concepts and practical mindfulness practices that conveys a message that our professional work and life has deep meaning and purpose, even in those moments when it doesn't seem to be the case. If you are serious about discovering calm and clarity in work and life, this book is a big help and a useful tool to become more mindful each day. I highly recommend this book. In both personal and business life, I will always remember going forward: 'It's time to balance the books.' "

—Reed Tinsley
CPA, CVA, CFP, CHBC

"*Beyond Balancing the Books* brings the practice of mindfulness into the office environment. Through mindfulness exercises and meditation, Marino shows the reader how to build resilience while navigating the business world. Chapter by chapter, he takes the reader deeper into practicing 'attention with intention' and living according to one's core values. I highly recommend this book!"

—Linda Sullivan
Owner, WORDsmart Word Processing, Inc.

"Marino's guidebook is a rich mine of helpful advice for anyone seeking a calmer, more spiritually focused approach to life's dilemmas. Discovering and practicing mindfulness changed Marino's life, and he desires to help as many individuals as possible. Highly recommended."

—Chanticleer Reviews
Full review online at: bit.ly/3uYBmDc

"I found reading *Beyond Balancing the Books* to be very beneficial and relevant in these tumultuous times. George has a way of being able to translate common business encounters into teachable moments. Let's face it—distractions are everywhere. Yet the value of mindfulness, being aware and in sync with your feelings, acknowledgment, acceptance—life skills that allow for fuller and more meaningful existence. I found the book to be very solid from a journalistic standpoint and well written. Glad that I took the time to read it."

—Ken Slivken
HR Director, A360media, LLC

"*Beyond Balancing the Books* is an excellent resource to help us achieve self-actualization. George Marino provides us with practical advice and tools in mindfulness techniques. I highly recommend this book for motivating you to reach your personal and professional goals and, contrastingly, achieve the delicate balance of work, coping with fatigue, and feeling renewed. Bravo!"

—Laurie Stanley
Senior Human Resources Professional, PHR

"A welcoming, comprehensive guide to practicing mindfulness and presence in professional life."

—Publishers Weekly
Full review online at: bit.ly/BBBPW

Beyond Balancing
the Books

Beyond Balancing the Books

Sheer Mindfulness for Professionals in Work and Life

George Marino, CPA, CFP®

First paperback edition: 2021.
Library of Congress Number: 2020925863
ISBN: 978-1-7363802-1-5 (p)
ISBN: 978-1-7363802-0-8 (e)

Edited and formatted by Joseph VanBuren—jvbwriteon.com
Cover art by Pagatana Designs—pagatana.com
Publishing consulting by Geoff Affleck—geoffaffleck.com

Published in conjunction with One Heart Coaching, LLC.
www.oneheartcoach.com

Download Your Bonus
Companion Guide to
Beyond Balancing the Books

This FREE nine-page bonus companion guide is a practical tool to help you apply the principles in this book to your daily work life. It includes five empowering questions for self-reflection plus exclusive guided responses from the author.

Download your copy at http://bit.ly/mindfulnessworkguide.

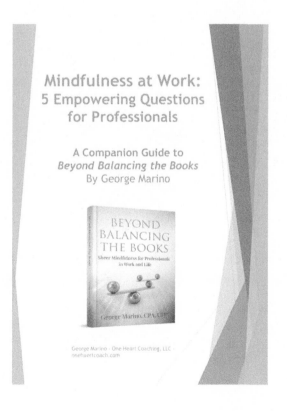

Dedication

For my life partner,
Pemari Ancheta,
who taught me about diversity and inclusion
and so much more...

And
for my mother and father,
who encouraged me to go to college
and so much more...

Table of Contents

Acknowledgments

Many people have helped me make this book a reality. Assuredly, the interconnection was the greatest pleasure in preparing the manuscript. It is now my pleasure to name some of those who have contributed their talents and support to the project.

Joseph VanBuren provided superb editing and coaching at every stage of writing and production. His intelligence, understanding, sense of humor, and invaluable support significantly enhanced the book. Joseph's skill is further appreciated in guiding me on pursuing permissions and shaping references, which are gratefully acknowledged at the back of the book.

The initial impetus for this book came to me about three years ago while attending a year-end tax seminar, as I note in the introduction. I want to acknowledge all the CPAs who have helped me stay current with tax and financial accounting standards and healthcare consulting, especially Chip Santye, CPA, and Reed Tinsley, CPA.

To the late Barry Kopp, CPA, who hired me out of college to work for his firm. I thank all of the partners at this firm who gave me a start in the profession and granted me superb experiences.

To all of my accounting and tax professors at Pace University, New York and Baruch College, New York, especially the late Anthony R. Pustorino, CPA, and the late Samuel A. Dyckman, CPA, JD, LLM. I thank each of you.

To Jean A. McConochie, PhD, Professor Emerita at Pace University, who introduced me to the art of writing and the enchantment of theater and poetry. I am deeply grateful.

Introduction

It is precisely the god-like in ourselves that we are ambivalent about, fascinated by and fearful of, motivated to and defensive against.

—Abraham Maslow

A Tale of Two CPAs

Larry

Larry is an early riser, up at 5:30 a.m. He hasn't needed a wakeup call for a while now. His cellphone is on his night table right next to the bed. The phone has been charging all night so that it will be ready for the next day. Unfortunately, the same cannot be said for Larry. He has been up several times during the night, checking his e-mail and texts. He sleeps about five hours a night on average. When he awakens during the night, his mind quickly starts ruminating over work-related issues and personal problems, his thoughts like crickets in the room loudly frolicking all night long. His wife complains often, so he has agreed to shut off all sounds from the phone and leave it on vibrate—which it does throughout the night.

Larry's sleep is clearly irregular and deprived, yet he won't admit it. When his wife asks him, he shrugs it off as if it doesn't bother him. Moseying to the bathroom, he looks in the mirror and sees that his eyes are a bit red. His balance off; he is in a fog. As he scans his e-mails in the bathroom for client and firm issues, he starts to feel energized with an adrenaline rush. He dresses and heads to the kitchen for a quick bite to eat as well as another coffee and a scan of today's world news—the first check since 2:30 a.m. He quickly hugs his wife and child and is off to the office. He'll see them at about 7:00 p.m. if he is lucky, later if it's tax season. His anxiety over disputes in the firm related to compensation, power, and succession planning comes back in the form of negative thoughts and emotions as he heads out the door.

Occasionally, Larry has some time to work out in the gym at lunch time. He is out of shape but determined to regain that youthful physique he had when he joined the firm right out of college twenty years ago. Larry made partner early. After eight years of experience, he rose up and gained the credit he deserved by advancing his technical skills, business development, and firm relationships. He is serious but likes to kid around once in a while, especially when he joins a few senior partners after work for a few drinks at the bar.

Larry has one child and another on the way. He is starting to worry about college funding and child care. His wife has a good career as a marketing manager at a mid-sized publishing company, and she too is under relentless pressure at her work with the office politics and in-house back-stabbing.

On the bus, heading through the Lincoln Tunnel to his Midtown Manhattan office, Larry responds to more e-mails and sends a few texts to his clients. His adrenaline is flowing; this is what he enjoys. He keeps score of his progress in income, status in the firm, new client opportunities, committee appointments, and networking. Being in the game is the key. It's all about wins and losses. The more he wins, the more alive he feels. Larry (and other accountants like him) gauges vitality by pressure, billable hours, compulsivity, addictions, anxieties, and feelings of superiority and entitlement that compose most of his business dealings. This shows up in countless ways, but mostly in an inability to sit quietly in a room and be alone in stillness. Whenever he is alone, Larry reaches for a device or the TV, reads, listens to music, sorts and organizes things—anything to keep him from being in stillness and facing his own emptiness.

Larry walks into the office ready for the games of the day. His tax department is one of the best in the industry. His motto is, "If you don't work on Saturdays and nights in tax season, don't bother staying in this profession." He is a Type A personality with a drive for power and an overly competitive stance. When he meets with other partners in the firm, it is a slugfest over who gets the best staff for engagements that he leads. In the firm, mistakes are frowned upon, especially within the quality review department that is even more Type A than Larry.

Larry's anxiety is concealed and never openly addressed. He sidesteps his emotional pain, often projecting it onto others. He is especially anxious when tax returns are near their due dates. He becomes overly bossy to his staff, constantly over their shoulders, watching how much time they are spending on each tax return. He would never admit that he is fearful and nervous most of the time. His feelings are never discussed except for his anger, which is quite noticeable. To openly discuss emotions and feelings, especially to staff, would be a sign of weakness. Occasionally he has private thoughts of becoming jaded and wondering what his career is really all about.

Due to the firm's arrogant environment, Larry and most of his partners and senior managers have become masters at turning ordinary situations into some kind of drama and conflict among the staff accountants. They would ardently dismiss such claims as hogwash. But deep within, most of the partners would acknowledge that they rarely, if ever, expose how they truly feel about their firm. They keep their poker face on all the time because in this game, information is key, and control comes by manipulating people while maintaining the mask.

At the end of the day, Larry grabs a drink with a couple of his partners as they shoot the breeze about current work. Their conversation is a debriefing and storytelling filled with bravado, strategy, and lots of gossip. Of course, it's all about the other partners, managers, staff, and their clients. It is never an opening up of some internal struggle or personal problem.

Larry catches the train out of Penn Station back to New Jersey at 7:35 p.m. He is home by 8:45 p.m., in time to say goodnight to his child, have a bite to eat, and watch Monday night football with another beer. His goal is to decompress. He makes his way to the bedroom to join his wife and sets the phone on vibrate. The evening shift of checking e-mails and scanning the net will begin in about three hours.

It's been another great day.

Larry is a successful partner in a prestigious CPA firm.

Larry is mindless.

Amy

Amy begins her day lying in bed and looking around the room as the sunlight pierces through the windows. She has had a good night's sleep, fully rested as she steps onto the bedroom floor with a gentle mantra that marks a new beginning with peace and love. She prepares some tea for herself and begins to meditate for fifteen minutes before taking a shower. She likes to call her meditation a "centering" as she focuses on her breath and bodily sensations. This centering is followed by fifteen minutes of spiritual reading and some journaling.

When her husband returns from the gym around 7:15 a.m., Amy has already showered and is getting breakfast ready, which they will share together at the kitchen table. They both agreed that their morning time together will be cellphone-free. They bond and check in with each other for anything that is blocking their connection. She is committed to making her second marriage one based on a close, loving, and playful partnership that supports them both in bringing their greatest gifts to the world. The marriage is successful, but it is not without periodic episodes of drama fueled by past emotional pain. However, both Amy and her husband have been doing their own respective inner work and cultivating mindfulness in their daily lives.

Her two kids join them for breakfast around 7:30 a.m. The kids are in fifth and sixth grades, and they lead full and active lives. Amy practices *presence* with her children. She makes a clear distinction between being with her kids and being present with her kids. She credits her alone time without any devices, during which she connects to the stillness within and cultivates a mindset of curiosity and openness.

Amy leaves for her office around 8:15 a.m. She travels by subway into the city from Forest Hills, Queens. A senior manager in the tax department of a well-established CPA firm in Midtown Manhattan, she is dedicated to spending her time doing what she is uniquely gifted to do and is aligned with what brings her the greatest joy. She finds tax to be an avenue to express her desire to make a difference in people's lives—helping them maximize their tax deductions, discussing financial planning opportunities, and making recommendations that serve them and the greater good.

During her train ride into the city, she listens to an Eckhart Tolle talk that he has given at retreats, which she has attended with her husband. Each time she listens to Eckhart, it is fresh and new to her. She is able to shift in and out of a deep abiding state of *presence* in her daily commute to work. She is fully aware of her surroundings and alert to the ordinariness of things around her. This carries over to her day in the office, where she cultivates this practice even further while dealing with complicated tax issues for her clients.

Amy's schedule is full today, and she has identified her top five priorities. Aware that she does her best work in the morning, she completes the more complex tasks and then meets with a tax and audit partner to discuss the tax implications of various transactions. At these meetings, Amy focuses intently on the person she is speaking with and rarely becomes distracted, although she is fully aware of the environment and the sounds around her. Her listening skills are multi-dimensional. She practices self-focused listening, including paying attention to her thoughts, body, and emotions before she speaks.

She brings awareness to what is happening in the moment, such as when one of the partners is anguished over the effect a transaction will have on the cash position of a client. Amy is in touch with her emotions and body, so she feels the tension build at the moment of seeing this in the partner. The reaction, although slight, could be an underlying fear that has not been fully processed. She internally acknowledges this feeling by giving it attention for a few seconds, and then she responds to the partner's angst by providing her with a few alternative tax treatments to consider for the transaction. Amy's pause and quiet listening to her internal reaction and attention are transformational. She is aware and awake to both her internal world and her external world and found a solution without effort and stress. She is mindfully listening. She also knows those times when she is not conscious, such as when her mind is in a progressive stream of past failures or future worries. When she notices this happening to her, she gently acknowledges it and returns to her present moment awareness.

As Amy's day progresses, she feels a sense of satisfaction with her work, mainly because it is aligned with her state and purpose, which is to bring conscious awareness to this world in a business setting. Although no one recognized this explicitly, that is perfectly fine with her. Amy is in alignment with her inner and outer purpose in life.

Amy leaves the office at 6:00 p.m. and is home by 7:00 p.m., where she reconnects with her husband and children at dinner free of devices. She helps her children with some homework before bedtime. She makes the evening matter for her and the family. She is usually in bed by 10:00 p.m., where she rests peacefully for a solid night's sleep.

It has been another integral day.

Amy is a successful CPA in a prestigious accounting firm.

Amy is a mindful professional.

My Journey with Mindfulness

> *Mindfulness has never met a cognition it didn't like.*
> —Daniel J. Siegel, MD

I love what I do as a CPA, and even more so when I am mindfully present.

I worked at several public accounting firms of various sizes before launching my own practice in New York City in 2000. For more than thirty-five years I have been an accountant, consultant, and financial planner for individuals and businesses. I discovered a niche in the healthcare industry. My clients are healthcare organizations, professional service firms, and small businesses, and together we try to make sense of the business environment from a financial and operational perspective.

I began a mindfulness journey in 2006 after experiencing many years of acute anxiety and stress that, like Larry, carried over into my work as an accountant. At times, it was very difficult to get through a day without a high level of stress, which would then spill over into my personal life. It was a vicious circle of anxiety at work and stress at

7

home. It was affecting my ability to focus and give attention to the things that really mattered to me—my "essential values." I was plowing through my workday filled with stress and short-lived moments of distraction, followed by ever-increasing levels of anxiety and boredom—not a healthy way to live and work.

In the spring of 2006 while browsing in a bookstore and in a state of acute anxiety, I noticed a book: *The Power of Now* by Eckhart Tolle. As I picked up the book, I thought to myself, "That is a strange title. I never heard that before, let alone no one really teaches this in school, institutions, or in mainstream culture, that the Now has power." Rather, I pondered that most of us have come to believe that the future is what matters most and the past is what makes us who we are today. Stepping way out of my comfort zone, I read the introduction while standing there and quickly moved to the checkout counter to purchase the book.

The teachings in *The Power of Now* and Eckhart's other books, *A New Earth* and *Stillness Speaks*, were just what the doctor ordered. Subsequently, I began to read other spiritual texts and poetry, finding deeper meaning as I began a contemplative practice. I noticed my reading was much more than conceptual understanding or knowledge gaining. Rather, I found incredible joy and peace reading so many like-minded books and started to realize how they all pointed to the "one thing necessary" (Luke 10:42): the indwelling divine nature within all creatures and the universe.

It wasn't until 2008 that I had a profound awakening after another intense period of internal turmoil. This shift brought forth a latent higher self that was ready to emerge as the ego identity began to gradually diminish. In other words, I became less identified with the ego in me. It was a little bit like handing over the turmoil to a higher power, feeling an internal acceptance and a letting go. These experiences are beautiful when they happen. After a while the intensity fades, but remaining in the background is an underlying peace and a sense of connection and harmony. In my case, I felt a

8

strong pull to continue with the practice of *presence*, holding that frequency in my daily work as an accountant and in my personal relationships. I came to more fully understand the nature of my experience and how others have also had these experiences. My love for the natural world intensified even while walking in Midtown Manhattan, where I work.

I spent the next twelve years practicing mindfulness and meditation in my daily activities and life situations. I also have participated in numerous retreats and workshops with some of the most well-respected mindfulness teachers of our time.

I started to realize a dramatic change from being like Larry to being much more like Amy. The practice of *presence* has affected all areas of my life, including my work as a CPA. I found good success in my healthcare niche working with small business clients and individuals performing traditional accounting, tax services, and consulting. Mindfulness has greatly helped me in both my personal and business relationships. I am still a work-in-progress, but I also know that the step I take in the present moment is the "one thing necessary." That one thing changes everything when it is fully embodied and not just a mental abstraction. I feel I am on a continuous learning journey in mindfulness and *presence* practice—now and now and now!

Why I Wrote This Book

In 2018, I attended a year-end tax seminar where more than 200 CPAs had gathered to learn and update their skills regarding the new tax reform legislation. This year I noticed a different vibe in the audience. The Larry-like CPAs already seemed worn-down, exhausted, and troubled—before the busy season had even started! In a New York City ballroom filled with very smart people, the collective energy field seemed to be full of worry and dread.

I stopped to recognize what was arising in the present moment and allowed it to just be. This acknowledgment and acceptance brought about a shift in awareness. In that moment, the awareness in me created an opening for my heart to connect to a sense of our common humanity. I felt a bond and a connection to each CPA. After this experience, I knew that I wanted to help my colleagues learn how mindfulness can benefit them in their practices and in their lives.

Weakness in Internal Controls: The Unique Challenges of Accounting

As accountants, we are trusted as highly trained advisors to our clients. Accounting work is largely numbers-oriented, detailed, and technical. With the issuance of new standards, laws, and regulations, accounting is always changing. Accountants are asked to be objective and independent, communicating findings in a clear, concise manner. They take pride in enhancing knowledge through continuing education, peer review programs, and other formal and informal processes and procedures.

Maintaining knowledge and running a successful CPA firm is no easy task. The work pushes, tests, and challenges at every turn. A partner calls you into the office and tells you to take early retirement, you aren't assigned to prestigious clients, or your billable hours are not meeting firm standards. Maybe a co-worker is putting unrelenting pressure on you and your emotions start to take over the day. Or your yearly review goes poorly, costing you that key promotion given to your prime competitor.

In addition, accountants are faced with the ongoing challenges of staffing, succession planning, merger mania, busy season, job stability, heavy workloads, multiple layers of review, commoditization of core services, tax reform, cybersecurity, and the search for relevance in a world of rapid technological change. When you put out one fire (April 15: tax due date), the next one rolls around (June 15: tax due date). The angst that CPAs experience takes a toll and feeds the discontent, stress, and irritation that lurks, if only in the background.

It is your ability to adapt to this relentlessly changing landscape that makes you a "professional."

Whether you are starting out as a junior accountant in a CPA firm or are more experienced and on staff at a private company, the challenges are immense and exist not only in the marketplace. Sometimes they manifest in the firm, and sometimes they reside closer to home—in your personal life. Examples include relationship challenges, family stress, juggling kids, financial hardship, and health issues.

You may shrug these feelings off as just normal stuff—especially work-related stuff. "After all," you tell yourself, "I get paid for all of these headaches, or maybe I can look for a better job—and actually find it this time." The famous saying "the road to hell is paved with good intentions" has some meaning here. You start out each day with good intentions, and yet how many times during the day are you thrown off course with what appears to be your external circumstances?

Most CPAs are trained to use their analytical minds to navigate their workday and personal lives. The analytical mind is a gift and a tool; in many practical ways, it helps to earn a living, make plans, manage the business, and much more. However, the analytical mind is often running on autopilot. It literally develops a mind of its own. It thrives on repetition and is filled with useless and compulsive thinking, which can actually interfere with the accounting work. Scattered attention, ruminating on the past, projecting into the future, and self-flagellation prevent access to creativity, resourcefulness, and efficiencies that the present moment brings. Furthermore, this kind of mind absorbs all attention, creating an attachment to work and making it difficult to take a step back and sense your true nature. Because it is so common, it is considered normal by just about everyone.

There is another kind of challenge that arises, one that is more internal rather than external—the challenge of our minds, emotions, fears, and frustrations. For many accountants (and almost everyone you come in contact with), there's no training to manage our inner operating systems (IOS) like the way we are trained to manage external circumstances. No matter where you come from, including background, education, wealth status, or otherwise, your IOS has most likely not been given the attention, compassion, and love that it deserves—especially while at work. But if you notice closely, your IOS is mostly a conglomeration of internal, repetitive, and reactive patterns.

Accountants often get lost in this maze of thoughts and emotions, especially during the busy season. The mind-chatter, as it is called, tends to criticize, judge, complain, and wander off. An unobserved mind can lead to stress, worry, anxiety, boredom, fatigue, and fear. Vices and behaviors (alcohol, drugs, social media, etc.) temporarily cover up this uneasiness to distract from what is actually happening in the moment, both within and without.

Does any of this sound familiar?

Waking Up: The Internal Audit and the Discovery Process

We all lose touch with ourselves at some point in life—it's normal—but have you ever looked into the mirror and performed an internal audit, saying, "Who is this person?" or "What happened?" I am not referring to physical appearance, status in the world, or rank in your firm. I am pointing to the sense of who you truly are deep down. You may have a relatively satisfying career and personal life filled with family, friends, health, and financial security, and yet, like Larry, the discontent, worry, and frustrations are there as your constant companions.

This is where mindfulness comes in. Mindfulness is all about accounting for what really counts—embarking on a discovery process in knowing who you are in your essence. With practice, it becomes your new normal.

As you work with the debits and credits on the ledger and in your personal life, with mindfulness practice you begin to notice that they become more balanced, like with Amy. You begin to acknowledge both the ups and the downs with equanimity and compassion and learn to savor a newfound peace and joy in your work and everyday life. You stay fresh, alert, and ready to continue learning new approaches.

It is vital to ground your mindfulness practice in your own experience. There is nothing to believe in with mindfulness practice.

What is Mindfulness?

The past has no power over the present moment.
—Eckhart Tolle

The clinical definition of mindfulness, according to Jon Kabat-Zinn, PhD, is "paying attention to something, in a particular way, on purpose, in the present moment, non-judgmentally." Paradoxically, mindfulness is not what you think it is. You can't think about mindfulness, and the mind can't understand it. Understanding mindfulness is being present.

Breaking down Kabat-Zinn's working definition would look something like the following:

"Paying attention" is attuning to certain things that surround you in the here and now. And, as you journey on with your practice, you will start to pay attention to the attention itself. If you look closely, your mind is typically wandering—thinking about other things and concerned about what might go wrong or how to make things right for desired results. These thoughts and feelings have a physical effect on you in ways that you are sometimes conscious of and at other times not. You may adjust your seating position, clench your teeth, and speak abruptly. When you bring attention to these actual experiences, you start to see what is happening. "Oh, I spoke loudly." "Oh, I am ruminating about the past." "Oh, I am feeling anxious." Paying

13

attention allows you to become comfortable with what is rather than struggling with how you want it to be.

"On purpose" means you intentionally decide to pay attention to something specific, and that can be an external situation like a conversation or an internal focus such as a thought or emotion. When you begin to practice mindfulness, you begin to train your mind and heart and expand your capacity to be present with all that is happening. Being mindful "on purpose" can also shift your awareness from external stimuli to what's happening inside, providing an opportunity to know yourself in a fresh way.

"In the present moment" is a shifting of attention to the here and now and a letting go of any thought about the past or future. This shift resembles a light that is redirected from facing a window looking outside to a mirror facing inward toward your thoughts, emotions, heart center, and body. The ability to be present in this moment is an important quality of mindfulness since life only happens in the *Now*. It doesn't happen in the future, no matter how much strategic planning you do. And it doesn't happen in the past, no matter how much you think about the error you made in that financial statement. You often miss this every day in the busyness and stress of work, but when you bring yourself into present moment awareness, you can actually enjoy each moment as it is arising. When your annual review is not going as you hoped, you can see what is occurring in the moment and offer clarifications and suggestions since you will be present to what is happening in the moment. A rainy day may not be what you ordered, but you can still see the sunlight beneath the clouds.

"Non-judgmentally" fundamentally means rising above thought into a state of open awareness. You engage in your experiences without judgment, whether you like them or not. In mindfulness practice, there is nothing wrong with judgment per se, except when you become overly identified with the subjective, judgmental mind. A non-judgmental stance opens to new experiences as habitual likes and dislikes have less sway on you. When you start to practice mindfulness, you often bring a lot of judgment and analysis to the practice. You ponder, "Am I doing it right? When will I see results?" You are constantly gauging yourself and holding yourself up to some notion of perfection, but mindfulness is not about perfection or achieving a certain state. Instead, you bring a welcoming attitude of non-judgmental awareness to each moment—preparing a tax return, visiting a client, or consulting on the phone with an auditor—reducing struggle and accomplishing more in less time.

In other words, to be mindful is to be aware of your moment-to-moment experience in a non-judgmental way and to acknowledge—without resistance—whatever you are facing in the present moment. Mindfulness allows you to find space to open up, to take stock of yourself, and to respond from a different perspective. Mindfulness is innate to us as human beings. It is our true nature. It just needs to be uncovered.

The Science of Mindfulness

Practicing mindfulness is an art. However, it is also supported by scientific research, as evidenced by the number of scientific journals published each year. Dan Siegel, MD, author and clinical professor of psychiatry at UCLA David Geffen School of Medicine, writes in *Aware: The Science and Practice of Presence* that developing focused attention, open awareness, and kind intention in a mindfulness practice leads to the following benefits:

- Improved immune function
- Optimized levels of enzymes and healthy cells
- Enhanced gene regulation to help prevent life-threatening inflammation
- Modified cardiovascular factors and improved cholesterol levels, blood pressure, and heart function
- Increased neural integration of the brain, enabling more coordination and balance in both functional and structural

connectivity within the nervous system including self-regulation, problem solving, and adaptive behavior that is at the heart of well-being

Practicing mindfulness also reduces stress, increases job satisfaction, improves focus and attention, provides greater emotional resilience, and enhances interpersonal skills. It is an intangible asset that does not amortize!

I will be highlighting some of the science surrounding mindfulness principles throughout the book and have included references in the appendix for those who would like to explore further.

The Essence of This Book

A primary aim of this book is to bridge evidence-based mindfulness findings with practical exercises for the busy professional. Another key aim of this book is to help you go deeper and align your outer purpose with inner meaning. Your true self is deeply connected—ready to emerge, embrace life, and create. In this book, going *beyond balancing the books* is primary, and traditional accounting is secondary, for it is the instinct in you to be creative that competes with the things that hold you back and shut you down. Mindfulness generates awareness of the higher self and its possibilities, including discovery of the compassionate voice within that integrates all of your parts, even those that you may not like. Through this practice, you get to know more about who you are.

Throughout the chapters of this book, I will guide you on a journey to discover a little bit more about who you are and to let that lead in your life. When I say a journey, I am referring to the potential shift from a mindset that is often based on worry, frustration, anxiety, competition, and a need to be right and critical (Larry) to a mindset that is open, aware, intuitive, clear, creative, compassionate, connected, and inspirational (Amy). I call this the higher self.

16

I detail the following tools throughout the book:

- Mindfulness practices and exercises
- Mindfulness skills specifically tailored to professionals
- Simple questions, exercises, and guided meditations
- Journaling your mindfulness journey

In this book, I use the term "mindfulness" interchangeably with "presence," "stillness," "attention," and "awareness." As a reader, feel free to substitute these terms in a way that is meaningful to you. Ultimately, these words are only pointers to that state of consciousness that can only be experienced in the present moment.

Also, I draw on my experiences as a CPA, business consultant, and professional coach to highlight questions and case examples throughout the book from these experiences. Many of these questions and cases are transferable to other professions and business settings, and so I use the terms "CPA" and "accountant" in a way that is mostly interchangeable with other professions and work settings.

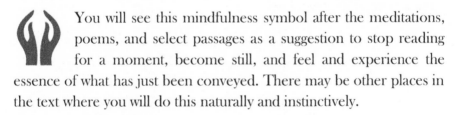 You will see this mindfulness symbol after the meditations, poems, and select passages as a suggestion to stop reading for a moment, become still, and feel and experience the essence of what has just been conveyed. There may be other places in the text where you will do this naturally and instinctively.

My Coaching Journey

I decided to embark on a path to be a life coach in a helping capacity with a formal training program titled "Coaching for Transformation" with an International Coaching Federation (ICF) accredited program. After finishing this training, I successfully completed a thorough accredited training program to teach evidence-based mindfulness meditation for enhancing people's well-being and resilience.

I am a certified professional coach (CPC) and certified mindfulness meditation teacher (CMMT), a poet, an urban nature guide, and I completed a certificate from the Eckhart Tolle School of Awakening in 2019. My journey also includes becoming the founder of One Heart Coaching LLC, where I work as a professional coach with diverse clients who often feel stuck in their life situation or are in transition. The people I work with are often experiencing stress, anxiety, and difficult emotions in their work, relationships, finances, and living situations. I help individuals discover their authentic voice, finding meaning and purpose at work and in life. With my CPA and consulting background, I also provide executive coaching and work with businesses as a transformational coach, helping to build a more conscious, resilient, and fulfilling work environment. Additionally, I volunteer as a mentor/coach for accountants through the New York State Society of CPAs and for students at Pace University.

If you would like to learn more about my coaching practice, feel free to watch my introduction video at oneheartcoach.com or on my YouTube channel (where I also have several guided meditations): bit.ly/oneheartyoutube.

Beyond Balancing the Books

While this book is geared to the professional, the practice of *presence* is beyond anything anyone can really say about it. With this in mind, I will attempt to convey some of the mindfulness practices that have helped me go beyond balancing the proverbial books of what culture, family, and institutions say about who we should be and what a successful career and life should look like. There is a place for these influences in our lives, of course, and it is part of our journey. But, unfortunately, having a degree and license, moving out of the house, making money, acquiring property, raising a family, and attending religious services often do not foster the kind of internal shift that is absolutely necessary for each one of us. For those of you who have recognized this shift or at least had glimpses of it, this book offers guidance on the challenges you face living and practicing *presence*, especially in a world with only a relative minority of individuals who know, or even want to know, about it. Although, in the *Psychology*

Today article "The After-Effects of Awakening," Steve Taylor Ph.D. states that the number of people living a more awakened life is increasing.

Carl Jung depicted the first half of a person's life (0–40 years perhaps) as the sun climbing to the meridian, and in this period one establishes oneself in the world (often repressing one's own shadow nature). The second half of a person's life he depicted as the sun completing its curve, and in this period one proceeds—or should proceed—"to go beyond oneself" (*beyond balancing the books*) or as it is known in other languages, to practice the *Tao* or the *Way*. "On this individuation" journey, one needs to deal with the shadow part of oneself and truly meet and live the archetypes. The full human spiritual experience is a "negotiation" with these archetypes. "Between them," Jung wrote, "the patient iron is forged into an independent whole, an individual." The end of the journey is a union with one's highest (Divine) self.

The Practice of Presence is the Way and the Tao

"There comes a time," Aldous Huxley wrote, "when one asks even of Shakespeare, even of Beethoven, is this all?" What is the goal of personal development? Is it the mastery of your experiences so that you are freed from childhood habits, adolescent feelings, and cultural ideas? I don't think so. *Beyond balancing the books* and personal development lies spiritual development, and what the mystics tell us is to unite in consciousness with God. This requires, in some measure, for us to "die to self" in order to "make room" for God.

Meister Eckhart, the great thirteenth-century mystic, writes about this union in this way: "For nothing is as opposed to God as time. Not only time is opposed to God, but even clinging to time, not only clinging to time but even having contact with time." To live from this space of "no-time" is both our challenge and our purpose here on Earth. The practice of mindfulness is one way to help you live out your purpose.

19

Give yourself space as you make your way through this book. Try completing one chapter at a time, take breaks and put the book down, then begin again fresh when you are ready. The exercises, questions, and answers and short guided meditations are designed to augment and ground you in the present moment—the space of no-time. The content of this book is thus secondary; your relationship to the content and yourself as you progress in the mindfulness journey is primary.

As you work through the chapters, you will be asked to answer questions. I haven't included any space directly in the pages of this book to answer. Instead, use what works for you—a journal, diary, tablet, loose paper, or print this out and write directly on the back. You can even use a blog to explore your answers to personal questions. It is, however, important that you answer the questions in written form so you actually see your thoughts and feelings on paper or a screen.

This journey is like a love affair with yourself and the world, so much so that once you start, there is no turning back. As you experience a gain in consciousness, it is never permanently lost.

What CPAs do in their lives and careers is relatively important as they grow and serve the public. The profession is based on trust, integrity, and objectivity. Collectively, accounting work is already serving the greater good. How accountants do their work is absolutely important. The art of stepping in and out of the stream of mental and emotional conditioning to know yourself on a deeper level at work and in the world is vital. In essence, mindfulness is your deep, abiding sense of identity. It is the essence of who you are.

Chapter 1

Getting Started with Mindfulness Practice

You are not a drop in the ocean. You are the entire ocean, in a drop.

—Rumi

Mindfulness practice is something you can do at any time. Even noticing that you are not practicing mindfulness is mindfulness—it's that simple. You'll reach a point when mindfulness is no longer something you do but rather what you've become. You know that a description of China is not China, nor is a map of China. To know China, one has to go there, and to know mindfulness, one has to live it daily. Not perfectly, of course, and that is one of its defining features. We return again and again to mindfulness.

I learned about the beginner's mindset and how simple mindfulness meditation can be one day on a retreat. Halfway through the meditation, the teacher guiding our group said, "Now let's begin our meditation." She was pointing to the present moment. We are all beginners, you and I, and that makes mindfulness so much fun. The newness of each moment is a metaphoric "big bang." Now, now, now.

That said, it is helpful to consciously remind yourself, in a way that suits you, to incorporate mindfulness into your daily routine. I provide you with some exercises in this book under the heading of "Informal Practices" so you can take what you learn and bring it to your work as accountants. This can help you bring mindfulness into your workday and relationships. You are not required, nor is it preferable, to have a goal in mind as you start practicing mindfulness. The practice itself is the goal, and you can return to it again, literally moment to moment when distractions happen, as they will.

Mindfulness cannot be done in a right or wrong way. When the mind is distracted, gently and kindly accept this as part of your journey. This is a mindful act of self-compassion. The moment you realize you are not mindfully present, you are in fact already present. This book will give you a basic idea but is not intended to be an official reference guide.

It is helpful to acknowledge in yourself that you are walking around with so many thoughts swirling around in your head at any given moment in time. These thoughts are very often repetitive. This thought chatter, as it is called, can make you feel unfocused, in a fog, and often overwhelmed. This mind movie is withholding creativity from you and sometimes keeps you up at night and anxious during the day as you perform your accounting work and live your life. Research has shown that much of people's thinking and many of their behaviors are automatic. Research findings illustrate that when the mind is running on "autopilot," our behavior and decision making often follow habits and routines. In this process, the mind is preoccupied with other thoughts (1). It does take courage to honestly assess and recognize the fact that much of our thinking is repetitive and useless. When was the last time you had an original thought?

Here is one way you can tell. Your body is like a jar, an instrument that plays music. It has different tones in response to your thoughts and emotions. The value of the jar, of course, can sometimes differ quite remarkably. How do you assign worth to your body's musical sounds? It is a little bit like this: what you say or do in mindfulness becomes memorable to another person in need. Then you will know you had an original thought. Jesus put it this way: "Out of the fullness of the heart the mouth speaks," and there you will know an original thought in a state of stillness as an integration of mind, body, soul, and spirit.

What is the Problem Now?

One of the first aspects of mindfulness that I found to be extremely useful, especially when some kind of worry or anxious thoughts and feelings come up in my work as a CPA, is to ask myself this question: What is the problem now? Then, I get very curious. To my surprise, the problem I thought was important was only a thought in my head—a "what if" kind of thought. This is very common. Here is a good example.

Let's say you completed a financial report and released it to your client. While at home later that night, a thought swirls around in your mind that you may have missed a footnote disclosure. You start to feel a contraction in your body, a reaction to the thought you just had a second ago. But it is also a signal for you to become more alert and present. When doing so, you are becoming mindful. I call it "catching yourself mindfully." Then, kindly ask yourself: What is the problem now?

As you look closely, you will see there really is no problem now, as you sit at home, otherwise enjoying your evening. But wait, I can hear your mind saying, my client will spot this error, and I will feel embarrassed, or maybe the client will lose confidence in my abilities. This relentless thought chatter will try to trick you into believing that you really need to worry about this footnote disclosure now. After all, as the mind believes, you aren't truly professional if you let it go and get back to your peaceful evening. Fortunately, as we practice mindfulness we discover awareness behind or above this thought, so to speak, that can see the thought for what it really is: a distraction. The distractive thought is an aspect of the inner critic (2).

The inner critic is a component of the ego-mind structure that has been inherited and passed down for generations; everyone has it to a greater or lesser extent. So there is no need to take it personally. What a big relief that was for me! Gradually, and with practice, this inner critic can be heard, embraced, and perhaps even transformed into something more helpful and positive in your work and personal life. This process of kind attention can create room for a more dynamic sense of self to emerge, which can be described as an ever-present observer aligned with your life purpose. This is evidenced by the growing body of empirical findings suggesting that mindfulness practice can lead to lower levels of impulsive reactions and higher levels of self-control (3). When this happens, you are more attuned to your life purpose. More about this later on.

For now, I would like you to recall a problem in the recent past. Pick one that is moderate in intensity and won't cause you any pain or discomfort. As you bring this problem into your awareness, place yourself in the situation, sensing the words and atmosphere that you felt back then. Take a moment, and then ask yourself: What is the problem now? If you are like most people, there really was no immediate problem. Yes, there might have been some concern or disturbance brewing in the background, but again: What is the problem now? As the poet Rumi writes: "In the blackest of your moments, wait with no fear."

Stress

According to the Cleveland Clinic, stress is the normal bodily reaction when changes occur. Our profession is undoubtedly changing all the time, not only with new laws, standards, and regulations, but also within our firms and organizations. Like you, I have experienced stress and acute anxiety as a CPA, sometimes working 70 hours a week in public accounting firms under tight deadlines and pressure to ensure that everything is completed on time and under budget. During the non-busy season, it is much less hectic, allowing time to take the required continuing education courses and handle projects that were postponed.

One thing is for sure: each of us has a different tolerance level for stress. For some of us, it can be helpful to see a licensed therapist when our anxiety elevates for a sustained period. Prolonged stress is associated with headaches, weight gain, elevated blood pressure, chest pain, and panic attacks. Therapy coupled with mindfulness practices can be a very potent antidote to higher levels of anxiety and an opportunity to be in a safe, secure environment to discuss circumstances.

That was the case for me in the middle of my career. Fortunately, I was able to leave therapy and continue on with mindfulness, which I continue to practice. Sometimes I go back to a therapist or coach to help me with certain circumstances. I find this very valuable. However, many accountants and professionals experience acute anxiety without seeking help for various reasons. This is unfortunate as there is no longer a stigma to seeking counseling, especially for males. Today, you can have a session online, which makes it much more accessible than ever.

According to AICPA, nearly 98% of CPAs report feeling some level of stress. Nearly 47% are frequently stressed and 11% of CPAs indicate they are at a "crisis point." Clearly, the excess of overtime hours can greatly impact the overall stress of the accounting profession. Another contributor to stress for accountants is a lack of autonomy. None of us want to be micromanaged. We all desire some level of flexibility and choice in our work responsibilities. However, most accounting-related work requires multiple layers of review. The documentation requirement is often very tedious and laborious. This sometimes leads accountants to feel they are micromanaged or their independence is being stripped away. Mindfulness practice can help you when these feelings come up. You will discover new tools in this book to help you cope with these situations.

Another factor that can cause stress is the emotion of boredom. I know from my own experience that some of the work is just not that interesting. Digging into the details of a general ledger to find out whether an expense should be either written off or capitalized as a fixed asset can cause both stress and boredom. This often leads to a wandering mind. Without mindfulness, the wandering mind can quickly make up stories and conflicts, causing further pain. We might even feel a loss of meaning and dignity when this happens. We may feel our firm does not value us or desire us to grow professionally. In turn, we may lose our motivation to perform or put in the extra hours required for promotion. In mindfulness, we refer to this as "internal thought chatter." This is normal, but it can also be very disturbing. You will learn new skills later on to help you with the wandering mind and its chatter.

Being an accountant can be stressful at times. Mindfulness can help you with this and even more—*beyond balancing the books.*

Question

> I'm rarely in my office. I am typically at the client's location and find it very challenging to wrap up jobs when I am out in the field. Besides, I feel like I don't even have an office to call my own—I am always on the run, anxious and frustrated. What can I do?

You are not enjoying what you are doing. However, you can change your energy vibration by simply accepting that this is what you have to do for now. By performing your work in an act of acceptance, you will notice a change from anxious to calmness, from frustrated to tolerable. That is a big first step. You will have taken responsibility for your inner state. From this place, see what happens. You may find more space opening up to complete your tasks and be more comfortable not having a steady office. You can choose to seek other opportunities and talk to your firm about your workload, all while maintaining acceptance of what is for now.

Informal Practice: The Three-Minute Breathing Space

These pains you feel are messengers. Listen to them.

—Rumi

For most of us, our busy schedules and tax season can prevent us from spending thirty minutes sitting quietly in meditation or focusing on the breath with eyes closed. The three-minute breathing space exercise is a good way to start incorporating mindfulness practice into your workday, especially during busy season.

This exercise is a direct way of coping with challenges characterized by the awareness and willingness to experience what is present. It consists of three components, each one about one minute long.

1. First, ask yourself the question: How am I doing right now? Focus attention on your inner perception. Notice which thoughts, feelings, and physical sensations you are experiencing. Try to translate your experience into words such as "I have self-critical thoughts" or "I feel anxious." What are you feeling in your body? Perhaps it is tightness in the chest or belly area. Allow yourself to feel whatever is arising for you in this moment. You can acknowledge the feeling with self-care and loving kindness.

2. Next, focus attention on your breathing. Follow the flow of the inhale, the pause, and the outflow.

3. Finally, allow attention to expand to the rest of your body. Feel how your breath moves throughout your whole body. With every inhale you can feel your body expand a little, and with each exhale you can feel it shrink a little.

You can do this exercise several times a day, even when you are not being challenged. You will be building mindfulness credits! Here is a guided meditation for the three-minute breathing space from my YouTube channel: bit.ly/3minutebreathingspace.

Discovering the Deeper Dimension

At the deepest level, mindfulness practice cultivates a different relationship with the self. This observing "self-stance" becomes stronger after repeated and consistent mindfulness exercises, allowing you to take a step back from all kinds of inner chatter, including identity-related thoughts. You can ask yourself, "Who am I?" The answer: the "inner I" as the aware observer and the "outer I" as the object of observations—namely your thoughts, emotions, and physical sensations. We all know what happens when we get caught up in a mental and emotional stream. We are taken over, and the thoughts and emotions are imbued with a sense of self that we take as who we are. This temporary identity often feels finite and rigid, which is not a comfortable state to define ourselves in.

Mindfulness will help to unclutter and clear your mind, calm your brain, and allow it to settle down. Mindfulness will also aid you in distinguishing between your life and your life situation. Finding the life in your life situation and your function as a CPA is one way to begin your mindfulness journey. That's exactly what happened to me when I started out practicing mindfulness. When you are full of "problems" like I was at work and home, there is no room for a real solution. True solutions come from a space within, where you can recognize your life underneath your life situation. All creativity, peace, and joy arise from this place inside yourself as you merge with the originality of it all.

Everyone has experienced this space at one time or another throughout their life. You may recall this to be a beautiful moment in your life. Maybe it was the birth of your child, a sunset, a deep connection to another, the day you made partner, an awe-inspiring glance at the stars at night, a beautiful garden, landing a new client, or passing the CPA exam. What would it be like to be in this state when nothing extraordinary is happening to you externally?

The Present Moment is Awareness

One of the key components of mindfulness practice is focused attention and listening. Focusing on your breath or inner body can shift attention from thinking to awareness. This self-focused listening can bring about a change from automatic reactions and judgments to the wisdom of the entire body system (more about judgments later). This heightened awareness makes intuition more accessible while you are present. It is a highly satisfying way to be as you go about your day

29

and your function as a CPA. You are more effective in your ability to respond to situations, and you'll listen more deeply.

Attention plays a key role in listening. When we meet a client or colleague, we narrow our focus so that all of our attention is on the other person, like Amy did when she met with the tax partner. Keenly listening to word choice and content helps clarify what is most important to our client. You can also listen to the gaps between the sounds of each word. This space, very subtle when you first begin to notice it, is like a living stillness that is the essence of any conversation.

Another aspect of attentive listening is being aware of all that is happening within us and the client simultaneously. With attentive listening, you'll notice openings and pauses in the conversations where transformation is possible and real solutions to challenges can happen. To be effective, it is vital to maintain some attention to your own inner stillness and the inner energy field of your body while you are engaging in the conversation with the client. In these moments, we also recognize the wholeness and resourcefulness of the other person. You'll sense a connectedness within and without, even if the other person cannot sense this in you. You'll bring another dimension of consciousness to your encounter.

Another way to begin this practice is to use your senses fully. Be where you are completely. Look around and listen without interpretation. See the lights, shapes, colors, and textures of things. Meister Eckhart writes about this very topic in the following way: "If my eye is to perceive color, it must be free of colors." In other words, drop your conceptual understanding and labels from time to time and just perceive. Listen to the sounds of car horns, the air conditioning humming, or birds singing. Listen to the silence underneath the sounds. What does that stillness mean to you? Realize that it is always there for you as you are working on a financial statement, tracking your time on a client, or discussing a client with a partner. Try to get more and more comfortable with the stillness.

Touch something, like a table, chair, or your feet on the floor—anything. Feel it and acknowledge its existence. Try it now. You can also focus on the rhythm of your breathing—one of my favorites—feeling the air flowing in and out. You may gradually begin to feel life energy inside your body. You are beginning to awaken to a deep, abiding peace and joy—even as you are challenged and snapped at—allowing things to be as they are in the present moment. You are leaving behind the fog of mental distractions: layers upon layers of stuff, most of which is unnecessary and draining you of the energy needed to enjoy your work as a CPA and be more engaged with the people around you as equals, no matter what their level in the firm. You won't need to believe this from a mental or practical point of view. It doesn't matter anyway. Posturing and self-promoting fall away. Your CPA work is fully raised to a greater good beyond a mere paycheck, retirement plan, and satisfied client.

Have you ever picked up a snow globe and shook it until the entire globe became so full of snow that you could barely see the object inside? That is what is going on inside your mind when absent of conscious awareness. Once you start to practice mindfulness, it will be as if the snow has settled to the bottom of the globe and you can think and see more clearly.

Informal Practice: Focused Attention

To further help you get started in practicing mindfulness, the focused attention exercise can provide a jumpstart and an overall feel for what mindfulness is and how it can help you. Here are the elements of this practice:

- Choose something to focus attention on.
- Choose how you will focus: using your visual, auditory, or tactile senses.
- Focus "on purpose."
- Focus in the present moment.
- Focus on non-judgmental awareness.

- Write your definition of mindfulness and what it means to you.

Let's break down each of these components and review the applicable process.

Choose Something to Focus Attention On

By focusing attention with intention you are using mindfulness to tap into your own needs and values. What do you need? What do you really want as a CPA? What is even more important? What stops you from creating what you want? Daniel Siegel, MD, writes:

> *If kind intention, emphatic joy, and a compassionate state of mind are so helpful in our inner lives and body, and it helps in our approach to others in making us more open and caring, how can we develop such states in our lives? The answer is simple: with the cultivation of intention, as it sets out a particular direction for energy and information flow.*

Pause and reflect on that for a moment. It seems to me medical science is informing us that when we set intention and choose to invite feelings of love and kindness toward ourselves and others—and really incline our hearts in the direction our intentions are pointing toward— we ought not expect something in return but give ourselves over wholeheartedly, or even just a bit, to see what already resides within us.

Routine functions are a good place to start. In preparing a tax return for a client, focus attention with intention on each step in the process, such as gathering the client data and sorting it out. Pick up all of the income components with not only your thinking mind but also your senses of seeing, hearing, and touching. Your entire energy body is working on the tax return. You'll want to keep some attention on your body, and then pick up all the deductions with your body's entire inner energy field. Pause for a few seconds. As you walk across the office to talk with an audit partner about a client you are working on, listen to each breath you take. In doing ordinary tasks such as these, you are mindfully present and alert to every cell in your body.

In focusing intent on the task at hand and that task alone, the tendency for the mind to wander is reduced significantly. If it does become distracted, as it will, you can return again and again to the task at hand. So the mind's distraction is neither good nor bad; in fact, it makes mindfulness practice possible. By staying with this practice, you are dissolving ordinary unconsciousness and the many ways in which your mind tries to make you feel uneasy, discontent, and tense. These mind patterns typically don't go away overnight, but they weaken with consistent practice, and you will find joy in walking to the partner's office without any expectations of outcome. You will be fully prepared to meet any challenge, not just doing things as a means to an end. Each step will be filled with the light of your presence. You are a mindful professional.

Make it a habit to focus attention with intention on something, especially your mental-emotional state, through self-observation throughout the day. "Am I at ease in this moment?" is a very good question to ask yourself periodically. Be as aware of what is going on internally, such as feelings, as you are about the client work you are doing. If you get the inner operating system right, the client accounting work will be more fulfilling. CPA will take on the meaning of Conscious Professional Advancement!

You may sometimes feel resentment concerning the particular client work you are doing. You may rationalize that this is only temporary and will pass, and this is true to a certain extent. However, unless you focus attention with intention and bring compassion to the feeling of resentment as it arises, even if only a few seconds at a time, it will come back in another setting, sometimes even stronger. Would you choose resentment? Of course not. Do you have a choice? Yes, you do.

Maybe you are being slighted at work. Perhaps the work is tedious and boring, or maybe the people you are working with are irritating and obnoxious. All of this is irrelevant. Your thoughts and emotions, whether justified or not, make no difference to the situation. The fact is you are showing resistance to what is. You are not present and thereby creating stress for yourself. The situation is actually neutral and not really the cause of your stress. The skill of separating your thoughts about the situation from the situation itself will keep you in the flow even if there is some turbulence. This skill is a little bit like the CPA code of conduct surrounding independence. In this case, I am referring to independence from the often complaining, conflicting, and judgmental mind. From this place of real independence you will see clearly and take actions as necessary.

Even further, your stress is polluting the collective human psyche of the planet, of which you are an inseparable part. Now that is a responsibility, isn't it? Eckhart Tolle writes: "The environmental destruction of the planet is only an outward reflection of an inner denying of a psychic contamination: many people not being accountable for their inner world." The good news is that this outer world will provide you with many opportunities to practice non-resistance to what is!

To some, this may sound negative and imply loss, becoming lethargic, not rising to meet the challenge, and so on. Actually, true non-resistance does not mean passively accepting situations or people. Rather, non-resistance, or if you prefer "letting go," is strictly an internal phenomenon. You can still take action on the outer level in a focused manner now that you have cleared the inner pathways through letting go to what is. Your actions are much more likely to be peaceful, dignified, and effective as you walk through the door, so to speak. Your feelings of peace come from your connection to your inner body even though the externals may not have changed.

As an example, your client sends you an IRS notice assessing interest and penalties on a late filing tax return. If you look closely, there is likely to be some irritation going on inside you. That is a sign of resistance and is normal. Not a problem. However, if you ignore the irritation time and time again, start commenting and complaining, it will build its own energy and create havoc in ways sometimes subtle to you and your environment.

Or, you're a staff accountant in a mid-size firm, and you are feeling frustrated and bored. You start to feel unease as you look around, and there is no one in your firm with whom you can openly discuss your sentiments. You may have a network of peers outside the office, but it still doesn't help discover what is really bothering you. You explore further and begin to notice a small opening in your inner energy field which provides a glimpse of the underlying meaning and purpose of your emotions. You seek a mentor or coach outside the office who can be a witness for you in your own internal development. You start to be accountable for your inner world.

In mindfulness, it is helpful to focus on your breathing to break the stream of resistance. Then, gently feel into the irritation in your body. Take note of where in your body the irritation is located and focus on that irritation even for just a few seconds at a time. Acknowledge the emotion and name it. Move back into your ordinary functioning and repeat this cycle periodically until you sense that the emotion has subsided. From that place, you are better able to respond to the IRS notice and speak with your client—you will have cleared any inner pollution.

Question

Do I need a new job? My current role as a tax manager in my firm is not satisfying me. How can I be mindful in this situation? What should I do?

The primary starting point in this situation is acceptance of what is. You are only accepting the present moment, not the situation. By doing so, you are removing suffering from your internal state.

Acceptance is the present moment. You are not accepting your role as a tax manager for next week, month or year, only this moment. After all, you cannot change it. Right now, this is your job requiring you to do certain tasks. You turn up the internal dimmer switch of attention with self-compassion. This does not mean you need to accept external conditions. Performing your work in a mode of acceptance will bring peace to what you do. This is not passive resignation, but rather an active aliveness bringing a new mindset to what you do—for the moment.

Then, start to look at what type of work will serve your life purpose more fully. Write down some of the issues that are bothering you at your current job. For example, you feel outraged at your firm's rejection of your ideas and recommendations. This may reveal your need for understanding, freedom of expression, and the desire to make a contribution to your clients and firm. Once you are aware of this more deeply, many strategies will surface to meet that need. You could discuss this with a partner at the firm, take a course to learn new skills that help you fulfill your creative impulse, or you could decide to seek a new job. In looking for a new job, you will do so with mindful awareness that your primary need is to make a meaningful contribution to clients and the firm of your choice.

Choose How You Will Focus: Using Your Visual, Auditory, or Tactile Senses

You can use mindfulness in all areas of your life and surroundings. We pass up so many beautiful moments by listening to all the noise inside our heads and not fully appreciating the beauty of any given moment, even while working. How you focus begins by setting your intention to have present moment awareness. Take a deep breath and follow the air flowing in and out. You become conscious of

36

spaciousness directly and indirectly. First, you recognize direct openness within—no internal chatter, just presence. Indirectly, you focus on the outer realm and a connection to sights, sounds, and touch. Inner and outer are united in your focus. Here is an exercise that can help you focus.

Informal Practice: Acute Sense Perceptions

Before you start this exercise, decide what your intention is. I like the mantra "let present moment awareness be with me." You can choose any mantra that is most helpful to you to set an intention, and then drop the mantra. Now start by observing the colors of the object of your focus right in front of you. Notice everything about this object. Let's say you're at your desk. Observe the colors of the items on your desk: pen, file, cup, and computer. Notice everything about these objects.

Next, listen intensely to the sounds in your office. Not the details of any conversations around you, but just pure sounds. The footsteps of people walking, the sound of the computer keyboard as you tap a key as a letter pops up on the screen in front of you. How do these sounds inform you?

Moving onto the sense of touch, are your hands active? Are you feeling the pen in your hand, the chair you are sitting on, and your feet on the floor? As you are fully engaged in the present moment, ask yourself: "What do I hope to accomplish today?" Write it down in a state of acute presence. Goal setting and presence practice are linked; with the step you are taking now, you know full well what you want to accomplish today.

Mindful seeing, hearing, and sensing can be practiced almost anytime and anywhere because our sense perceptions are available to us continuously. If something is particularly unpleasant, such as loud music, car alarms, or office chatter, bring attention to the sound itself without analyzing it. On a more basic level, the mind simply hears the sound waves. Auditory sounds are ubiquitous; you can't escape them. Even if you isolated yourself in a soundproof room, you'd still hear internal sounds of your heartbeat, your pulse, or ringing in your ears. Whatever you see, hear, or touch in your environment, try not to judge it as good or bad. Notice how these sense perceptions come and go as transient events.

Question

I believe I listen—what are you referring to when you write "listen to the sounds intensely and not the details of the conversation"? What is the purpose?

All creative and genuine solutions to problems come from silence. The stillness within. You have the potential and deep desire to learn, grow, and evolve when you tap into the stillness. When you notice the stillness, you aren't actually listening to anything in particular. Your primary focus in listening is the silence within, and the secondary purpose is in the details of the conversations. Anything that is really important for you to hear, you will hear when you have your ear primarily turned internally. Get the inside right, and then the external will flow with a birthing of something brand new.

Focus "On Purpose"

By focusing intently, you are establishing a framework that makes it a little more difficult for your mind to wander. The difference between this type of focus and concentration is that in mindfulness we focus in an open and non-judgmental way. So it is the quality of attention that is vital, not the actual focus itself. That is why it is important to identify your intent before you begin.

While focusing, notice what is happening in the moment and acknowledge it by letting go of any distractions. Try to remain aware without wanting to change anything. That is being open in a non-judgmental way. Observe and take in any and all observations. When you become aware, you will eventually change unwanted patterns. Have a look inside. What kind of thoughts is your mind producing? What do you feel? Direct your focus into your inner body. Is there any tension or contraction in your body? Once you detect this unease or tightening, explore the ways in which you are denying or resisting life in this moment. With practice, your inner state will become sharper and more resilient.

Question

> How can I manage my time at work, especially during busy season? The day is filled with distractions, and I find it hard to account for my billable hours. What can I do?

So, you think you are not managing your time properly. What are you feeling? "I am irritated and frustrated." What can you delegate? "I do that but it doesn't help." What do you want? "I want to feel light and release the pain in my shoulders." What else? "I want to be more organized and ask for what is necessary to do my job." Have you spoken to someone at your firm about your frustration? "No, I am concerned about how that might be interpreted." "I see that my frustration is causing the pain in my shoulders." "I sense that my own blaming and anger is in part creating the frustration."

Your focus on your body and listening to the warning signs has helped you become aware that your story about managing your time has placed restrictions on yourself. You now have the choice to remove those restrictions and create space to take the next steps. Becoming aware through purposeful, focused attention enabled you to be open and non-judgmental to your situation. You discovered a new mindset and a commitment to be more assertive. You have transcended and yet included your "to-do" list, which was put in place by the person you were yesterday. You have touched your authentic voice. What is really important to you now? A practice that may further help you manage emotions like resentment and irritation is self-compassion. We'll talk more about compassion in Chapter 7.

Focus on the Present Moment

The world we live in is filled with distractions. We have computers, tablets, iPads, cellphones, all of which serve to fill our life with "noise." We are so distracted these days that we aren't even aware of how much noise there is in our lives. Our work environment is not much different, unless we can use some of the tools mindfulness makes available to us.

When you practice mindfulness, you are letting go of the noise. You are paying attention to your thoughts, feelings, surroundings, and physical sensations. These distractions are not wrong in and of themselves; it is how we pay attention and the quality of our relationship to them that is vital. What is your relationship with these devices at work?

I have noticed that an intention to make the present moment the primary purpose of my life is enough to help me stay focused in an open way. In doing so, I am letting go of my internal "protectors," the time-honored egoic strategies, or shadow elements, that are the root of being stuck. Einstein said, "The formulation of the problem is often more essential than the solution." What is important to you in your work? What is holding you back? Try to contemplate something other than the technical and business aspects of your job. What is stopping you from realizing this? Write down your answers in a journal.

Question

> My accounting career has provided me with a very good living, wonderful relationships, and a lifetime of successful achievements combined with a sense that I made a difference in some of my clients' lives who have told me so. Why should I practice mindfulness? I don't feel I need it.

If that is the case right now for you, let's talk next year. What you refer to as very good living, relationships, achievements, and client accolades are transient by nature, to be enjoyed when they come to you. But they don't last. In mindfulness, the present moment is the central portal into a deeper state of being.

Think back to when you started out in the accounting profession. How much has changed? Quite a lot. Now, sense within yourself by going deeper and ask: Who am I now? Then, do the same back to when you first started out as a junior accountant. Who was I back then? If you look closely, you'll notice that you are the same; yet, the surface level of things, including your personality, has changed. Mindfulness helps you get in touch with the life force that many people ignore throughout their lives, especially at work.

Deep down, each of us wants to experience our connection with the Divine essence, not just on special days or when sitting alone. We can bring it to our workplace and see it all around in people, places, and things underneath the surface level of personalities. Mindfulness can

41

help you build that muscle, which is infinite. Mindfulness can also help you recognize the obstacles to living in a state of presence and going *beyond balancing the books.*

Informal Practice: Open Awareness

This exercise is about helping you make the present moment your primary focus and goal through open awareness: being mindful of whatever happens during each moment in the continual progression of present moments. It includes whatever arises in your mind and body, whether sensory perceptions or thoughts and emotions. On the surface you may be very still, or not, while internally you are having an influx of physical and mental experiences.

Working together, your mind and body interact through constantly changing mental and physical stimuli such as thought, emotions, physical sensations, sights, sounds, smells, and tastes. With open awareness, observe what is presently forefront in your mind and body.

If nothing is especially dominant to draw your focus, remember you can always go back to your breath, sensations, sounds, thoughts, and emotions to anchor yourself in the present moment.

Here is an exercise in open awareness that will help you become aware of the judgmental nature of the mind. The goal of this exercise is for you to experience for yourself the following:

- Nothing is 100% good or 100% bad.
- Everything has some good and some bad.
- By judging, we ignore the endless complexity of situations.

Recall a painful event or some loss in your career as a CPA, and respond to the following questions by writing your answers in a journal.

- What were the most negative consequences of this event?

42

- Now, focus on the positive aspects and the ways in which the experience has benefited you as a person and as a CPA. For instance, how has the experience helped you better meet the challenges of the future?
- What did you learn from the experience?
- How have you changed or grown as a person and as a CPA as a result of the experience?

Here is a guided open-awareness meditation from my YouTube channel: bit.ly/meditationopenawareness.

Non-Judgmental Awareness

Without distractions, we can allow ourselves to set our intention to pay attention. When you allow yourself to focus on one thing, you notice everything about the moment and the object of your intention. You are in a state of non-judgment awareness. Your mind is not cluttered, and you are open to sensations that you might not have felt in a while. You are not being distracted by your thoughts, feelings, and physical limitations.

When judgments are negative, the inability to see through their relative and subjective nature can have a negative effect on well-being. When judging, a comparison is made between how reality is perceived and how one believes reality should be according to one's conditioning. A construct that is closely linked with subjective judgment and further illustrates its possible downside is dichotomous thinking. Many judgments are characterized by dichotomous categorizations of terms: things are labeled as good or bad, beautiful or ugly, or a success or failure, for instance. Likewise, dichotomous thinking involves the tendency to think in terms of binary opposites (e.g., all or nothing) and involves making judgments along the end of the continuum. This particular inclination leaves people evaluating the world in a static, mutually exclusive, either-or mindset.

Write What Mindfulness Means to You

After you practice mindfulness, write down your experience. What does it mean for you? What did you notice? You can start slow; you don't have to start out practicing mindfulness one hour a day. Gradually build up your mindfulness practice a little at a time. Write down your observations each time so you can look back and reflect on where you began and where you are now. Researchers have convincingly argued that mindfulness is a natural human capacity that untrained laypersons can experience (4).

Mindfulness has both formal and informal practices that can be learned and integrated into your ordinary daily experience.

Formal Mindfulness Practices

Body Scan

The body scan, as the name suggests, entails bringing awareness to each part of your body. During this practice, you move your awareness, starting on your feet, paying attention to physical sensations present in each area. After focusing attention briefly on a particular region of your body, you move on to the next region. During this exercise, you will be distracted by thoughts, feelings, sounds, and bodily sensations. All of that is normal. When this happens, as it will, gently guide attention back to the focused area without self-criticism or reacting in frustration. Sometimes you might become aware in certain regions of a particularly painful or unpleasant sensation (i.e., back pain). Instead of altering, ignoring, or suppressing these sensations, you simply notice them on a moment to moment basis.

Here is a guided meditation for the body scan from my YouTube channel: bit.ly/meditationthebodyscan.

Seated Meditation

Just as the body scan uses your body as an object of attention, the seated meditation uses breath as the main focus of attention. Sitting in an upward position with a straight back, eyes closed or head tilting downward, you begin by noticing your breath. You notice the physical sensations of breathing, such as the air moving into your nostrils and your chest expanding. As soon as your mind begins to wander, you notice the distracting thought without evaluating it and kindly return attention to your breath.

Informal Mindfulness Practices

Awareness of Routine Activities

Routine activities are performed regularly, often daily. Most routine activities require little conscious attention because they are highly automatic. Some examples include driving to work, taking a shower, eating lunch, or walking to the copier. Bringing mindfulness to daily activities at work, including your body movements, sights, and sensations, takes ordinary daily activities and makes them more alive and enjoyable.

45

Taking a morning shower is a good example. I often think about the day's to-do list or the previous day's conversations while taking a shower. When this happens, sadly, I miss the soothing touch of the water on my skin, the real sense and smell of the soap, the sheer flowing of the water, and, more importantly, the sense that I am present and awake during this experience. Of course, thoughts and distractions emerge, so we notice and bring attention back to the feeling and sense of the experience of taking a shower. You are present.

Body Awareness

The awareness of your body that is cultivated through the body scan meditation can be implemented in daily life by paying attention to your body regularly throughout the day in various circumstances. When you pay attention to your body, you are more likely to enhance early detection and prevention of physical complaints. I have discovered that body awareness contributes to calmness, clarity, and less stress.

Awareness of Impulses and Reactive Patterns

Many daily patterns of thinking and action are habitual (unconscious) reactions to experiences and events. Failing to perform well may immediately trigger negative self-critical thoughts and judgments. The experience of sadness can result in a direct attempt to push away unwanted feelings. You can ask yourself: What is hiding underneath the sadness? The loss of a client can make us feel sad. But underneath the symptom of sadness, there may be fear. Becoming mindfully aware of the fear helps to lessen it and build resilience. I have found that lessening the gap between the emotions of sadness and fear and mindful attention directed at these emotions is the key for transforming the negative feelings into a sense of calm and peace.

Receiving a snide remark from a colleague may cause you to raise your voice and say things you might regret afterward. In this example, automatic patterns guide your behavior. Mindfulness is awareness of these patterns moment to moment. Even if you become aware of these patterns afterward, it is still beneficial.

Here is a guided meditation for facing challenges from my YouTube channel: bit.ly/meditationfacingchallenges.

Business Settings

Practicing mindfulness in a business context involves interacting with another person as a single point of focus. Instead of multi-tasking during a conversation with a colleague or thinking about what to say next, attention is paid to the current conversation, in contrast to identifying with your own assumptions and reacting impulsively. This book is filled with many examples of practicing mindfulness in a business setting as well as other environments.

Informal Practice

Pick a few daily office routines and practice them mindfully. Some possible examples could be setting a single point of focus while preparing a financial statement, listening to the pause in a conversation (the silence in between sounds), walking across the room or to the copier, or riding the elevator and noticing the sounds and space inside the elevator without any thoughts, comments, or opinions of your fellow elevator companions.

The Science of Mindfulness

Mindfulness is now popular not only in mainstream culture but also in science, as evidenced by the number of monthly publications in scientific journals (5). These studies provide valuable insights about the effects of mindfulness and the underlying attributes that give rise to the positive effects on individuals who practice presence. Mindfulness is not simply relaxing; it aids in observation, attention regulation, emotional coping, and time perception. In other words, mindfulness practice can help you detect when attention wanders and strengthen your capacity to monitor thoughts and emotions, a significant aspect of successful self-regulation (6).

Science has confirmed that mindfulness involves focusing attention on the present moment. When mindful, you direct attention to the internal and external phenomena occurring at each moment of awareness (7). In contrast, when you ruminate—such as when your mind is preoccupied with a negative experience at work like unhealthy competition—you are drawn away from the present moment. By cultivating mindfulness skills, you become skilled at focusing on the present moment, which may facilitate directing attention away from ruminative thoughts.

Worry about work situations and careers can have all sorts of negative consequences to well-being. Sometimes, our work situation causes us to feel less in control of our lives. Research has shown that mindfulness helps to reduce these effects by decreasing the number and duration of worry episodes and decreasing worry-related anxiety and depressive symptoms (8).

On a physiological level, mindfulness is characterized by lower respiration and heart rates, longer exhalation time, and increased heart variability. On the other hand, worry is characterized by higher respiration and heart rates, shorter expiration time, and decreased heart rate variability (9).

Mindfulness training has resulted in a significant decrease in rumination in otherwise healthy individuals experiencing significant amounts of stress (10).

Research has demonstrated that much of people's thinking and actions are automatic (11). A growing body of empirical findings suggests that mindfulness practice can lead to de-automatization. For example, past research has shown that higher levels of mindfulness are associated with lower levels of impulsive behavior and higher levels of self-control (12). Mindfulness training has also been found to reduce the automatic process of stereotyping (13). We will address mindfulness, diversity, and inclusion in Chapter 10.

The Three B's of Beyond Balancing the Books

As we begin this journey, the three B's of *beyond balancing the books* will be our guiding light and the essential components for knowing who you are beyond what you do. The practice of presence and accounting can be integrated together like a seedling watered with your tender hand to help it grow. The three B's of this practice are as follows:

- *Beyond*: be your authentic self
- *Balancing*: merge human and being into one
- *Books*: accounting for what really counts—living your life with meaning and purpose

Mindfulness is the framework through which you can realize and sustain the three B's at work and in daily life. We will be diving deeper into the three B's throughout the book.

Chapter 2

Presence and the Vertical Dimension

Attention is like a flame that burns out past and present hurts.

—J. Krishnamurti

I love accounting. From the very beginning, it was love at first T account. What I love most about accounting is the rational, logic-based requirement that T accounts need to be balanced.

According to accounting theory, the debits on the left should equal the credits on the right. From that balanced vantage point, accountants can then help their clients make business decisions, often leading to sustainability and growth while maintaining their objectivity and independence. The work you do as an accountant is meaningful in so many ways, and you are very talented in what you do. Your training has prepared you well.

As your clients look to you for guidance, especially during challenging times, it is vital for you to provide self-guidance and compassion toward yourself. Most of us have not been taught how to take care of ourselves mentally, emotionally, and spiritually. Instead, we tend to be hard on ourselves, especially during busy season when expectations of our performance are much higher. Your rational and logic-based training does not help in this or in discovering what is really important to you.

Mindfulness is the framework through which you can realize and sustain the three B's at work and in daily life.

In this book, I will use the T account as a metaphor for accounting *beyond balancing the books*, which is ultimately the balance inherit in the present moment. If we are honest with ourselves and look closely, our attention each day in providing accounting services is dominated by past and future thinking and the corresponding emotions that accompany those thoughts, often stressful, anxious, and sometimes filled with irritation or anger. The internal dialogue in your head might be: "What if this happens?" "I should have been more guarded." "Did he really mean that?" "I may have missed that item on the supplementary schedule." And the list goes on and on. You'll notice that these thoughts are oriented toward the past or future. Accounting is by nature past and future oriented, so it is easy to slip into the trap of the wandering mind.

As we navigate our way through each day dealing with money matters and using the gifts of conceptual, rational, and logical thinking to balance the books in a traditional sense, you do a great service for your clients and the public. Of course, accountants do so much more than balancing the books. So, it is important to understand at the outset that I am using that phrase to encompass all the services that accountants provide to their clients and their organizations.

Let's return to the T account theory. In this metaphor, the debit side of the T account represents the past. There are many ways your past can show up in your work, especially with unprocessed pain. In reviewing your client's books, your mind may start to drift. This is a very common occurrence when your work is focused on past events through conceptual thinking and you start to develop a "story" about such events. Before you know it, your unconscious mind picks up on signals that trigger a reaction in you, often irritation or sadness. The credit side represents the future. You may worry about what your next project might be—"Will I be able to complete it within budget?" "Will I be micromanaged again?"

Or, let's say you are forecasting business operations and budgeting, and a sense of anxiety comes up for you when the numbers don't meet budget. In these instances, you do your best to maintain a professional stance. As you do this work, you may unfortunately notice your mind drifting, often caught up and drawn into past and future thinking without realizing it. This is normal. Our thinking is sometimes scattered, and the internal dialogue might ask, "Did I miss that adjusting journal entry on XYZ client?" or "What will I eat for dinner tonight?" or "Will my documentation pass muster with quality review?"

While these thoughts can be useful and help in a certain sense, they are often accompanied with anticipation, worry, and anxiety. This internal voice chatter fuels corresponding emotions through which we call on our habitual reactions to solve problems or to address issues, often without awareness. This is where mindfulness comes in. What if you could "look" at client problems through the lens of both awareness and conceptual thinking simultaneously without the added layers of habitual reactive patterns?

Unfortunately, these habitual patterns often lead to irritation, anger, worry, and boredom, especially when things don't go your way or you face a challenging situation. Let's say a banker is restricting funding to one of your clients due to certain financial ratios not meeting benchmarks. This surprising news brings up some underlying emotion in you surrounding the scarcity of money. Perhaps when you were younger, your family had scarce resources and you experienced some form of trauma around money issues that you have not fully addressed in your body with awareness. Or, you may have personally been denied credit from a bank, which brings up fear and anxiety. You may experience a remark from a senior partner as a micro aggression. More about micro aggression in Chapter 10.

These situations and others like them cause pain and suffering, but they can also be learning opportunities when you use mindfulness to tap into the wisdom of the body. As accountants, we bring our entire self to the job, and though very few will admit it, people and situations affect us. Accountants may sometimes not want to show their own weaknesses surrounding money due to pride, fear, or shame. This unhealed wound affects well-being, even if you can "handle" the client issue on the surface level. This past and future orientation, often unconscious, automatically starts to take over. Before you know it, your mind is wandering and you are not present.

Hafiz, the well-beloved fourteenth-century Sufi poet, writes about money in his poem "When Your Portfolio Takes a Hit." Here is my translation:

> Contemplate this over some morning coffee
> or tea or when your portfolio takes a big hit:
> Zero is where the real fun begins; there is too much
> counting everywhere else!

Yes, our clients sometimes get rattled when they take a financial hit. Accountants are no exception to this emotional roller coaster concerning their own financial situation. Mindfulness helps us go beyond a merchant transactional mindset, where there is a tit-for-tat engagement with others and even with ourselves as we track wins and losses. The zero point is the present moment where new beginnings and the fun really starts.

With mindfulness, the same picture can look much different, as Hafiz writes regarding the zero point. Let's say you are analyzing a new tax provision, and as you read the regulations, you apply your conceptual thinking mind in a focused and clear way as we discussed in Chapter 1. With focus, you then step back out of thought and into awareness for a few seconds, and then back into thinking as you read the regulations. This process of stepping in and out of thought is the basis for creative solutions to client matters and our own financial issues. I wasn't taught this in business school, studying for the CPA exam, on the job, or in mainstream culture. Were you?

Albert Einstein pointed to this very process when he wrote, "You can't solve a problem with the same level of consciousness that created it." In other words, when you look closely, problems are created from the unconscious thinking mind. So, in order to find a truly creative solution, as pointed out by Einstein, it is vital to direct attention to another state of consciousness to solve it. The state of consciousness he was pointing toward is awareness.

Mainstream science takes the position that consciousness is a byproduct of brain activity. However, findings in quantum physics and "post-modern science" suggest otherwise. Physicist Lothar Schafer writes in *Infinite Potential: What Quantum Physics Reveals About How We Should Live*, "The discovery of quantum phenomena signifies an evolutionary metamorphosis of the human consciousness, a leap of the evolution of life into a new human species." Eckhart Tolle points out that "the physical brain is more like a radio receiver for consciousness." In other words, consciousness uses the brain, but that is only a tiny aspect of consciousness. You cannot look in a certain place and find consciousness. *Presence* arises as experiences (or, more accurately, as "non-experiences") and can't be reduced or explained away in terms of brain activity. *Presence* is the primordial essence in which everything else arises: your true nature.

Returning to our metaphor, the gap between thoughts is the center, right down the middle of the T account—the vertical dimension. It is called "the present moment," where awareness always dwells, now and now and now. Mindfulness is the key to knowing who you are in a deeper and fuller way. It is not necessary that you believe this. Try now to sense where these words are pointing you toward. You have been doing this throughout your life, but now you can make it more conscious through awareness. As a byproduct, it will help you minimize any anxiety, stress, or boredom while building *presence* power, so to speak, within yourself. This practice of mindful attention will heal old wounds. And on top of that, it will make your work as an accountant and your personal life much more enjoyable at the same time. The practice itself is the reward; everything else is an add-on.

Instead of just focusing on the debits and the credits in this metaphor, you'll shift attention to that line right down the center of the T account as a focused point of intention and attention, which in this metaphor is the *Now*: awareness itself. Drawing a vertical line through the center of your being, you establish a vantage point centered and rooted in mindful *presence* while visiting the debits and credits of your work and life as required. **You'll be accounting for what really counts. You'll be going *beyond balancing the books.*** This does take some practice because of our conditioning, but it is much more enjoyable and has far greater rewards than constantly labeling and evaluating. Let's turn now to the five core components of mindfulness.

The Five Core Components of Mindfulness

1. Attention and Noticing
2. Open Awareness
3. Acknowledgment and Acceptance
4. Detachment
5. Conscious Choice

1. Attention and Noticing

An essential aspect of mindfulness practice is focused attention on the present moment. You can do this right now. Attention can be focused internally such as your thoughts, feeling, emotions, and physical sensations. Attention can also be directed on an external situation such as a conversation or other sense perceptions.

You'll notice that I don't call attention "your" attention. To do so would make it something you have like any other object. Attention is not a possession of "yours" or "mine." Attention is unconditional spaciousness, freedom, and at a deep level, love. You can't claim ownership to it. To know things is to know them in their first cause. Attention is like the light of a lantern. In making it "your" attention, you would become the lantern rather than its light. That is the shift in consciousness that can change everything for you. Can you sense into this right now as you stop and pause the reading? We will use the lantern metaphor throughout this book.

As you set your intentions in practice, distractions normally occur that will draw attention and take you away from the present moment. As you notice this happening, it becomes part of the practice to gently return back to attention. For this reason, setting intention on an anchor such as sense perceptions, breath, or inner body—whichever one you prefer—will greatly help you to be present. Then, when distractions happen, you'll gently guide attention back to your anchor right down the center of your being (heart center). Picture the T account again. In other words, mindfulness practice can help you learn to detect when attention wanders to either the debit or credit side of the T account, thus strengthening your capacity to monitor thoughts and behaviors, a crucial aspect of successful self-regulation (14).

The process of focused attention can be compared to using a lantern. Attention is the light of the lantern that you are holding. Mindfulness practice and exercises help you build the muscles in the hand that is holding the lantern. Most of us have not been trained in this way. Rather, we become the lantern, not its light. As you direct attention to a specific area (i.e., thought, emotion, physical sensations, conversation, or even your detailed accounting work), you make the object visible to the one who is holding the lantern—namely you. In other words, attention allows you to make things "visible" and for "you" to become aware of things.

You may ask, "Wasn't I doing this anyway?" Yes, when you are aware. You have the ability to direct attention in your accounting duties, while being aware of the awareness (the light) anchored in the present moment. This is a very pleasant practice and can change everything for you. As you read this now, focusing attention on the words on this page, kindly invite attention to notice the space in between the words on the page and after each sentence. You may notice a slowing down. This is a good practice to help you get started and train the muscle of awareness.

By slowing down your reading and many other activities, you'll continue to build the attention muscle on your balance sheet. Your mind won't like this, but do it anyway. Attention is a little bit like a young child, wanting your hand to care for it and some love to grow more fully. When you do this, you become like a little child. Not in the sense of an adolescent or preschooler. Rather, you will have taken a leap and transcended thinking as your primary state by entering into a deeper state of attention. This state has similarities with a child's mindset before conceptual thought first develops. J. Krishnamurti puts it this way: "The day you teach the child the name of the bird, the child will never see that bird again."

However, since all of us are moving through the egoic state of consciousness at some level, which includes identification with thoughts and emotions, when we come out of a stage, so to speak, we now sense a deeper wholeness. This is what physicist Lothar Schafer is pointing toward when he writes about an evolutionary leap into a "new human species." This wholeness includes everything that came before. In other words, it has been transcended and included.

As we transcend and include thought as our primary way of being in the world, we become a little bit like children. Yet we have gone through the conceptual thinking state of human development and come out with far greater knowledge than any IQ test can quantify. In fact, IQ tests and scores pale in comparison to the depth of intelligence available to you with awareness. When you look at a tree with the pure perception of awareness and without labels, you can sense the life of the tree and a kind of connection. In my opinion, this post-thinking state is the destiny of each one of us filled with wisdom, kindness, and gratitude as our true nature. These virtues are then guided by the flame of attention, which we could call love, as the virtue of virtues. Paradoxically, this is all available to us now.

The Compelling Forces of Attention

There are two primary forces at play as we focus attention. On the one hand, there is the object that is demanding attention (thought, emotion, conversation, etc.). On the other hand, there is you: the one that can regulate attention in holding the lantern—that line in the center of the T account. When we are not mindful (lost in thoughts, emotions, conversation), these two forces become a single phenomenon, leaving little or no space for yourself. Your consciousness is soaking in thoughts, emotions, and the content of your conversations. You really are not there, although it may seem like it because this state is so normal. You are unaware (unconscious) when this is happening to you.

I use the term "unconscious" to mean that you are totally identified with your thoughts and emotions to the extent you are willing to fight, argue, defend, and so forth, to prevent being hurt in some way, such as getting fired or attacking back. We all know what can happen when this occurs as we get lost in a vicious cycle of thinking and reacting, and it is very often negative. It is not a pleasant place to be.

Everyone has the ability and the will to focus attention. Let's say you're sitting at your desk preparing documents for a client who is under audit by the IRS. As you focus attention on the documents, a conversation right outside your office is distracting you away from your work. At first, you hear the sounds, and then attention draws you into the specifics of the conversation. You merge with the conversation. You really have no choice; it is an automatic unconscious response.

In mindfulness, we become aware of the moment when attention moves away from our focus. We can "catch" ourselves and guide attention back to our work and to the vertical line in the middle of our T account. This is called attention regulation. According to some researchers, attention regulation is the most important form of self-control. Attention plays a key role in all forms of regulation including regulating emotions, impulses, and thoughts (15).

Meister Eckhart, the thirteenth-century mystic, teaches how to deal with distractions when he writes:

Now some good people maintain that they have progressed so far that the presence of physical objects no longer affects their senses. But this is not the case. I shall never reach a point where a hideous noise is as pleasing to my ears as sweetly sounding strings. But this much is possible—that a rational, God conformed will (presence) may be free of all natural pleasures and, upon hearing such a noise, commands the sensual will (mature ego) not to be concerned with it so that the latter replies: "I gladly agree!" Then conflict will turn to joy, for what we must strive for with great effort (work) becomes our heart's delight, and only then does it bear fruit.

Frustration, boredom, and lack of energy at work have their roots in unfocused attention and distractions. There is a much more effective way to deal with difficult people and situations than reframing your thoughts about a situation or wishing it away. With reframing, you are still in the thinking mind, which by nature is always transient, relative, and subjective. Wishing for a problem to go away doesn't work; rather, it compounds the problem.

With attention, you are in a state of non-resistance to whatever is occurring in this moment. You'll discover an abiding peace in the midst of your work and any "outside" turmoil. You'll be in a mindfulness moment. The only absolutely true moment. You don't have to "do it" all the time. Touching base with the here and now naturally strengthens your resolve and brings peace to you shedding a new light on your day. You'll notice that mindfulness is a state of being and not something you do.

Through open and focused attention, peace is present even if just in the background. Research illustrates, to the extent you focus mindfully, attention largely gauges your overall well-being (16).

Mindfulness teaches us to focus attention on what is happening in the moment. This can be the first step into a deeper dimension of consciousness. As you hold the lantern, instead of turning the lantern to objects in consciousness such as thought, emotions, and sensory perceptions, you direct the attention of the lantern onto the light itself. Ask yourself: "Who is aware?" There are famous inscriptions at the temple of Apollo in ancient Greece: "You Are" and "Know Thyself." The conceptual mind can't understand the deep meaning of these words. These two phrases direct your attention to attention itself or awareness of awareness, whatever words you prefer to use, to know yourself as the timeless and formless mindfully aware *presence.*

Mindfulness has been practiced for thousands of years in all parts of the world under different names, approaches, and traditions. However, it all comes down to knowing yourself at the deepest level of your being. *Beyond balancing the books.*

Now, we are stepping into an area that is even more difficult to put into words, so as you read this, I invite you to slow down and pay more attention to the gaps or spaces in between the words on this page. What do you notice? How is the space opening up for you? When you focus attention on attention itself, the past and future fall way—you have discovered pure awareness.

This simple yet profound practice is a game changer. It seems like nothing, yet it encompasses everything. You discover that you are the light—the light of the present moment—and your accounting work shines brighter, is more engaging, more joyful, less stress-based, and worry-free. You discover that deep down your role as accountant is not who you are in your essence. You are the attention that guides your work right down the center of the T account.

You have discovered the essence of love, and your work and relationships helped you do that.

You are no longer run by outer circumstances constantly on edge for the next attack from someone in the office or an unruly client, no matter how technically good you are. Rather, your inner state determines your outer state and how you respond. In mindful consciousness, accounting services are not really about what you do: needing to do right, providing the quickest turnaround, issuing the most comprehensive financial report on the planet, or making the top 100 firms. Rather, it's all about how you provide your services in the present moment in an open, non-judgmental way and knowing yourself and your true nature.

Question

> I have been assigned to several clients, and I am finding the work to be boring. I am only staying in public accounting to get my experience and then move into private industry. In the meantime, the boredom is causing me to seek other activities to make me feel better. What can I do?

What does boredom feel like to you in your body? Where in your body does it show up? Once you notice this, place attention on those areas and sense into the feeling if you can. What does the boredom really want? "When I do that, I feel I want to run away from it. It is uncomfortable." I understand. Boredom is not used to attention. It wants you to run away and seek other activities to temporarily make you happy. However, this practice of mindful attention, even if only a few seconds at a time, will help you. You'll start to become more aware of the feeling, and it will shorten in duration little by little. You may reach a point that your relationship to boredom is friendlier, and you'll know it is serving a purpose for you. Be compassionate with yourself. We'll be addressing compassion in the workplace in Chapter 7.

Formal Practice: Awareness of Awareness Meditation

Dr. Dan Siegel developed the Wheel of Awareness practice as a way to practice becoming mindfully aware (17). The wheel offers a visual metaphor (see Exhibit 1) for the way the mind works. The center of the wheel, the hub, is the area that we become aware of.

Exhibit 1: Wheel of Awareness

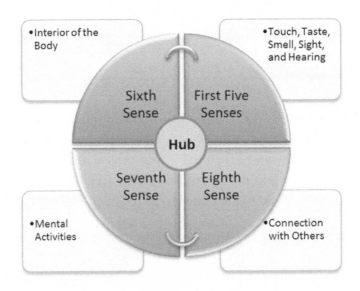

Source: Dan Siegel/Mind Your Brain, Inc.

From the hub, we can choose to focus our attention on (i.e., become mindfully aware of) both internal and external experiences. Awareness of internal experiences is represented by the areas of the wheel that park our thoughts, images, feelings, and bodily sensations.

Awareness of external experiences is represented by an area of the wheel that parks our sense of connection to others. In essence, within the metaphoric hub is the sense of knowing; within the rim of the wheel is that which is known, such as our five senses, the sixth sense of our bodily sensations, our mental life of emotions and thoughts, and our relation to people and the planet.

In this *presence* practice, you start by visualizing a wheel. This wheel has a central hub, an outer rim, and four quadrants in between. In this metaphor on how the mind is structured, the hub represents our awareness, and the quadrants represent anything that we can be aware of, including sensory awareness (i.e., what we see, hear, smell, taste, and touch), bodily awareness (what we can sense physically), mental activities (such as emotions, thoughts, memories, and sensations), and our sense of connection to things outside ourselves (such as other people and the natural world).

The aim of this practice is to bring forth a full sense of connection and awareness to both yourself and the world around you. I invite you to read each step in this practice and then pause and drop into what these words are pointing you toward. Then, when you are ready, move on to the next step. Journaling your observations at the end can help you in reflecting on your experience.

To start, find a comfortable meditation position, sitting straight and in a position that signifies dignity. Allow your spine to be straight and long, and let your shoulders drop and relax. Rest your hands in your lap, and, if you wish, gently close your eyes.

- Become aware of the flow and rhythm of your breathing. There is no need to adjust your breathing in any way; simply notice it exactly as it is.
- Now, bring to mind the image of the wheel. Imagine the hub in the center and the four quadrants surrounding the hub. See the rim that includes everything. For each part of the practice, you will focus in on one aspect of the wheel, and become

aware of its contents. I guide you through the four quadrants in a meditation that can be found on my YouTube channel: bit.ly/oneheartyoutube. For now, let's continue with the guided meditation as you read this and pause periodically.

- I'd like to invite you to first turn attention to the top right quadrant, which parks your five senses. Focus in on this area of your wheel by engaging your sense of hearing. What do you hear? (Pause.) And now your sense of touch. What do you feel? (Pause.) And now your sense of smell. What do you notice? (Pause.) Now, gently open your eyes for a moment. What can you see? (Pause.)

- That is very nice. And now close your eyes again, and bring the wheel back into your awareness. Take a deep, slow breath here. Feel the air flowing in and out. Now I'd like to invite you to turn attention to the top left quadrant, which parks your sixth sense, the inner sensations of your own body. Take a few moments to scan through your body from head to toe, becoming aware of any and all physical sensations throughout: tingling, heat, contractions, tightness, numbness, and so forth. Take your time to move through every part of your body. Just notice, be open, and simply observe. (Pause.)

- You're doing well. Let's take another nice deep breath here. Breathe in through the nostrils, noticing the pause at the peak of the inhale, and then a letting go of the breath as you release the air with the exhale. And now, I'd like to invite you to turn attention to the bottom left quadrant, which parks the activities of your mind itself, including your emotions, thoughts, memories, beliefs, attitudes, and intentions. First, simply become aware of everything that is entering your mind at this moment. Welcome this mental activity into your awareness. What thoughts and feelings are showing up right now? (Pause.) Then, begin to notice how these internal experiences arise and pass. Do they come up quickly or gradually? Do they stay the same or move in and out? Do they have a certain vibrational frequency? Are there gaps between the different mental activities, or do they exist as one long mental stream? (Pause.)

- Beautiful. Let's take another nice deep breath here. Gently breathing in through the nostrils as your body expands and then gently exhaling and letting go. And we'll now bring attention to the center of the wheel, the hub, which is where awareness arises. The hub is "you" that has noticed everything so far in this practice—the part of you that is observing, listening, looking, focusing, and sensing. Take some time here as you bring forth this "awareness of awareness" (attention of attention) practice. This is the secret that is no longer a secret. Thank goodness!

- Wonderful. Let's take another deep, slow breath here, noticing the air flowing in and out of your body. And now turn attention to the bottom right quadrant of your wheel, which houses your sense of connection to the outside world. First, notice your connection to the people physically closest to you right now. (Pause for 15 seconds.) Expand this to people further away. (Pause for 15 seconds.) Then tap into your sense of connection to your loved ones, wherever they may be right now. (Pause for 15 seconds.) Finally, widen your sense of connection step by step to include those who live in your neighborhood, city, state, country, continent, in the whole world, and finally to all living beings on Earth and the natural world.

- As the meditation comes to an end, simply bring attention back to your breath, as you did at the beginning of the practice. You might want to take a few deep breaths here to ground yourself back into this moment. Then, when you are ready, gently open your eyes.

Reflection

- What did you feel during the exercise?
- Did you sense anything new or different about yourself?
- When do you think this practice could be usefully applied in your accounting position?

You can implement aspects of this practice during your busy day, perhaps between clients or right before a meeting.

As you continue to practice and start to develop your own sense of what mindfulness means to you, it will bring a clarity and harmony to your work as an accountant and life without separation. You will no longer have this strict dividing line. You will practice discernment, of course, and know what is true for you in the moment. You will begin to sense an authenticity that is with you wherever you may be, like Amy in the introduction to this book. The role-playing and storytelling resembling Larry will gradually fall away. This can bring up some fear as you will have stepped out of your comfort zone and into new territory. This new-found land is the interior dimension of being that is no longer neglected, especially during the work day.

Informal Practice: Attention and Striving

There is no need for striving. One of the common obstacles to mindful *presence* and practicing the essence of love is looking forward to a more perfect version of yourself. If you continue to think about this, you can be sure it won't happen. Instead of striving for your next promotion, pay raise, or client acquisition, let go of this deep-seated "striving" mindset, and go deeper into the present moment. Be aware of the mind's tendency to continue to strive for a better and more complete version of yourself. Inquire into the things you may be striving for and whether or not it is becoming a source of discontent for you. If this moment is unsatisfactory or unpleasant to you, make it a practice to simply accept things the way they are. This does take courage as you step into the unknown. From this vantage point, you may find it easier to move into a better relationship with your experience. This is vital and will change everything for you, including your ability to adapt and make real sustained changes in your work habits. You'll be more open to your environment because you'll be more open to yourself and therefore much more likely to achieve your goals.

2. Open Awareness

The practice of open awareness occurs when we drop the notion of opposites and let go of taking sides. In other words, we become aware of our judgments (good vs. bad or right vs. wrong). Rather than judging everything inside and outside ourselves, we bring forth a mindset that is aware of judgment. We see things in a fresh and new way instead of through the lens of our conditioned past. Typically, our minds automatically judge everyone and everything around us.

For instance, as an accountant working on a tax return, you may sometimes feel unpleasant emotions surrounding money if you believe a client is earning excess income. The accountant in this situation can act "professional" on the outside, but inside have a different perspective filled with negative emotions. The experience and relationship to money gets mixed up with the work done, and sometimes this conflict causes emotional pain. So, we form a judgment as an unconscious strategy to alleviate the pain. This is projecting pain silently onto another (the client) but keeping it to ourselves, where it lodges inside our body and wreaks havoc on our internal operating system.

We could simply suppress the feeling and ignore the pain. Both of these strategies are unhealthy. In open awareness, total attention is given without the observer (you, the holder of the lantern), and attention (light) observes the client's income situation in open awareness without division between the observer and that which is observed (the high income). The subjective judgment that caused you the conflict is transcended in an act of open awareness. You are not relinquishing your ability to apply conceptual thinking and logical reasoning in your work. In fact, your thinking is clearer and without the judgments that are subjective by nature. It is helpful to practice open awareness when you are taking a walk in nature or when you are not being challenged. This will build up your proverbial balance sheet and strengthen your current ratio!

For example, when you look at a tree in open awareness, you are not looking to define the tree as tall, wide, in bloom, or an elm tree. You just look at the so called "tree" without any labels. With practice, open awareness will help you see things that you never noticed or that you once observed through the veil of your conditioning of likes and dislikes. You still have preferences and opinions, of course, but they no longer take over your consciousness in a way that disturbs you or hurts others.

The Flow of Energy

Energy is always in motion. It never completely stands still. The nature of energy is to flow. Our pain and suffering arises when we try to stop or block this energy movement. We do this in one of two ways. First, we try to hold onto the energy that we enjoy. We want to work on certain clients. We want our client relationships to always be the same. We want our bodies never to age. When we're met with the inevitable, we're surprised or upset. Second, we try to hold back energy we don't like. We suppress, reframe, and distract ourselves from painful emotions. We are rude to clients we don't care for. We avoid certain partners or situations that cause us nervousness and fear.

All of this takes a toll on our well-being. Even in meditation, trying to hold back energy causes us frustration. We believe in the common misconception that in meditation we can stop our thoughts.

We finally feel free when we stop resisting the true nature of energy. One good way to remember this is by paying attention to the continuous movement of your breath. The breath is always with us and is always energy in flux.

Formal Practice: Breath Awareness Meditation

To begin this meditation on breath and energy flow, please bring awareness to the following:

- The present moment—make it your ally.
- How do your belly, chest, and head feel when you reflect on this topic?
- What emotions can you associate with these visceral feelings?
- What positive or negative stories do you believe surrounding this topic?
- Know others might have similar feelings about this topic.
- Think of how you might feel with increased awareness around this topic.
- When can you apply increased mindfulness on this topic in your accounting work?

Now, this meditation can help you become familiar with an awareness of movement through the movement of the breath.

- Find a comfortable seat that allows for an upright spine and an open chest.
- Close your eyes or gaze downward and softly turn attention inward.
- Breathe slowly and quietly in and out through your nose.
- Notice your breath not through your thinking mind, but through your body.
- Feel the slight upward lift of each inhale; feel the release of each exhale.
- Recognize the ever-present movement of your breath and body.

- Notice the stillness, and pause in between the inhale and exhale.
- Your mind, too, is always moving. Each time you notice that the movement of your mind has drawn attention away from your breath, return your awareness to it.
- Allow the movement of your mind without trying to stop it.
- You do not have to follow or chase the movement of your mind.
- Each time you notice attention is on a thought, return it to your breath.

Reflection

- What is your general experience with the meditation?
- Where in your body did you notice the movement of breath most clearly?
- Did you find it challenging to stay present with breath awareness?
- Do you think it is possible to recognize that your mind is active yet choose not to follow this activity?
- Do you think that with practice, you could learn to return to your breath more quickly once attention has wandered?
- In meditation, we become still, and yet we notice movement. Why is that?
- In what ways were you trying to "stop movement" because something felt good?
- What would it be like at work to be still and quiet despite an active mind?

- Do you think this exercise might change your relationship to your own mind and your own thoughts with practice? If so, how?

- How might you benefit from a greater acceptance of movement and change?

I invite you to journal your experience.

Even that which seems stable and solid is always in motion. If we were to zero in on the office furniture at work, we would see movement on a molecular level. The oldest trees in Central Park are still growing and changing. Our computers and devices are all in the process of getting older and breaking down. We suffer when we forget that this movement of energy is irrefutable. We suffer when we expect things, people, and circumstances to remain one way forever, and they don't.

Breath gifts us the constant reminder of movement and rest. It's always with us, reminding us that everything is in flux; then there is a pause, and once again everything is in the process of change.

The Nature of Reality

Mindfulness can help us realize that thoughts are just thoughts; they are not reality. By focusing attention on the present moment, we free ourselves from the tendency to obsess on thinking, and therefore make contact with our direct experience rather than a mental story. In open awareness, we let go of judging ourselves and everything around. We bring forth a mindset that is aware of judgment, thereby opening us up to take a fresh look at what is arising in the present moment. Our mind automatically judges things, people, and events as we constantly look at reality through the lens of judgment. We judge our staff more than is required for a review of their performance. A big part of each person's suffering is their judgments. Unfortunately, this is considered normal by most.

In mindfulness, we become aware of this tendency of the mind as we label people, things, and circumstances as good or bad. Keep in mind that there is nothing wrong with judgment unless we become overly identified with our judgments which, by definition, are subjective. Open awareness helps you to cut the cord of judgmental tendencies and look at reality in an open and fresh non-judgmental way.

The 20th century teacher and practitioner of *presence*, J. Krishnamurti writes in his notebook about a peak experience in open awareness:

> *It's as though everything stood still. There is no movement, no stirring, complete emptiness of all thought, of all seeing. There is no interpreter (judgments) to translate, to observe, to censor. An immeasurable vastness that is utterly still and silent. There is no space, nor time to cover that space (conceptual thinking). The beginning and the ending are here, of all things (present moment). There is really nothing that can be said about it. (18)*

Eckhart Tolle puts it this way:

> *When you step into the Now, you step out of the content of your mind. The incessant stream of thinking slows down. Thoughts don't absorb all of your attention anymore, don't draw you in totally. Gaps arise in between thoughts—spaciousness, stillness. You begin to realize how much vaster and deeper you are than your thoughts.*

Formal Practice: Open Awareness Meditation

- Let's begin by taking a moment to allow your body to settle.

- Find a comfortable position that allows your spine to be long but with a natural curve in the lower back.
- You can close your eyes or keep them open with a soft gaze downward a few feet.
- Let your belly and shoulders relax.
- I will lead you through an open awareness practice. Before we start, take a full breath in and a long breath out.
- We'll work on opening our awareness to whatever arises; thoughts, sensations, feelings, and sounds will come and go.
- Cultivate open awareness by practicing meeting whatever comes, trying not to focus on or place more or less weight on any one thing, as you breathe in and breathe out.
- If you feel yourself following an unpleasant thought or feeling, labeling it can be helpful. Use simple words like "thinking," "work," "irritation," or "excitement."
- When you realize you have gotten caught up in thinking, just come back to rest in the simple clear awareness of what's here now.
- Let's finish this open awareness practice by taking a full breath in and a long breath out.

I guide you in a meditation on "open awareness" on my YouTube channel. Here is the link: bit.ly/meditationopenawareness.

Informal Practice

Take a few minutes today to go for a walk with open awareness. While staying connected to your breath, see how many colors, shapes, sounds, smells, and sensations you notice. If you can't go outside, try this when walking in your office from one meeting to the next, with an emphasis on seeing things in a new way.

Reflection

- Was there anything that surprised you on your walk?
- What impact might taking an open awareness approach have on your work as a CPA?

3. Acknowledgment and Acceptance

Rather than resisting experiences internally—such as when you are assigned to work on a client that does not interest you, working late in tax season, or on the weekend—mindfulness is about cultivating an accepting stance within the context of the present moment. In other words, unpleasant experiences are not accepted forever, only the present moment experience is accepted. This is not a trick of the mind. There is a dimension in you far beyond thought that knows. In mindfulness, we rise above thinking and are aware. Acceptance and awareness merge as one.

Sometimes, the situation is too difficult to accept, so we can instead acknowledge it first and then see what develops. Nothing is forced in mindfulness practice, and that is the art of *presence.*

It is important to recognize that you can still take action, if possible, to either remove yourself or change the situation. You do so in an open, non-judgmental way. For example, you speak with the partner in charge or Human Resources expressing your desire and goal to work on a certain type of clients, perhaps in another industry. You do so without a storyline or angst. When fully present, it will come from an authentic place within you: *beyond balancing the books.* Then you can see what happens.

Many of us often experience sadness or anger over this type of situation. We think it will affect our career path if we don't work on certain type of clients or late every night in tax season. This is called worry. If this happens to you, rather than pushing the emotion away and not wanting reality to be as it is, use mindfulness to cultivate a "friendly" relationship with the emotion of sadness or anger and "look" at it in a fresh new way. Acceptance has nothing to do with accepting everything that happens to you, as when someone steals your wallet or falsely accuses you of an error in a malpractice claim. Mindfulness helps us in accepting the fear or anger that comes up in such situations. This is a big difference and fosters well-being.

> *Surrender comes when you no longer ask, "Why is this happening to me?" Acceptance of the unacceptable is the greatest source of grace in this world.*

> —Eckhart Tolle

Formal Practice: Pleasant vs. Unpleasant Situations

In this practice, we'll deepen our awareness of the tendency to label each of our experiences as good or bad, positive or negative.

We'll begin by working on physical sensations in the body, and then apply this same awareness to thoughts and emotions. Once we label something or someone as negative, we solidify that thing in our minds as being just one way.

And yet, we've all had experiences of disliking something that we later discovered a love for, or the experience of an enemy or a stranger who later became a friend, or a client who refused to pay a bill who later paid it and more.

We have also had experiences of labeling something as negative, only to find out that others disagree. So who is right? In the following exercise, we'll use mindfulness of the sensations in the body to develop an awareness of the ways in which our mind colors our perceptions of the world. Through this exercise, we'll open our hearts and our minds to the possibility that nothing is just one way. If we can practice curiosity instead of judgment, acceptance instead of resistance, we'll cause ourselves and others less pain, resulting in a workplace and an accounting career of greater ease and happiness.

Let's begin with the following seated meditation:

Set a timer for three, five, or seven minutes, whichever you prefer.

- Begin in a comfortable seat (your meditation posture) with your spine tall and neutral.
- Close your eyes or keep a soft gaze toward the ground in front of you.
- Breathe deeply yet quietly in and out through the nose.
- Turn your awareness inward toward your physical body.
- Beginning with your feet, notice any sensations in your body that are calling for attention.
- Without lingering too long on any one sensation, quickly label what you notice, and then decide whether it's pleasant, unpleasant, or neutral.
- For example, "tight knee: unpleasant" or "rise and fall of the chest: pleasant."
- Slowly move from the feet to the lower legs, upper legs, hips, belly, lower back, middle back and chest, upper arms, lower arms and hands, and back up the neck, the jaw, and the face.
- Without seeking any type of sensation in particular, remain open to the arising of sensations within your awareness.
- Notice the sensation, and then notice the label.
- Continue until you've scanned the whole body, or until the timer stops.

Reflection

- What was your general experience during the meditation?
- Can you describe the experience of body awareness?
- What did you notice about physical sensations, or your labeling of them, that was new to you?
- Did the labels arise automatically with each sensation? Or separately?
- How often did you label a sensation as neutral? Why do you think that's the case?
- Which did you notice more, pleasant sensations or unpleasant ones, or did they both arise evenly?
- Do you think it is possible to be aware of sensation, absent of an opinion or thought about it?
- If so, how would that skill be useful outside of your meditation?
- What do you think is the difference between "my knee hurts" and an "unpleasant sensation is arising in my knee?"
- How might it be of benefit to create more separation between "my knee" and "sensation in my knee?"

Now we turn to thoughts. Each time you find yourself moving away from your breath toward a thought, simply label that thought as pleasant, unpleasant, or neutral, and then quickly return attention to your breath. Repeat this as many times as you need to. There is no need to go searching for thoughts; no need to keep yourself busy. If you can, spend most of your time on the breath. After this exercise on thoughts, do the same for emotions such as frustration, happiness, bliss, anger, sadness, contentment, or excitement.

Informal Practice: Creating Quiet Time

At the core of mindfulness is awareness. Practicing mindfulness helps us become aware of our internal worlds, our thoughts, bodily sensations, emotions, feelings, and needs. Applying a mindful focus can be a challenging task, and creating quiet time can be equally challenging. In our work as accountants, we are continually required to focus our attention outside ourselves: on a tax return, spreadsheet, financial statements, and more so interacting with others and replying to e-mails. Every day, we devote a significant amount of time to our interactions with the world outside. During these interactions, we are surrounded by a considerable amount of noise (people talking, traffic sounds, beeps on the phone) and mental noise (planning, thoughts about what's next, rumination). Most people believe this is normal; I guess, that is true in a way. But there is another way. The way of silence.

Silence allows you to become aware of what is going on internally. When the external noise stops, the sound of the internal world becomes stronger. By deliberating and creating more moments of silence, you can become more acquainted with it again. I know this can be very challenging—it was for me. But with practice and guidance, you will learn to become more comfortable with silence, using it as a tool to connect with ourselves again even while practicing accounting. Silence facilitates a connection to our inner world because we no longer have to move beyond the noise that generally prevents us from doing so. I invite you to deliberately create more "quiet time" to strengthen mindful attention to your inner experience.

With acceptance, everything we notice has an equal potential to be lovely or unpleasant. The quality of that which we notice is not fixed. The world is not black and white, and neither is any one thing within the world. By placing greater attention on our tendency to label things as good, bad, or neutral, we begin to understand how these labels can change. Everything that arises in our awareness does so dependently. It depends on our minds. Once we realize that labels can change, we also realize that we have the power to change our world, ourselves, and others by intentionally changing the labels we apply. One step further, we can drop the practice of labeling completely.

When we become present with what we notice without judging it, we break down the barriers between "me" and the "world I notice." By softening boundaries in this way, we experience a greater connection between ourselves and our world.

4. Detachment

In practice, mindfulness helps us recognize a difference between what you are feeling and thinking and you, the one who observes the feeling and thought. You are aware that you are not the feeling or thought. This was a huge revelation for me. When you experience anxiety, there is a space between the experience of anxiety and you, the observer of the experience of anxiety. This is detachment. There is a subject-object relationship. We all know what can happen to us when we identify with an emotion like anxiety. The emotion takes us over, and we start to take our thoughts seriously as some objective truth, sometimes leading to panic attacks. By practicing mindfulness, we learn that not everything we think is true. Thoughts are like passing clouds. What is your experience with thought?

Formal Practice: Dealing with Unpleasant Thoughts

No matter how much you try to think positive thoughts and be optimistic about the future, unpleasant thoughts will still arise. You cannot avoid them, and there is no use in pretending they aren't there. Mindfulness practice can help you approach these thoughts with curiosity. As you build an understanding of your unpleasant thinking patterns, they will no longer hook you in so strongly. You can learn to allow them to be present without letting them consume you.

Formal Practice: Awareness of Thoughts

This exercise is a practice in letting thoughts go so that you are better able to do it when negative thoughts arise.

- Close your eyes and tune in to points of contact in your body.
- Feel yourself grounded and stable as you sit.
- Breathe deeply, feeling your body supported by the chair.
- Pay attention to the experience of your mind.
- Notice any thoughts as they arise, and try to identify any emotions that accompany them.
- Pay special attention to negative thoughts, and note what you are feeling and thinking.
- Try to avoid the word negative, and instead identify each thought as sad, unpleasant, irritating, painful, or otherwise.
- Continue for five minutes, noting any thoughts and their accompanying feelings.
- Make impermanence the focus of this practice.
- See each thought and acknowledge as it passes.
- Continue to note what you are thinking about and how it feels, using noting phrases like "coming, going" or "arising, passing," if you choose.
- After five minutes, return to your body for a few deep breaths.
- Remind yourself that thoughts come and go, and you have a choice in whether or not you are identified by each one.

Informal Practice: Detachment and Letting Go

All the ancient wisdom traditions speak of the benefit of developing a sense of detachment to things such as possessions, situations, and even family. The underlying purpose in cultivating this practice is not that there is anything wrong with these things, but rather attachment to these forms will prevent us from realizing a deeper experience of who we really are and the B's in *beyond balancing the books*. The three B's are pointing you toward your authentic self, a "oneness" as you merge the human and being aspects of who you are, and an accounting for what really matters—namely, your state of consciousness at any moment. When we are attached to our sense of personal identity (i.e., CPA), that will become an obstacle to realizing the deeper dimension of our true nature, which is in the formless dimension beyond the reaches of the conceptual mind.

Start to practice detachment with little things, and gradually work your way to bigger ones. Basically, practice with whatever you are experiencing each day and let them go. Detachment is never about indifference; on the contrary, we can experience our lives because we are deeply present for the moment in front of us. "Everything in the world of form is subject to impermanence and disappearing," reminds Eckhart Tolle. "But finding that which is eternal, everlasting, brings 'the peace that passes all under-standing.' "

5. Conscious Choice

Dan Siegel, MD, writes in his book *Aware: The Science and Practice of Presence*, "When we harness the hub and access the plane of possibility, we expand that vessel of water and bathe in the beauty and expanse of eternity. We are fully present in our lives." That plane of possibility is choice. When we pause and allow ourselves to experience an emotion (providing it is not too overwhelming), a space opens up between you and whatever you are facing (i.e., difficult people, complex accounting matter, or leaving your firm). This space is freedom itself.

The main difference between reactions without choice and a response with choice is that our behaviors are no longer guided by impulse but rather conscious awareness. You begin to see that you are a big part of changing both your inner world and the world around you.

Informal Practice: Restoring Confidence When Negatively Impacted

In this exercise, we will practice how mindfulness can help you choose by restoring feelings of confidence that may have impacted you over time. Many survivors of very difficult circumstances will get to this stage of practice with an even stronger sense of themselves and a deeper appreciation for their own resources. But trauma and deep internal challenges can leave its mark on confidence, attitudes, relationships, and behavior long after the core wound has healed. Mindfulness practice can help you to feel more confident in yourself, restoring you to your original authenticity.

Over time, you may have developed the tendency to over-monitor everything in your experience. From competitive colleagues, slights from clients, disruptions to routines, tax season pressures, looking for signs of danger, harm, or anything unpleasant. Of course, a cornerstone of mindfulness practice is to be aware of our experiences moment to moment. But it can be unhealthy if we're not going *beyond balancing the books* and realizing we are actually okay in each present moment. So it is vital to learn to monitor without letting it take over and undermine your confidence in your current state of "okay-ness."

In opening up and bringing mindfulness to all the positive states of being throughout your day, your sense of self-confidence will grow little by little, drop by drop, until your water bucket of self-confidence is totally embodied and full. You'll know this when the next challenge comes your way and how you respond. But don't worry if doesn't work out exactly as you would like. The more you open up to your disappointments and start to realize that they are not really disappointing, the more you will grow in confidence.

The more you open up to your sense of well-being in this moment, and each present moment, the more your nervous system will settle and the more embodied you will feel. You are already resourceful. Peace and joy will automatically increase your self-confidence, and you will feel the same toward others.

Practices That Support Growth

Some of the keys to help support you in *presence* and creative manifestation include slowing down, breathing deeply, taking long walks in nature, journaling, practicing yoga, running in the park, noticing your sense perceptions, and meditation. These practices have helped me because they fuel intuition and insights. Stepping outside your comfort zone can support your vision, including new relationships and breaking old habits that don't serve you anymore. Humor is also a great source for new creation. Deep and heartfelt laughter releases tension and frees up space inside where *presence* is recognized and deepened. Telling stories expands the sense of possibility to create and opens you up to mystery. Reading spiritual books and works of literature and poetry can deepen your practice. Participating in spiritual retreats and related travel to holy places can have a huge impact on your life. There are many online courses and workshops offered by mindful organizations that help people with specific challenges and overall growth. Mindfulness fosters personal growth; paradoxically, it is also a kind of personal diminishment as you become more attuned to your own humble nature.

Chapter 3

Reactivity: Becoming Aware of Automatic Patterns

In the beginner's mind there are many possibilities, but in the expert's mind there are few.

—Shunryu Suzuki

Joe worked at a successful accounting firm, drove a BMW, and to the outside world, was a success. His parents always expected him to be a doctor or lawyer, but when he finally made partner he realized something was missing. He wasn't happy and didn't know how he had ended up living a life that was far from what he wanted. Joe loved cooking and would rather be grilling his favorite dishes than crafting footnotes on financial statements. While he dreamed of leaving the firm to become a chef, he was afraid of disapproval from his wife and parents if he did. Not only that, he felt the weight of his culture forbidding such moves. More so, he was terrified of failure, afraid of what would happen if he couldn't make a living as a chef or have his own restaurant.

Has anything like this happened to you at one time or another? If so, those are moments to assess your core needs and values. What are Joe's core values? The answer: freedom of expression, creativity, and meaning. In Joe's case, these needs were not being met in his present position.

When we are not aligned with our core values, we suffer. An important part of mindfulness is to be aware of our core values and noticing if we are living in accordance with them. In the process, we cultivate discernment and give ourselves only what we truly need.

Joe eventually sank into acute anxiety and started to see a therapist, who told him about mindfulness. If he was going to take care of himself, Joe realized he needed to start participating in activities that he enjoyed. Joe was an early riser, so he began setting aside an hour each morning to meditate and read spiritual books that helped him connect to his true nature. After some time, Joe enrolled in a cooking class, in which he learned new skills that reignited a joy in himself that had been covered up.

This small change made him feel happier and more energetic. Joe discovered that his accounting work became less onerous. He joined a cooking group that met online, made some like-minded friends, started to explore international cuisines, and generally felt life was getting back on track. The internal pressure Joe felt to change his career subsided, at least for now. Joe was able to transform his pain into something that was deeply meaningful to him. He cultivated a mindfulness practice, fueling an energy in him that connected to his true nature held dormant through the incessant mental and emotional streams that he took to be himself. This is so common, it is considered normal by most.

Making Up Stories

The mind automatically creates a story about what happens to us, almost immediately after events occur. Certain feelings, emotions, and body sensations may automatically arise based on the nature of the story. Let's take Joe for example. He felt "something was missing" in his life after making partner and started to ponder how he ended up in this position. When unobserved and not faced in the moment, this negative self-talk led him to feelings of acute anxiety. For instance, the thought could be "How boring is this job" or "How obnoxious is my partner" or "She must be upset at me" or "He makes too much money." These and other similar reactions may automatically trigger feelings of anger. This is commonly referred to as "reactivity."

These emotions can be unsettling. When Jesus taught "turn the other cheek," he was not only referring to one's outer circumstances when confronted with unconscious individuals, but also to the internal negative reactive patterns in us. To turn your cheek means to step out of the stream of unconscious thinking and emotions and enter the *Now* fully, facing what is in front of you with conscious awareness. This mindfulness approach to emotional balance involves contacting and living our emotions fully and simultaneously, developing the habits of the heart, mind, and body that cultivate peace and joy within and around us.

From a mindfulness standpoint, Joe could direct attention by turning to his thoughts and feelings in the moment they arise and "catch them" before they spiral into something else. It is not easy at first, but with trust and patience this skill can be cultivated. Even if you don't "catch them" right away, the minute you start to pay attention to what is going on inside you, this creates a pause in the stream of mental and emotional reaction, however slight. That pause is like a "field" where something else can emerge that is more helpful. Jesus taught to "look at the lilies in the field how they grow, they toil not." He was pointing toward an open field of awareness, where you look and are aligned with the present moment in which love is born. Anything else that is needed will be an add-on. When doing this, Joe disrupts his cycle of negative thinking and emotions and takes a step back from his circumstances.

This awareness offers the sole possibility to observe the interplay between thoughts, emotions, and body sensations. You are not attempting to change the emotion, feelings, or sensations that are present, but only trying to observe them. Your acknowledgment and/or acceptance of the experience fosters an opening in you. This opening is the basis for choice. Mindfulness doesn't dictate to you what to choose; rather, it allows the possibility of conscious choice. Without it, your actions will be based upon your conditioning.

In turning attention back to the present moment, to the feeling itself, we allow ourselves to connect to the reality of the present moment rather than our mind's version of it. The *Now* offers the opportunity to step out of the continuous stream of thinking and the emotions that follow your thoughts. Mindfulness can help you become aware of how thoughts, emotions, and body sensations automatically influence you and vice versa. This was a huge revelation for me. When I started to observe my thoughts, I realized that in most instances thoughts are related to some aspect of the past or future. Thoughts are typically not about the present, unless you come up with an original thought! When that happens, you'll notice an energy inside you that encompasses many positive feelings. This is intuition and a sense of empowerment.

Science and Emotions

Science has confirmed that much of people's thinking and many of their behaviors are automatic (19). The internal "story" in the head that often accompanies decision making is frequently on "autopilot" while the mind is occupied with other thoughts (20). Paying mindful attention to your reactive patterns and ways of thinking is a redeeming means of reducing their effect on you. Mindfulness is all about creating room for you to choose actions that are in alignment with your life purpose. What is your life purpose? How do the automatic reactive patterns in your life prevent you from experiencing deep meaning? What is the meaning of your accounting career? Is your life purpose in alignment with your accounting work, or is your accounting work just a means to an end? I invite you to write down your answers in a journal.

There are certainly some benefits to automatic patterns and thinking, which allow us to work on a tax return while tracking our time for billing purposes. On the other hand, automatic patterns of thinking and reacting can negatively influence well-being. For example, when a client notifies you that they no longer need your services, an automatic and unconscious reactive pattern is likely to come up for you. Or maybe something more personal triggers a reaction. The self-talk might sound something like: "What is happening to me?" This produces emotions such as irritation, anger, and anxiety. Over time, these reactions can influence you in a way that reduces your self-confidence, which in turn leads to various problems like anxiety disorder (21). That is why it is important to understand your emotional triggers.

Emotional Intelligence

What are emotions? According to psychologist Paul Ekman, "emotion is a process, a particular kind of automatic appraisal influenced by our evolutionary and personal past, in which we sense something important to our welfare is occurring, and a set of

91

physiological changes and emotional behaviors begin to deal with the situation" (22). According to Ekman, emotions evolved as part of our survival mechanisms, which he called "automatic appraising." That is why it is difficult to change what we become emotional about. Mindfulness does not require us to change emotions; in fact, just the opposite is true. Mindfulness helps us foster a friendlier relationship to our emotions, even the more difficult ones.

When these emotions react, it's without our consent and often without our awareness. Did you ever instruct sadness to visit you? Or say, "Hi happiness, come join me at my office today?" Understanding the emotional process deeply, we can forgive both ourselves and others, in due time. Of course, there are other ways that our emotions can be triggered besides reactivity. Talking about and remembering past emotional scenes or thinking about the future can trigger emotions. Even watching characters in films or theater or reading a mystery novel can elicit strong emotions.

Regardless of the circumstances, our emotional responses can either be functional or dysfunctional (unconscious). British clinical psychologist Paul Gilbert proposes that humans have three main emotional regulation systems: the threat-protection system; the drive-resource-seeking and excitement system; and the contentment, soothing, and safeness system (23). For now, it is important to realize that no matter the emotion, we can accept it in the present moment as we notice and feel into the emotion. There is a field between the stimulus and response where the lilies grow called mindful *presence.*

Exhibit 2: Emotional Intelligence

Mindfulness is the foundation for emotional intelligence. At the top, we're equating mindfulness with self-awareness, which is the basis for self-regulation, motivation, social skills, empathy, and loving kindness.

In this field, we go *beyond balancing the books* and align with the vertical dimension of our T account in the present moment. Now, that is accounting that truly matters.

Leading with Emotional Intelligence

Do you remember something happening to you that you didn't expect—a surprise and not in a good way? Maybe you passed two parts of the CPA exam and your parents, rather than celebrating with you, questioned you about the other parts you didn't pass. Or maybe it is something more recent at work, when your supervisor berated you for not completing the work within budget. How did you feel? Or the time you were passed over for a promotion or were not asked to join your colleagues for lunch. What emotions came up for you?

Now think about when your child was born or when you met the love of your life. What emotions did you feel then?

A growing body of research has convincingly illustrated that emotional intelligence is essential for leadership. You can see why this is the case as you look around at institutions, businesses, and informal group gatherings. But before anyone can increase their emotional IQ, they first have to become emotionally literate. In responding automatically, we often have an opportunity to not only identify the core emotion but also to develop a clear, accurate meaning of what that emotion means to us on an experiential level. In doing so, we can shift what might otherwise be a negative experience into a quality learning opportunity for enhancing our emotional IQ.

Most people struggle with defining their emotions, mostly because it was not taught in school or at home. I like thinking of emotions as the process of energy in motion. At a fundamental level, emotion is energy moving in and out of the body, and feelings are the corresponding physical sensations that come up. Imagine that. Every time you experience an emotion, you feel a sensation in your body (images, sounds, etc.). Thoughts may be present, but not every time. Irritation has a certain sensation, as does shame and anger. Your feelings are these sensations (24).

In my opinion, understanding this basic definition is vital. If we agree that emotion is energy and feelings are sensations moving through the body, then we can drop binary thinking of good or bad and realize the emotion "it is what it is." Knowing this and taking it a step further implies that you are no more your emotions than you are your toothache or broken finger.

Next, it is essential to identify the core emotion. Just like molecules are made up of a group of atoms, all emotions come from five primary emotions—fear, anger, joy, sadness, and sexual feelings—each with a unique energy pattern and set of sensations in the body. Underneath these five basic categories is the plethora of sub-emotions. For example, under anger we can include emotions like upset, frustrated, and irritated. I won't get into all of the various combinations and sub-categories here.

It is important to be aware that your feelings are too often repressed in business settings, as they are unfortunately viewed by many as distractions for making good decisions. This reasoning is starting to change as more and more business organizations are placing high priority on conscious leadership and development. In our everyday work as accountants, we can lead by example by not only using our mind as the go-to place for solving our client problems, but also include our heart center and gut in an integrated mind, body, soul, and spirit connection. Mindfulness is one of the paths that can foster that connection. Mindfulness is the basis for conscious decision making in an empowering way.

In my coaching practice, I like to pause in the conversation and ask my clients, "What are you feeling right now?" This empowering question invites people to stop and take a "look" inside and see what is happening in their heart and gut. This simple noting is more profound than you can imagine. Often, when I ask this question in an executive coaching session, I'll usually hear something like, "if I do that, I feel that I won't know who I am anymore," or "I feel that I am anxious about the results," or "I have a resignation toward another busy season."

If you look closely, these honest statements are more like judgments, opinions, or beliefs rather than true feelings. Feelings are followed by one of the five core primary emotions, such as "I feel angry," "I feel sad," or "I feel joyful." Once a client identifies a feeling, then I would ask my client, "Where is that feeling in your body?" This practice takes you out of your head and into your body. Remember, as accountants we often spend much of the day using our analytical minds, so tapping into your body when a feeling comes up shifts your focus from thinking to awareness, which is a core aspect of mindfulness practice. By doing this, you'll be moving from understanding basic emotions to emotional maturity—a key aspect for success as an accountant and for life in general.

Emotions and New Tax Laws

Quite often, we tend to believe that outer circumstances are the cause of our difficulties. When a new tax law is passed, for the tax accountant it means learning the new rules, attending webinars, reading articles and commentary, and discussing the changes with colleagues and clients. This can be a stressful time, but it doesn't have to be.

What are the causes of stress? Is it the new law, extra commitment to learn the new tax provisions, responding to anxious clients or firm pressure, updating tax plans? Or maybe it is office politics that get in the way and trigger your stress. I would suggest, in most cases, it is none of these. Rather, it is the automatic unconscious reactive patterns in you that the change in tax law triggers. The new tax law is a new circumstance. Why resist it? The important question is: What is your relationship to the new tax law? Can you apply mindfulness to your reaction to the new law? Who will you be if you don't criticize or complain about it? For some, it may mean stepping out of their comfort zone, even when you are well-versed in tax.

Taking a mindful stance surrounding any change will bring up some discomfort, like my coaching client who told me "if I do that, I won't know who I am anymore." What do you prefer: working with constant stress, most of which is self-created, or would you rather develop new approaches to the triggers in you that give you a choice?

Under these circumstances, cultivating a non-resisting attitude is the first step in freeing you to choose how you are in relation to these tax law changes. I suggest practicing the three-minute breathing space exercise augmented by formal meditation as frequently as possible during these times, before or after work, and see what happens.

High Performance Emotions

While all emotions are valid, and all emotions are important because they provide you with important information, some emotions help you to perform better at work. These high performance emotions are enthusiasm, confidence, tenacity, and optimism. High performance emotions increase our drive while maintaining a wide and open focus. For example, when you are very enthusiastic about helping a client maximize their tax position, it is common for your thoughts to race. This indicates a high energy level involved in the high performance emotions. Keep in mind, however, that not every emotion with high energy is helpful for performance. The other key factors that mark the high-performance emotions are mindful *presence* and open awareness. Mindfulness is the foundation for emotional intelligence, as previously highlighted in Exhibit 2.

Mindfulness and Leadership

As you develop a greater awareness of the interplay between thoughts and emotions, you will notice that the people around you don't quite have the same awareness. This can be unsettling, but it is normal. Seeing this clearly and without judgment is a reward in itself as you practice aligning with whatever arises in the present moment. Practicing *presence* actually helps make you a better accountant and leader, and modeling mindfulness for the rest of your co-workers helps make your corporate culture and firm a more positive and productive one. While I would recommend practicing informally throughout the day, engaging in formal meditation for ten to twenty minutes a day, before or after work, is a good introduction. As you sense into the joy this practice will bring you, then you can extend the session.

Noticing the stillness inside and around you will paradoxically enhance your approach to leadership and accounting work. This in turn will profoundly increase your mental toughness and ability to focus selectively on that which is important while improving your capacity to feel compassion (we'll go into this in more detail in Chapter 7). In letting go of the constraints you naturally place on yourself, you will feel more creative. What inside you wants to create something magical? It could be as simple as noticing the stillness in the background of your day.

While mindfulness is about helping you focus attention in a neutral and accepting fashion, as a CPA who handles multiple clients, you will constantly find yourself having to decide what to focus on. Discovering your core needs and values is a potent way to gather the wandering mind and "come home" to yourself and what matters most. This in turn will enable you to take action, which is aligned with your essential values, bringing about greater fulfillment, energy, and passion. You will discover more than meets the eye.

One way this comes up for accountants is when documenting your work and getting it ready for the multiple layers of review. Let's say you are presented with five pages of review notes, all requiring you to go back into the files and reevaluate your work and conclusion, knowing you are already slightly over budget on the job. In these moments of stress, your automatic reactions can inform you about your core needs and values. Your automatic reaction might be to go right back to the office and start working on the open items. In doing so, you can sense the stress build up.

Explore your needs first by asking yourself, "What is underneath the issues and the stress?" You can eventually take action that is informed by a deeper sense of what is important to you. Digging deeper, you discover the need for understanding, freedom of expression, and making a contribution to your firm become evident and even more important than the action of finding a new job. In mindfulness, you become much more attuned to your emotions, allow for the pause, feel into your body, and listen to what your mind and body are asking of you. From this place, soak into your core needs and values. Finally, you'll notice strategies that will surface to meet your core needs. You are a mindful professional.

Formal Practice: Understanding Your Emotions Meditation

To begin, bring kind awareness to your belly, chest, and head as well as the emotions you associate with these visceral feelings and the positive or negative stories you believe regarding this topic. How many others might feel similarly? How might you feel with that increased awareness around this topic?

Emotions are complex occurrences that can be most simply understood as a combination of physical sensations and thought patterns. When you mindfully tune in to your emotional experience, you can begin to break it down and separate yourself from its power. With wisdom and care, you'll be able to let go of your feelings rather than allowing them to rule you.

- Find a posture that feels comfortable and conducive to mindfulness.
- Take a few moments to examine your body and what is present.
- Bring to mind a recent experience of joy or happiness in your work as an accountant.

- Try to recall as many details as you can about this event.
- Visualize the experience, and give it space to be present in the mind and body.
- As this emotional experience is with you, investigate it closely.
- What is the joy?
- Notice what you feel in your body.
- You may notice a relaxing of your shoulders, gentler or deeper breaths, or warmth in your chest.
- There is nothing you should or should not be feeling.
- Just recognize your own experience of joy/happiness.
- Tune in to the mental state that accompanies this physical sensation.
- As you rest with the memory of joy, what is happening in your mind?
- Notice if it is calm, active, agitated, or at ease.
- There isn't a right or wrong answer.
- Familiarize yourself with the experience of joy.
- Now, do the same with a recent experience that was unpleasant.
- It may be a time in which you were stressed, anxious, frustrated, or sad.
- Steer clear of experiences that are powerfully charged, like an intense argument or workplace conflict.
- Instead, start with something minorly unpleasant, like waiting for your client to show up or tying in a spreadsheet.
- Investigate the experience in both mind and body, resting with each for a few minutes.
- Return to your body and breathe for a minute at the end of your practice.
- Allow the mind to relax for a few deep breaths before opening your eyes.

Case Study

Tom is an audit manager in a mid-sized accounting firm. He made plans to meet his audit team in the office at 5 p.m. to prepare for the upcoming audit. Tom raced through the afternoon facing deadlines with some of his other clients. He was feeling pretty confident and knew the work he did would be well-received from the partner. Before he could make it out of his office, he received a text from the partner asking him to address another issue concerning the accounting treatment of a lease transaction for one of his clients, and he needed an answer in the morning. Tom shrugged his shoulders and felt a contraction across his body. Tom began to draw a blank, realizing he wasn't prepared to answer that question. He started to feel anxious, and his confidence faded. Tom decided to call his audit team members and tell them he wouldn't be able to meet with them until 6 p.m. He then went back to his desk to work on the lease transaction.

Questions

What emotion was Tom feeling before he received the text from the partner?

   a) Anxiety
   b) Confidence
   c) Overconfidence
   d) Anger

What emotion motivated Tom to go back to his desk and work on the lease transaction?

a) Confidence
b) Anger
c) Overconfidence
d) Anxiety

Tom is under significant stress about 50% of the time at work. He asks, "How do I know it is best for me to allow myself to feel these negative emotions vs. anchor in the present moment and not address the emotion right now so as not to get 'stuck' in the cycle of thinking and feeling? Also, how can I allow myself to feel the emotion of anger without getting lost in the story?"

These are two very good questions. What does Tom mean by "not addressing the emotion right now?" Is he mainly trying to create space from the emotion? There is nothing inherently wrong with that approach as long as it is a result of a conscious choice (rather than a reactive response) and does not reflect an intention to not experience the emotion. Here is the reason. Mindfulness is not about blindly applying acceptance but more about bringing forth a more accepting relationship with emotions and increasing awareness so you can make a conscious choice from a place of awareness rather than be guided by impulses. The emotion is there after all; why not take a look and give it some compassion?

Sometimes, allowing emotions to be fully present might not be the best alternative. For example, I was about to make a presentation of financial statements to a board and received a distressing phone call from a dear friend. I became mindfully aware of the emotion that started to build in my body. I decided to not focus my attention on the emotion but rather on the content of the presentation. I anticipated that fully allowing the emotion to be present would greatly interfere with the quality of my presentation to the board and result in sadness later on. However, I intentionally created time and space for this emotion to take place after the presentation. So, in this example, I used mindful awareness to make a choice about how to deal with the emotion. I was not avoiding the emotion because I didn't want to feel it. Rather, I allowed the emotion to be present later.

Nobody but you knows what the best thing is for you to do. There is no right or wrong way to respond. Don't look to mindfulness in terms of right vs. wrong but in terms of conscious choice. Whatever choice arises from conscious awareness is the "right" choice. Again, mindfulness is not about doing or not doing something. It is all about increasing freedom by increasing awareness.

It is important to note that a more friendly and accepting relationship with the present moment is key. The good news is that this relationship with the *Now* can be built incrementally; even a few minutes at a time can be a starting point for a less antagonistic relationship with whatever arises for you. I would focus on developing a friendlier relationship with your emotions, gradually building a willingness to experience them, rather than making a "right choice."

Tom's other question is about rumination or, as he put it, "getting lost in the story." Rumination means all our attention is focused on thinking. Recall the lantern metaphor I used earlier to explain the process of directing attention. When we are ruminating, the lantern is pointed at our heads all the time. It's stuck in traffic!

A powerful way to get out of rumination is to point the lantern at something different than our heads. Focus attention on your inner body—that midway point between your outer physical body and the deep abiding *presence* you are. Sense into the feeling. Your emotions are halfway between these two dimensions, so to speak. Maybe you have tension in the shoulders. If you notice that you are ruminating again, gently turn attention back to your body. Select a specific part. I like to start with hands. If the thoughts are too overwhelming, turn attention to your breath. Stay connected to the present moment by focusing on your breath. This response is all part of our understanding of the emotions meditation we did earlier.

Multi-tasking

Mindfulness has sometimes been referred to as doing "one task at a time" and can be considered the antithesis of multi-tasking. If you are writing up a financial statement and answering texts at the same time, every incoming text is an interruption of the writing task and requires a reorientation, which leads to increased stress levels (25). The practice of *presence* enhances skills that can counteract the negative consequences of multi-tasking. According to one study, participants who received eight weeks of mindfulness training switched less frequently between competing tasks, experienced fewer negative emotions, and spent more time on each individual task (without increasing total time investment) than those in the control group. The mindfulness group also experienced improved memory for the details of the work they performed, an important element of accounting (26).

Many mindfulness practices require the participant to focus on one thing, such as a conversation, thereby promoting single-focused attention. For example, instead of talking to a client and at the same time checking one's phone for new messages, mindfulness cultivates attention for the conversation with the client as the main and only object of attention. In this way, it is similar to the breath and body meditations in formal practice we discussed earlier.

I have found that keeping some attention in the body serves as an anchor and a reminder to continuously come back to a single-focused attention whenever I am interrupted by e-mails and texts. Since accounting is detail-oriented and uses the analytical mind most of the time, it is easier for us to be distracted by the incoming alerts, beeps, and flashes on the screen. By keeping attention in the body, there are fewer tendencies to be distracted without missing any details.

Automatic Accounting

Repetitive work consists of influences outside of our conscious awareness. That is, we are not consciously aware of our own actions. It may be hard to fathom, but research led by Melanie Vella ("How to Engage the 90% of Our Brains that Resist Changing Behavior") suggests that about 90% of our behavior is carried out automatically. A clear example of this is in the accounting work program; while necessary, such programs can be a trap for automatic responses. As accountants, we follow certain procedures and routines as we go about conducting our work on our clients' financial statements.

For example, as an experienced CPA, you are aware of the process and procedures involved in the review and reconciliation of accounts. You know it so well that it is done automatically, which reduces the need for your complete conscious attention, especially thanks to automation. Unfortunately, repetitive patterns are not limited to tasks like reconciliation of accounts, but they also play out into your thoughts concerning changes in your environment or stress. In some cases automatic behavior can be useful and productive; however, it can also cause serious problems. With mindful-ness, we can become aware of our automatic patterns without losing conscious awareness and without losing time to perform the audit function within budget.

Exhibit 3 displays how a certain feeling, thought, or sensation can automatically lead to reactions like suppression or worry. In these situations, we are not in conscious control of the reaction. The reaction is a result of an unconscious tendency. There is no room for consciousness between the trigger and our reaction.

Exhibit 3: Automatic Reactivity

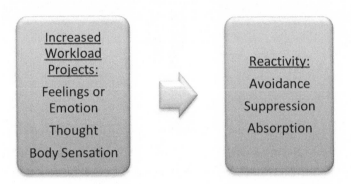

The only way to change automatic patterns is with attention. Austrian neurologist, psychiatrist, and Holocaust survivor Victor Frankel writes, "Between stimulus and response there is a space. In that space is our power to choose our response. In our response lies our growth and freedom."

Mindfulness cultivates awareness for the space that is created between what is happening in this moment and the reaction that follows. In that space is your freedom to be a creative human being. Your internal thought chatter will try to tell you otherwise. Just notice it and move on past the clouds in the sky. Repeat the following so that your subconscious mind will hear it, and there it shall rest:

Why I AM Here (A Poem)

I am here to create and manifest what truly matters
And what I really, really want
In the present moment, the deep now,
In its own time and place.
So be it, and so it is.

106

Managing Anger: Off Balance Sheet Awareness

Sometimes, an automatic response can be fueled by anger. This comes up at work often enough, especially during stressful times like busy season. The first step is to understand the anger at its root. It is not often thought about in a positive way, anger is actually the emotion of self-preservation through which you wish to maintain your sense of worth, legitimate needs, and fundamental convictions. At its core, anger has a high purpose and reasonable function when managed properly. Unhealthy management of anger consists of suppression and either being openly or passively aggressive. On the other hand, being assertive and standing up for your dignity, needs, and convictions while showing civility to others is a healthy form of managing anger.

In addition, letting go of any anger in its own time with awareness and kind attention frees you in so many ways. If you experience anger when confronted with multiple deadlines and little room to finish, mindfulness helps you to pause for a second and devote attention to the experience of anger. By giving attention to the emotion and staying connected to the experience, the chance of reacting impulsively is reduced. This off balance sheet approach to anger paradoxically enhances your self-worth and long term equity position! I have done this on many occasions, and each time anger is managed in this way it brings about a strengthening—an inner resilience and a peaceful joy. You could say that you are taking a break to allow some consciousness into your working life. Ultimately, the reaction that follows will be guided by a conscious choice, not an automatic reaction.

So, the next time you are confronted with multiple deadlines and colleagues breathing down your neck for answers, employ a pause followed up with assertiveness and a letting go. Science supports this approach. Research findings show that mindfulness helps reduce automatic responding. Consequently, behavior is guided to a greater extent by conscious choice and less by automatic, unconscious reactions (27).

The Cycle of Reactions: The Debits and Credits of Emotions

Automatic reactions can also cause you to become stuck in a negative cycle of feeling and thinking. Exhibit 4 depicts an example of such a cycle. Imagine your client calls you up complaining about your fee in a rude and condescending manner. An immediate result of hearing this news is a feeling of sadness and frustration. Often, we automatically start thinking in familiar ways. Our thoughts may concern the feeling ("this is no good, I don't want this, this must stop") or the situation ("How could this happen?") or the self ("Maybe I am not a good accountant"). These thoughts can cause feelings or emotions that can lead to further thoughts, and the cycle continues.

Exhibit 4: The Cycle of Reactions

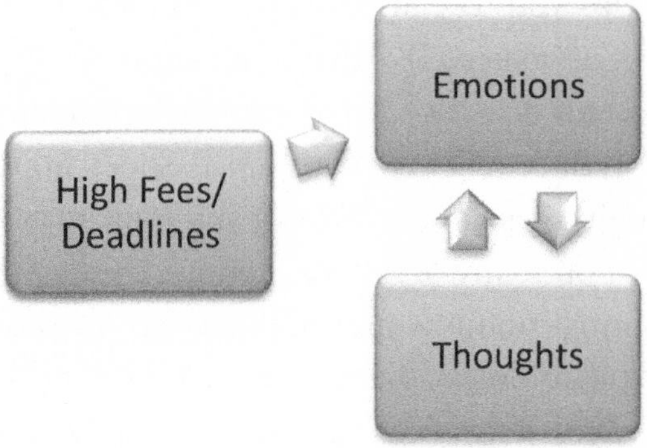

It is also possible that this client may first trigger thoughts ("This can't be true," "I made a mistake"), which in turn result in negative emotions, like embarrassment or frustration, that cause new thoughts to emerge, and so on. Whatever is triggered first (thoughts or emotion) by a situation, the point is that we are not aware of this automatic interplay between thoughts and emotions; we get caught in a cycle of thinking and feeling for a very long time. Because we are paying attention to our thoughts, we lose awareness of what is happening: (the line down the center of our T account). We are caught in a game of feelings and thoughts as illustrated in Exhibit 4. This is an example of how we sometimes can get lost in worrying or ruminating (repetitive and negative thinking about the past).

When we are confronted by multiple deadlines and impatient clients and colleagues, we can get completely lost in a train of thought. As accountants, we devote so much attention not only to our work but also our peripheral environment, often triggering us to get lost in our thoughts. Then, all our attention goes to the content of our thoughts. We are not present anymore but living in our heads. Our thoughts determine how we feel. We are slaves to our thoughts and barely notice how we are being moved between thoughts and feelings.

Realizing this was happening to me was quite a revelation. When I get lost in thoughts and emotions these days, and I am in the grip of a vicious cycle. I "catch myself" and remember a writing from St Paul: "For in him we live and move and have our being." Simply, Saint Paul is pointing to the dimension of conscious *presence* or awareness, where we are connected to the Source of all life or whatever name you prefer to use. When lost in thoughts and emotions, we are not aware of this connection. I recommend that you too find a "go-to saying" from an inspirational being or from our natural world to help you reconnect to the present moment.

Question

> Sandra is a CFO for a large hospital system and often notices that she is "lost in thoughts and emotions." When she notices this happening, she feels it won't stop. It's like being pulled along by a train wishing for it to stop. What can she do?

Even when we notice that we are in a cycle of negative thoughts and emotions, we often use strategies like suppression or putting things in perspective. These strategies really don't work well long term; rather, they pull you back, if not now then at the next earliest opportunity. The more you attempt to avoid or get rid of the thoughts and feelings, the more they will persist.

By paying attention to the here and now and the related thoughts and emotions, you can disrupt the cycle and create room for awareness. This awareness provides the sole possibility to observe the cycle between thoughts and emotions. For instance, if the medical director comes into your office with some "bad news" concerning some compliance issue triggering automatic thoughts, mindfulness involves taking a step back and noticing the thoughts. Just pause for a moment and focus on your breath. Then, become aware of what is going on inside you. What thoughts are currently running through your mind? You can name them, such as "I feel worried" or "I feel nervous." Where in your body do you notice these feelings? By taking the role of a curious observer, the automatic cycle of thinking and feeling is disrupted.

If you notice that you are not observing anymore but are drawn away by thoughts or feelings again, simply focus attention on your breath once more, and use this neutral point to take on the role of observer again. This ancient breath awareness practice works because you connect back to the present moment. It works because the present moment is the only place where life exists. It works because of a trust you evoke by continuously turning back to your breath. That is the deeper meaning of the first beatitude when Jesus says, "Blessed are the poor in spirit, for theirs is the kingdom of heaven." The word "blessed" points to a goodness and a ripeness, your soul self, where you connect to the *Source* in the *Now* moment and a different dimension of consciousness opens up. There is a grace. Our breath turns to something more than just a physical movement.

Lunch and Work

Eating with Awareness

Everyone eats, and accountants are no different. Eating is a necessary daily habit. It is no wonder that it involves many automatic processes. Eating does not always require focused attention. We can easily have lunch while sending an e-mail, reading a blog, shuffling items around our desk, and so forth. When we do so, we become less aware of the process of eating and tasting the food. Our attention is not focused on the sensation of eating but on the e-mail, blog, and items on our desk. When this happens, we tend to enjoy our food less. In Mindfulness Based Stress Reduction (MBSR) training, each participant is asked to taste a raisin—I mean really taste the raisin, as a way to bring in our whole sensory body to the experience and be present. This training started by Jon Kabat-Zinn in the 1970s and is a very powerful way to connect more fully to yourself.

When you experience the taste, smell, and texture of food that becomes your anchor for *presence*. Similar to making your home in the breath, anchor yourself in the actual experience of eating with attention. You can still have a conversation with a client or colleague and enjoy your surroundings. When you eat mindfully, you will notice how many times attention is drawn away from eating by thoughts and other distractions. The practice is to gently direct attention back to the experience of eating. I am amazed how sometimes we can discuss the most complex of accounting and tax provisions while eating at the same time. When the lunch is over, do we really remember the taste, smell, and texture of the food we just ate? If you're like me, then sadly you often don't. But once you realize this, remember it and guide yourself back with some mindful self-compassion.

This exercise can show you that even when attention should be focused on eating the food in the present, it is quite frequently directed to the future; you take a bite and before you swallow, your mind is already paying attention to the next bite. This is a pattern that is often present when eating sweets, chips, or other desirable food.

Mindful eating can contribute to a healthier pattern of eating. Research has shown that mindfulness reduces emotional eating and can help contribute to a healthier weight. Science tells us that mindful eating reduces the speed of eating, and one is satisfied earlier and eats less. This reduces the chance of overeating and, thus, the consequences of high blood pressure, diabetes, and cancer (28).

Routine Activities at Work

Informal Practice

This week, I invite you to choose three activities at work and try to do them with as much undivided attention as possible. Notice how attention is automatically drawn away from what you are doing by thoughts, emotions, and body sensations. Write down your experience in a kind and gentle way.

If you notice this week that you are worrying, ruminating, or brought out of balance by certain situations, try to pause for a moment. Can you refocus attention on the experience in the present moment? Can you let the feeling be and become aware of the thoughts that automatically arise? Can you become aware of the cycle that is detailed in Exhibit 4? I invite you to journal your experience. The Poet Rainer Maria Rilke writes about it in this way: "Reflect on the world that you carry within yourself. And name this thinking what you wish. . . Your innermost happening is worth all your love."

Chapter 4

Open Awareness and the Judgmental Mind

Knowing yourself is to be rooted in being, instead of lost in the mind.

—Eckhart Tolle

Good living and good work are two sides of the same coin. Hildegard of Bingen, a twelfth-century mystic, put it this way: "When humans do good work they become a flowering orchard permeating the universe and making the cosmic wheel go around." What is good work to you? Hildegard presumes that we are not bound to a human-focused comprehension of work, and that our work is cosmic when we turn attention to the wonder and awe of the universe. What is the fundamental nature of the universe when you look up in the sky and experientially sense what it is?

For me, I look up and see space and "things" in space. Mindfulness is all about creating that space within you, so that your work (things) is an outward reflection of your inner space. Unless you move, live, and breathe in this internal space, accounting work will seem like the leaves of an ailing tree—dry, boring, or perhaps just a paycheck. With all the information available to us as accountants, we can now transcend and include our technical abilities and conceptual understanding, providing accounting that takes us *beyond balancing the books.*

You are being asked to redefine your relationship to accounting work, not just by keeping up with all the technology, new regulations, firm mergers, commoditization of core services and so forth, but also by becoming a mindful professional, living and working in open awareness to your internal and external circumstances in a non-judgmental way. Accounting work then becomes a creative expression of the soul, the inner being unique to each one of us. As you well know, we don't need creative accounting, we need creative accountants, even if you are reviewing bank reconciliation or tying in a general ledger account. Creativity begins in a moment without thought, now and now and now. You need to know this as experience.

Open awareness is about the quality of your consciousness. Essentially, it is about stepping through its evaluative, judgmental nature and becoming fully receptive to experiences as they occur. By becoming aware of our judgments, we set aside a large obstacle to *presence*.

One of the ways to make open awareness a practice is to set daily rituals throughout the day. Simply noticing a moment without thought—to "preserve single moments of radiance and keep them alive in our lives," as Rabbi Heschel puts it—is a ritual to be praised. To keep them alive is not just to remember wonderful moments but rather to sustain mindful *presence*. And as shamanistic teacher Joan Halifax said, "When you reach very deep states of consciousness, you see the mind includes not only your entire nervous system, but the entire cosmos." The here is expanded to not only include the physical space surrounding you but also the reflection of a continuum of space extending far deeper than we can imagine. Contemporary author Matthew Fox writes, "These are things that must be experienced and not just talked about. They are things of ritual." What is your daily ritual?

Accounting in Open Awareness

Good accounting and good decisions come from the same coin. Without a clear picture of the business, financial position, and results of operations, it would be almost impossible to make decisions such as purchasing equipment, adding new employees, finding a strategic partner, analyzing financial ratios, or obtaining capital. For example, as an accountant, you prepare financial statements that are among the documents submitted to a bank in which a decision will be made regarding whether or not to extend credit to your client. In this process, there are many judgments that will be made from the perspectives of you as the accountant, your client, and the bank involved in the credit application. The judgments are a necessary aspect of the process that facilitates the business decision at hand.

But what happens when things don't go as planned during the application process? For example, the banker is not responding to your e-mail for a status update, or the bank is requesting further documentation and support for the numbers on the financial statements, even though the financial ratios are within acceptable benchmark levels. Or what if the bank declines the application? What judgements come up for you when this happens? Does it trigger irritation, frustration, or even anxiety? If so, how do you manage the underlying emotion of anger or fear?

Sadly, I have noticed that when a client reacts angrily, there is sometimes a tendency for wanting to be drawn into that emotion and ride its wave. If you notice this happening to you, what can you do from a mindfulness perspective? In this chapter, you will learn about the judgmental nature of the mind and how it colors reality and creates conflicts. You'll come to recognize the difference between practical judgments, as in the case of preparing financial statements, and the unconscious judgments that arise when negative or even positive experiences happen in the course of your work as an accountant.

An essential ingredient of mindfulness is open awareness, which refers to the quality of attention that is not evaluative or molded by pre-existing ideas or intentions. In open awareness, there is instead receptivity to allowing experiences to simply happen as they do. After all, things happen. This allowing of experiences is a key component of mindfulness, as pointed out in Chapter 2, and is in itself a rewarding practice. As a byproduct of maintaining this open awareness stance, you will be able to respond in a more open and non-judgmental way to the client and banker fostering equanimity rather than condensation.

A common misconception about open awareness is that you'll be a "doormat" and be viewed as weak. This is unfortunate and prevents people from experimenting and realizing their innate goodness. Rather, many people are constantly on guard, preventing them from taking a leap of trust into a new dimension of being. I would suggest that small simple steps around routine activities can build your confidence and strengthen your open awareness muscle so that you too can be a light shining bright in your work and relationships. Some of the practices and exercises in this book can help you do that.

While open awareness involves non-judgment, if you're like me when I started to practice mindfulness, it may be easier said than done. I noticed most of my daily awareness was clouded by numerous judgments and evaluations. However, with a combination of teacher training, spiritual reading, meditation, and simple informal practices, they occurred less and less over time. Now, I recognize judgments for what they are: simply subjective passing thoughts with perhaps some relative truth, but not absolutely true. What has your experience been at work and in your accounting function with judgments? Can you notice the difference between effective practical judgments and unconscious evaluative thoughts that are often a negative commentary about yourself, others, or situations?

As a reminder, it is important to know that in mindfulness practice, there is nothing wrong with judgments; after all, it's what the mind does. The practice is to gently notice the judgment and come back into open awareness as you let go of the unconscious judgmental thought pattern. I like to take a deep breath. This allows for the judgement to pass. You'll be giving attention to the breath rather than the judgment and become present to this moment. As a result, you'll feel relieved. When Jesus said "do not judge," he was pointing his listeners to this state of open awareness.

By becoming aware of our judgments, an obstacle to open awareness is removed. Keep in mind that the goal of mindfulness is not to get rid of judgments per se, but rather to become aware of judgments and see through them and their subjective nature. We do a disservice to ourselves, the client, and the banker in my example when we mistake our views about reality for reality itself. It's a little bit like mistaking the financial statement for the actual underlying assets, liability, and equity.

Working with Our Judgments

When working on an engagement with colleagues and clients, how often do you look at them from the perspective of your own beliefs? In other words, what lens are you viewing others from? Is it the lens of your beliefs and evaluations, or is it the lens of open awareness? Here is a case study followed by various applications of the judgmental mind in the context of our work as accountants.

Case Study

Allison and Marty both worked on the same stressful audit every year. When they first started, they had to deal with an extremely angry client. While both found it stressful, they could handle the client initially without it affecting their mood. Eventually, the daily negativity they dealt with during this audit began to seep into the rest of their lives.

Allison began practicing meditation, but Marty did not. Even though her work was still often stressful, she learned to detach herself from the demands of the angry client. She realized that her client wasn't directly angry with her, and this helped to relieve the stress. Marty did not do anything to handle the stress. He just toughed it out. He finally got fed up, and one day the CFO called Marty into his office and told him that he and his firm were "woefully incompetent." Marty lost it and began to curse out the CFO before exiting his office. Marty was reprimanded by his firm the next day.

Questions

How did Marty handle the stress of his job?

    a) He exercised.

    b) He didn't.

    c) He meditated.

    d) He beat people up.

How did practicing mindfulness help Allison deal with her stress?

    a) She became enlightened and didn't feel stress anymore.

    b) She became relaxed and didn't feel stress anymore.

    c) She learned how to avoid stress.

    d) She learned how to become detached.

Marty didn't handle the stress at all. His strategy was to tough it out, which led to obvious consequences. Allison, on the other hand, learned to be detached. Detachment is equivalent to *presence* and open awareness, through which she is able to take a step back and create space between herself and the situation she finds herself in. She has the attention or light shining on her experience.

Mindfulness is not about becoming enlightened, relaxed, or avoiding stress. Allison's ten-minute meditation is the 1% of her day that uplifts the other 99%. The uplift is from being totally identified with her thoughts and emotions to a higher, deeper state of open awareness. Her meditation practice has helped her mindfully respond to challenging situations.

Mindful Accounting for Technical Challenges

Whenever you feel emotionally ill at ease by not fully understanding some technical aspect of your job, it is completely natural for your thinking to become distorted as well. During these anxious moments, your thoughts race, trying to find a solution or gain some knowledge to help solve an issue. During these times, you will come up with both logical and intuitive solutions that may or may not hold up on further examination by your quality control department or your client. When your focus narrows, as when your mind is completely absorbed in conceptual thinking, you close yourself off to possible creative solutions. As a byproduct of this tendency, you circle around the same types of destructive thoughts and judgments.

Unknown to many, seeking solutions purely through the conceptual mind is only a tiny aspect of true intelligence. As you become more and more aware and curious about your circumstances, you'll begin to tap into what may be called a "potential receptivity" lying deep within the recess of your being. Dr. Dan Siegel writes about this same potential in *Aware: The Science and Practice of Presence*: "This position of highest potential of all options we can call the plane of possibility" (29).

This potential receptivity is a microcosm of the "big bang" and lies at the heart of creative intelligence. This internal big bang is available and unconditionally waiting for you from moment to moment. Resting into this feeling will be a little unsettling at first because you'll leave behind the judgmental mind. When this happens, keep your kind attention on this uneasiness in an accepting way. This is creative intelligence and energy formations moving around as inner energy in your body, resettling and restoring an alliance with your true nature. You can call it spirit, soul, essence identity, *presence*, or some other name that is comfortable for you.

Black-and-White Reasoning

Dichotomous reasoning means you think in terms of extremes such as black and white or good and bad. In mindfulness, we become particularly aware of thoughts such as always, never, everyone, nobody, best, worst, or either/or. Rarely is a client's financial condition the "worst you have ever seen," and no matter how difficult your peers may seem to be, this doesn't mean that "everybody hates you." In becoming aware of this tendency, mindfulness allows you the choice to reframe that thought in a more open way. For instance, "although it feels like everyone hates me, in reality it is only (these specific people), and the reason why they might disagree with me is..."

I used to magnify or minimize situations that would often lead to distortive thinking, which is a type of judgment. When you blow things out of proportion, often referred to as "making a mountain out of a molehill," you are distorting reality with unconscious thinking. Here are some examples:

- "If I don't make partner, I won't be considered a success in the eyes of the accounting profession."
- "If I leave the meeting early, I'll be ridiculed."
- "If that person gets promoted before I do, I am leaving the firm."
- "If the subway is late, I'm going to be late for work, and I'll be in trouble."

This type of catastrophic thinking occurs when you give added weight to the worst possible scenario. Catastrophic thinking is a form of judgment that includes an implied fallacy of the slippery slope, in which one thing leads to another all the way down to the worst possible disaster. Here are examples of the opposite of making a mountain out of a molehill:

- "It's okay to miss work today. It's April 14 and nobody will notice. I have plenty of absences to play with."

- "It's okay not to return a call to the client's lawyer. He can wait. The matter is not a big deal anyway."
- "With one month to go, I haven't earned any CPE credits this year. I have plenty of time."

The first thing to notice is how your body feels after having catastrophic thoughts like this. You'll then mindfully direct attention to the part of your body that might feel a contraction. This tightening up is the wisdom of your body sounding an alarm bell for you to notice and mindfully place attention on that area feeling pain. You then get very curious. Upon "looking" deeper, you may notice how your thinking became distorted without you realizing it. You are then free to place your focus on a sense of acceptance and compassion for yourself.

Fully recognizing that you are part of the human condition and naturally have this type of thinking is an aspect of the current evolutionary stage of human development. In other words, recognize your common humanity and try not to be hard on yourself. You'll notice as the observer of your own thoughts that they are like clouds passing by. From this place of open awareness, make plans to deal with the situation with the three C's of heart-centered thinking: clarity, connection, and compassion.

Filtering

In conversations with your client, you might sometimes discuss the balance sheet and income statement and present various financial ratios and statistics that summarize the operations of the business.

The client says: "You did a nice job. You gave us a lot to think about. Some of it is pretty complicated. You might want to shorten it, but I can tell you worked hard on it, and I appreciate your dedication." You hear: "The financial statements and analytical review was too complicated and long."

In this example, you are judging yourself negatively. This doesn't just happen out of the blue. It is an aspect of the ego that we will address in Chapter 8. With open awareness, you'll start to notice this pattern and a tendency for the mind to judge. The good news is that this "inner critic" can indeed be transformed into something more helpful for you. The various mindfulness practices can be your foundation for discovering a way to turn negative self-judgments into more realistic and practical steps to deal with situations and people.

Jumping to Conclusions

Did you ever draw a conclusion about what someone else thinks or feels and will do to you in the future with little or no information? Here is an example: You see your client frowning as you speak to her about your consulting project and think, "She must be angry at me because I didn't give her exactly what she was looking for." This type of judgment will be felt in your body as a tightening and contraction. The free flow of your energy gets trapped in a certain area of your body when the judgmental mind jumps to a conclusion.

In this scenario, your client may be angry for reasons that have nothing whatsoever to do with you. It's just that your consulting project allowed her an opportunity for her anger to come up and project it onto you. In open awareness, you'll notice the judgment, if not immediately then certainly when there is a change in your body's energy flow. If you apply Einstein's approach to solve this problem, you won't rely on your thoughts alone to help alleviate your pain and body contraction. You'll employ open awareness, which is taking a non-judgmental stance to your reaction and pain with kind attention focused on the area in your body that is feeling unsettled. Of course, if you can catch yourself before the negative reaction and judgment, that is all the better. But you get another chance, as I have illustrated when you notice the unsettling feeling in your body. This is mindfulness at work by a mindful professional.

Cleaning up the Shadow

Open awareness can help you recognize those instances when you base an entire class of circumstances, people, and events on one singular example or a relatively few examples. For instance, your clients are mostly auto dealerships, but over the years you have done work with some not-for-profit organizations. On these occasions, you did a good job, but your time exceeded budget on each occasion. You found the work fulfilling, but now when presented with another opportunity, you believe you won't make a profit on this engagement.

Notice how the judgmental mind comes in and zeroes in on the so-called negative factors right away. You know that this work is rewarding, but rather than looking at reality from an open awareness stance, you allow these judgments to distort your thinking. This is a pattern that most likely plays out in other areas of work and in your personal life. These "protectors" are part of the egoic mind structure and have a noble purpose in serving you. After all, the protector doesn't want you to "fail" and lose money on the job. Interestingly, the protector is really not personal to you; it is a common pattern in almost everyone. So, it is important to get to know your protector—have a conversation with it and embrace the shadow.

Carl Jung believed that "in spite of its function as a reservoir for human darkness—or perhaps because of it—the shadow is the seat of creativity." The shadow represents everything we refuse to acknowledge about ourselves yet project onto others. We hide these hidden parts because we believe they are unacceptable. It's a little bit like the caboose in the back of the train that is dragged along. In doing this, we disown part of ourselves and our personal power.

In mindfulness, we get very curious about our shadow parts. We begin to see these aspects of our personality with fresh eyes and listen to what they want to say to us, so to speak. Healthy personalities include many sub-parts; some we identify with strongly, and others we disown. Mindfulness does not attempt to change them or our personality, but rather to shine the light of awareness on all of them. We mindfully use our bodies to see where these parts have called home and bring loving awareness to them in an authentic way.

Our bodies store our experiences on all levels: mental, emotional, physical, and spiritual. It functions as a general ledger for the soul. You may have forgotten the grueling audit you worked on last month or the negotiation you had with IRS regarding some tax matter, but your body remembers everything. One of the reasons mindfulness directs our attention to our body through meditation and informal practices such as the body scan, breath meditation, and noticing our sense perceptions is to reclaim these parts when they come up as distractions. For without distractions, we won't really know who or where we are, as we gently return again and again to our anchor for *presence* and the *Now.*

Transforming Parts

Once the protector part, or the inner critic, is understood through the light of awareness, you may notice that it is a necessary part of you. As you work on your shadow parts through mindful awareness, you'll appreciate each aspect of your personality all the more, even the troublesome aspects. When we open the door and respect all aspects of our personality through *presence*, they gain confidence that allow the wounded child parts to heal. In this way, the untapped potential within us can grow and we can access creative solutions. This practice becomes a way of life through mindfulness.

When we notice our parts are in alignment with our core needs and values, we can bring them to our attention and allow them to speak. If you sense any contraction in your body or tension in your mental activities when doing so, it likely means that there are parts of you clamoring for attention at the same time. This internal conflict is a sign for the light of awareness to come forth and reconcile these warning aspects of your personality in an open, non-judgmental fashion.

This "parts work" as it is called, when filtered through open awareness and mindful attention, deepens trust in yourself, your clients, and your work as an accountant. Although still not taught in most business schools, when we learn how to listen deeply to all the voices in the head, we open up and become more effective in our business relationships and our work. We are the center of our T account. You don't have to wait until these parts are 100% effective. Start by honoring each aspect that wants to be heard, and keep welcoming them home. Your personality will love you for this. By doing the inner work necessary, you'll be less likely to hold judgment on parts of yourself that may have been problematic. It may be difficult to be an advocate for climate change when we haven't been an advocate for the climate change within our inner world. By doing the work, you are a mindful professional.

As you work with your parts, you may notice that you attract clients that have similar issues as your own. Their troubled parts act as a mirror to your troubled parts. That is one reason why our clients trigger us. When we leave the center right down the middle of the T account and get sacked by either our debits (past) or credits (future), it sometimes takes time to restore our balance and return to our authentic selves.

Suppose your client is overly conservative, providing very little bonus and raises to their staff. Your part may say, "You're a terrible businessperson" at the very moment when you are discussing year-end bonuses with them and preparing their budget. You ponder this and all of sudden another part says, "You're a terrible CPA." What can you do? First, while in the meeting, you can take a deep breath and show empathy to your inner critic. Then gently acknowledge the critic and ask it to take a back seat for now, knowing the voice will be heard later. When you have a moment later, it is not so much the technique you employ to engage your parts, but rather how you do in an open, non-judgmental way, including your open heart.

Mindful Strategic Planning

When we engage our judgmental minds and the various sub-parts of our personalities, we invite our souls to come forward in a very sacred way. We turn ourselves inward and invite *presence* to fill our minds and bodies, feeling an "aliveness" within that can't be described. You just know. When we have a heart-to-heart conversation with ourselves, we uncover what wants to be born in the present moment, and we sense awe both within and without. When you notice this, it is vital to pay attention with your whole being. As an old proverb says, "A vision without a plan is just a dream. A plan without a vision is just drudgery. But a vision with a plan can change the world."

This process of creation and manifesting what is most important to you starts with a vision. Let's say you want to start your own CPA firm. That is a big step for any accountant and one that requires you to have a heart-to-heart conversation with yourself. You will listen to all aspects of your personality. The aspects that say "You don't have what it takes," "You can't develop business, "You're too shy," "You will fail," and so forth. These voices can be very dominating; yet, in some way, they want to protect you. So, you need to listen carefully, as we have addressed. Once heard and fully acknowledged, you can work with your parts as they settle back and relax.

Now, you are ready for your strategic plan for starting your own CPA firm. A personal strategic plan helps you determine where you stand, where you wish to go, and a plan to get there. By tapping into the wholeness of who you are and your own resourcefulness, you'll begin to say, "I can do this."

Like any business plan, your personal strategic plan will include different categories. The key components are to be aligned with your values, vision, and purpose. You'll ask yourself, "How do I allocate resources, both personal and financial? How can I set priorities, deadlines, etc.?" What is most important during this process is to focus attention on the step you are taking in the present moment, being fully aware of where you want to go. We'll address mindfulness of goals more fully in Chapter 6. For now, I'd like to continue to address open awareness and mindful attention to the judgmental mind.

The plan is not the territory. Mindfulness will help you be more flexible in your planning. It will open you up to new frontiers. If you run into a detour, as you will, mindfulness will help you maintain an equilibrium right down the middle of your proverbial T account so you stay focused. You'll look at your whole life situation from the perspective of open awareness. I notice that when this happens to me, I bring in self-compassion to all the various aspects of life, including my accounting work. You'll fully recognize that you don't have all the answers, but you find ways that help you get answers, sometimes in unforeseen ways. You start to close the gap between where you are and where you want to go. The action you take is rooted in *presence* and linked to your core values, vision, and purpose—in other words, your T account.

Henry David Thoreau writes on this point: "If you have built castles in the air, your work need not be lost; that is where they should be. Now put in the foundation under them." Jesus put it this way: "Everyone who hears these words of mine and doesn't do them will be like a foolish man, who built his house on the sand. The rain came down, the floods came, and the winds blew, and beat on the house; and it fell, and great was its loss." In other words, find who you really are in your essence, your authentic self, and let your light shine on all you do. Bring forth your three B's: *beyond balancing the books.*

I am often struck by the phrase "hanging in there," signifying our collective struggles. I wrote this poem to help find a way through the daily grind and to discover a way forward through it all.

Hanging in There

Hanging in there.
We are hanging in there,
To our sense of being right
And our judgments that
Keep us stuck.

We are hanging in there,
To our assumptions and fears,
As if our life depended on it,
Shielding us from

The present moment,
Protecting us from living
The One life in the
Here and Now.

We are hanging in there
For our retirement fund,
In the empty hours of our time-tracking.
Hanging in there
To who we think we are
And supposed to Be.

We are hanging in there
Onto the railings of each day,
to the fractured bones,
to abandoned goals.

Where is time for living?
What time is upon us?
What can we do?
Be Present and Open to
Awareness of Awareness.

Open awareness will bring forth so much in your life. It can help you in busy season, during changes in your work environment, job insecurities, lack of autonomy, work-life balance, new business risks, and boring work. I wrote this poem, adapted from the style of St.

Francis of Assisi, to help me address these very issues in my own accounting and coaching practice:

The Lilies in the Field

Life Source makes me a lily in your field,
Where there is uncertainty, let me plant potential.
Where there is pain, healing.
Where there is trouble, trust.
Where there is loneliness, encouragement.
Where there is boredom, light.
Where there is gloom, hope.
O, Devine Master, grant that I may
Not so much seek relationships as to relate,
To fit in as to fit,
To do as to allow,
To coach as to be coached.
For it is in giving that we receive,
It is in sweeping away that we are polished,
And it is in releasing that we awaken to the Here and Now.

Formal Practice: RAIN Meditation for Difficult Thoughts and Emotions

RAIN stands for:

- *Recognize* what's going on
- *Allow* and accept the experience to be there, just as it is
- *Investigate* with kindness

133

- *Natural awareness,* which comes from not identifying with the experience

You can use RAIN with any experience, make it a stand-alone meditation, and easily return to daily work. It is especially helpful with difficult emotions, like the emotions and thoughts that your inner critic seems to bring forth. Let's begin the meditation.

- Sit comfortably and bring awareness to your present experience.
- Give yourself a minute or two after closing your eyes to notice what you hear, what you feel in your body, and what is occurring in your mind.
- Bring up a moderately difficult experience or emotion, starting with a recognition of what it is. Take care of yourself: if the emotion becomes too strong, put it aside for now.
- Recognize the thoughts coming up, the sensations in your body, and the critical inner voice you often hear.
- Spend a few minutes just acknowledging the presence of the difficulty, tuning in to the different ways it manifests in your experience.
- Move to the next phase: allowance or acceptance.
- With unpleasant emotions, the habit of the mind is to try to get rid of these experiences.
- Instead, allow it to be present for you.
- You may try offering this simple phrase of equanimity and acceptance: "Right now, it's like this."
- Continue to work with acceptance for five minutes, bringing the mind back when it starts pushing away the difficulty.
- Now begin investigating more deeply.
- Recognize what you were feeling in the first step of RAIN.
- In investigation, allow curiosity to take over.
- Ask yourself where you feel vulnerable, how this emotion serves you, and if you believe you can be free from this pain.

- For the final five minutes, turn toward your natural tendency to nourish yourself with mindful self-compassion.
- This whole exercise has been a practice of mindful self-compassion, as you are tending to the pain with awareness rather than denying it.
- Lastly, make a dedicated effort to offer a few phrases of compassion with an open heart.

From Judgments to Mindful Management

Learning how to mindfully manage your staff rather than boss them around is a skill that can transform your work environment and bring about a more conscious, productive, and fulfilling workplace. Here are ten transformational opportunities that you can implement in a variety of business settings and situations to bring about a higher level of awareness and connection in your firm or with your clients.

1. Instead of invoking fear, share power to stimulate clarity, connection, and creativity.
2. Rather than pointing out problems to solve, affirm the strength in people.
3. Stop making demands and instead make requests.
4. Let go of control and start facilitating empowerment.
5. You don't need to know all the answers, but you do need to seek answers.
6. Hold off pointing out mistakes and celebrate new learning.
7. Cease delegating responsibility; instead establish accountability.
8. Stop believing knowledge is power; believe vulnerability is power.

9. Say "no" more often to directives and "yes" to dialogues.

10. Refuse to see people as "costs" to minimize; see people as assets to develop, not only technically but adaptively to increasing awareness of who they really are. In other words, use your emotional intelligence.

In order to change a mindset, there needs to be an internal shift in each individual so that awareness becomes the primary driver for actions rather than the conditioned thinking mind. As a leader, you will either make this shift after a period of pain and suffering, or you can do so voluntarily. The framework for this consciousness is mindfulness. It is conscious leaders that actually take the lead in facilitating change within the executive ranks and lead by example rather than just "approving" a program like mindfulness coaching and development for the staff. In particular, CPA firms can do a better job and commit resources to mentoring their staff, who too often feel isolated, fatigued, and frustrated. Here are some business challenges that can present opportunities for mindfulness at all levels of an organization, one person at a time. Some of these are routine, while others occur during a transition.

New Projects

When new engagements come in, we sometimes go through turbulent periods until the dust settles, communication channels are established, and vision and goals are shared. Mindfulness can help support the development of these projects through *presence*. How is that so?

First, recognize your own emotions and feelings as you embark on a new project. There is often a sense of excitement about the new business. And that is good. But as you know, today's highs are tomorrow lows. By staying in touch with your sense of excitement and not getting carried away with it, you'll be practicing mindfulness. It's that sense of equilibrium at the center of the T account we have addressed earlier, which we call awareness.

Second, as you start to communicate within your firm and to the new client about the project, there will sometimes be disconnection or misinterpretations of roles and responsibilities, even with an engagement letter in the file. There will be individuals around you who are not conscious and will start to accuse and blame while feeling anxious and overwhelmed. What can you do? Of course, you can sit down with them and discuss the situation. However, these are moments when you will be tested. You'll need to raise your antenna so that the light of awareness is shining on your own internal struggles about the breakdown, and also on the immediate environment and people around you, in an open, non-judgmental way. Many people skip over their own internal feelings and brush them away as part of normal everyday existence. Unfortunately, that is an unconscious way of approaching struggle, and it limits one's capacity to expand awareness and tap into their creativity. This happens to just about everyone as the pain is too difficult. So we cope in a way that makes it lighter, or at least we hope it will.

Third, when we share vision and goals with other team members, sometimes we get "buy-in" and sometimes we do not. You'll know this when the first conflict comes up during the project. How one responds to conflict informs us more about the person than their reactions when things are going well. A healthy way to respond to conflict is based in trust, mutual respect, and civility. A healthy person will want to directly meet with another in a shared space of openness and connection where each person has an opportunity to speak and learn. The unhealthy way to respond to conflict is to close up and maintain silence, to send texts and e-mails as a means to establish a position. This approach, used too often in business settings, does nothing to build understanding and true resolution to matters that are important to someone in the conversation. Mindfulness is about connection and sharing in an open, non-judgmental way. We let go of our egos and realize we are here to go *beyond balancing the books.*

Mergers and Acquisitions

When a firm mergers, restructures, or downsizes, revised work responsibility can increase stress, decrease morale, and foster other interpersonal conflicts and anger. Mindfulness helps build resilience and trust while supporting vision and a blended culture through open awareness. It's about creating a resonant relationship in which each side is in tune with the other. As one study pointed out, "the return to mindfulness or retaining some degree of humility as one is never truly as mindful as one would like, at least a relative return to it, only seems to occur when one is able to build or rebuild a set of resonant relationships in one's life and work system" (30).

"The path to creating or maintaining resonant relationships is through mindfulness, hope, compassion and playfulness. Once one person in a relationship begins to invoke any of these experiences through the process of emotional contagion, the other person is infected and moves into that state—unless something is blocking or inhibiting them, such as their own fear, negativity, or defensiveness" (30).

Not every relationship is based on these ingredients, of course. The good news is it takes only one person to maintain the presence in a room filled with unconscious people, all positioning themselves to get a word in and an upper hand, so to speak. By returning again and again to a state of mindfulness during a merger, you will find it easier each time. "It is through practice that a person learns the techniques to change their own mood and activate related neural networks and endocrine secretions" (30).

Virtual Teams

When people are in different offices or need to communicate with clients that are geographically dispersed, mindfulness is the foundation in which perceived distance or differences no longer matter. Mindfulness is really creativity in action, and virtual meetings can be the very space to introduce meditation practices in the workplace. Start out each meeting with a three-minute breathing space meditation, which was introduced in Chapter 1. This not only settles everyone into the same virtual space, it also introduces a sense of playfulness too often missed in business settings.

Mindfulness is so much more than a wellness intervention. It is the basis for all that is good in life, like genuine connection, compassion, clarity, kindness, creation, and love. The key is to understand the link between mindfulness and creativity as you work together in a virtual meeting. As you gather information, pinpoint issues, develop solutions, and implement action plans, stay in touch with your inner dimension of thoughts, emotions, and feelings. Stay in touch with the stillness within and without by acutely listening, not so much to what is being said as to the underlying ground in which all words arise: the stillness.

In this state, anything you'll need to hear or say will be said at the right moment, and it will be a creative thought. You may not have said the most during these meeting, but what you say will have meaning and energy that will be felt at least on a subliminal level. You will be instilling the belief that one is capable of creative behavior, which is so important to accountants who have been misperceived in culture as having an uncreative profession. Through mindfulness programs in the workplace, creativity can be developed, sustained, and fun!

Performance Objectives

How leaders assess, communicate, and reward performance can be based not only on getting things done but also on qualities such as emotional intelligence, speaking candidly, practicing integrity, eliminating gossip, fostering creative perspectives, and taking radical responsibility. Management philosopher Peter Drucker writes, "You cannot manage other people unless you manage yourself first" (31). He acknowledges that his work is aimed at a particular type of manager, one that seeks to make a positive contribution through their work while also making a living.

Have you ever brought an upsetting emotional issue to the office? I have, and no matter how much I attempted to concentrate, there was usually a feeling of unease and a contraction in my body. Since I started practicing mindfulness, however, I have noticed that these unpleasant emotions are really not so impeding anymore, provided that I acknowledge them and remain open to the feeling. When I do that, it really is no longer a distraction, as I discover the emotional pain is no longer stuck energy but fluid motion.

According to Jeremy Hunter, Ph.D, Professor of Practice at the Peter F. Drucker Graduate School of Management, "contemporary management education has largely overlooked creating an educational process as systematic as accounting and financial analysis for managing oneself. Students are left to fend for themselves to know how to skillfully handle and transform their inner forces of emotions, physical sensations, thoughts and beliefs to produce elegant and effective results" (32). Mindfulness is supported by science and starts from within by noticing your internal state. Awareness and attention take you from exclusively thinking about what's next and getting things done to seeing what is in front of you and getting things right. You'll sense greater intrinsic meaning, personal responsibility, and social contribution in all aspects of your life.

As we become more aware of our judgments, we are often surprised by how much we judge. I know I was. Take heart, for this is common, and yet it does diminish our capacity for creativity and overall well-being. You can decide for yourself if the judgments you make of people, places, and situations are serving you well. It does take courage and openness to the unknown to let go of judgments, which often can bring up fear. In our culture, we have little or no training to access open awareness and this deeper dimension of our being—our inner state. Educational, social, religious, and family institutions have suppressed our fierce and feral creativity. However, even under these limitations—or perhaps because of them—*presence* practice is here and now a way to include and transcend all that came before.

I invite you to ponder what mindfulness means for you and how it can uniquely help you in your personal and professional life.

Chapter 5

Cultivating Acceptance as a Doorway into Presence

Seek not the things which happen should happen as you wish, but wish the things which happen to be as they are, and you will have a tranquil flow in life.

—Epictetus

How many times have you engaged with someone and felt that the way they treat and talk to you is just not acceptable, filled with double standards and hypocrisy? When this has happened to me, it has caused unpleasant feelings and sensations in my body accompanied by thoughts that are often unreasonable. In this chapter, we will discover and cultivate an accepting stance to situations, people, and events that a reasonable person's mind might conclude as unacceptable.

Let's take Sandra for example. She is a rising CPA financial planner serving high-net worth individuals. She has a blossoming practice in which she engages with her clients in personal and business matters. Over time, she has built relationships with a diversified population. She works within a large investment advisory firm where there is a rigid structure of reporting and review. Sandra has several partners that work with her, and she has come to me for coaching on some of her relationships and issues at work. One of her core values is a sense of freedom and equality. She wants coaching on how she can stay true to her values while working in this firm that is constantly putting her down and is oblivious to her emotions and feelings.

Sandra has been practicing mindfulness for some time, and she is connected to her inner state where she has cultivated a non-resisting stance, which has opened up doors in all aspects of her life in so many meaningful ways. One such way is her keen understanding and discernment of the people she works with in her office. For example, the partners always think they are right. They don't view Sandra as an equal and feel they don't have any particular need to address her concerns. In fact, the partners crave affirmation, believing their employees are there to serve them and then justify their own freedom within the organization simply by being a partner. How can Sandra possibly accept that which any reasonable person would consider as unacceptable?

First, Sandra is in touch with the unpleasantness of her work environment in a non-judgmental way. She is accepting of her emotions, feelings, and thoughts about the situation. She does not need to accept, condone, or approve the way she is being treated. Sandra is able to recognize the difference between the situation and her own reactions to the situation—she has cultivated an acceptance of her own feelings. This accepting perspective is the freedom she yearns for and that which is real and true for her. From this place, she has a choice to continue with this firm and talk with a partner and human resources or look elsewhere.

Sometimes, our paths lead to a crossroad, and Sandra met her crossroad. She is in alignment with her needs and values and is not afraid to ask herself the difficult question most people are afraid to ask themselves, because they believe the answer may be no.

What do you love?

Acceptance and Its Fruit

The fruit of acceptance is wisdom, and gratitude is wisdom. Of course, we're talking about gratitude for the big things in life like health, family, and career, but also gratitude for the little things such as when the air conditioning is working in the office and a warm smile from a stranger. In other words, the things we take for granted. Research shows that gratitude is linked to happiness. Gratitude and humility are closely linked cousins.

Did you ever try to be humble? If so, you may have found that to be difficult. Humbleness is not something we do; rather, either we are humble or we are not. Did you ever try to tell someone you are a grateful person? Of course not, because to do so is a mark of inauthenticity. True gratitude happens naturally out of a state of *presence* with a tender hand and some water to grow, blossoming into your very own gratitude garden! It means showing up and being there for someone when they are down, like a colleague who lost a spouse, or to discuss some conflict or hurt directly in an open and non-judgmental way. Melody Beattie writes: "Gratitude unlocks the fullness of life. It turns what we have into enough, and more. It turns denial into acceptance, chaos to order, confusion to clarity." In other words, real gratitude transforms you.

Richard McKnight, an organizational psychologist who works extensively with stress management, calls for a greater sense of spirituality in business, which he defines as "an animating life force, an energy that inspires one towards certain ends or purposes that go beyond the self." To go beyond the self in business and life is to have no ego attachment to your work, firm, relationships, your role as a CPA, family bonds, and so forth. To have no attachment is to cultivate mindful *presence* in all aspects of your accounting work. When we embrace ourselves and our experiences with loving connected *presence*, it feels good. The goodness is intrinsic to who you are.

Sometimes, however, we are challenged. For example, when you sit down with your quality control (QC) department, and your work is critically scrutinized, what happens to you in those moments? Mindfulness does not say you should become a doormat to someone's ridicule or condescension but instead aims to cultivate a stance of acceptance of what you feel in those moments, like Sandra did. With acceptance of your own inner turmoil, you can then respond from a position of strength, knowing full well what you feel and think about your work. In other words, acceptance of your experience actively generates positive emotions.

We may need an energy boost at times just to focus on our positive experiences, especially after sitting down with a supervisor. I like to take a few deep breaths and be still. Helen Keller puts it this way: "When one door of happiness closes, another opens, but often we look so long at the closed door that we do not see the one that has been opened for us." This is why acceptance is so important to your well-being. It helps you move on and open the next door—the sooner the better.

Wonderful things happen when we cultivate an acceptance stance to our experiences and step out of a "me mindset." We move beyond a cause and effect, quid pro quo, and merchant mentality, and discover a creative impulse in us that has its roots in acceptance. There is a letting go of control-based strategies, like pushing away unwanted experiences such as anxiety. When you try to push away anxiety, does it work? Usually, it doesn't.

I often would succumb to anxiety attacks in my early days as a CPA, and it wasn't pleasant. This anxiety was usually self-created and involved some worry about the future. Back then, I didn't have the tools to cope adequately, so I tried to hide these feelings of uneasiness. Sometimes it worked, and more often it didn't. Eckhart Tolle writes: "Whatever you fight, you strengthen, and what you resist, persists." Anxiety may come up when you are asked to work overtime during non-busy season. How do you relate to these types of situations? If you can't accept it, then at least acknowledge your feelings and opinion in a non-judgmental way. In other words, take care of yourself. Paradoxically, research has consistently demonstrated that trying to control and avoid these negative emotions often increases their intensity (33).

Accounting for Acceptance

Using our T account metaphor, I invite you to imagine on the debit side a negative experience at work that brought up an emotional reaction. Correspondingly, on the credit side imagine a positive experience in your accounting career that elicited a positive emotion. As you know, both positive and negative experiences are a natural part of our working environment. However, we usually don't have a problem dealing with the positive experiences. The debits can be more challenging.

The negative situations, such as when we are understaffed on an audit, are generally experienced as challenging, not because of our actual experience but due to our mindset and relationship with those feelings. We tend to resist these situations and want them to go away. Although being understaffed is sometimes a natural part of our work in accounting, most of us have developed a completely different relationship with these debit-based negative experiences than we have with the credit side of experiences, such as when we are fully staffed and the job is flowing with equanimity. We tend to embrace positive experiences and fight against and resist negative experiences. William Shakespeare writes to this point in this way: "There is nothing either good or bad, but thinking makes it so." Your perspectives, beliefs, and opinions make things good and bad to you. One client might think a profit margin of 30% is good and a sign of growth, but another client in the same type of business may think it is a sign of weakness.

In many instances, these negative experiences arise when feeling a loss of control over the engagement. Sometimes, this causes internal conflicts among your peers, which can be overbearing and argumentative as you discuss staffing a job. This may be done quietly with somebody winning and others losing. In the long term, this tendency to deal differently with both the negative and positive experiences fosters a certain type of relationship to each of them.

Treating Positive and Negative Experiences with Equanimity

Joe is the partner on an audit, and one of his staff members is standing right outside of his office. The staff member is in a good mood, smiles, and has a positive attitude. She is a rising senior accountant at the firm. Joe has a nice chat with her, and then she leaves. The next day, she stops by to discuss the upcoming audit. Joe invites her to sit down in his office to have a cup of coffee and discuss the audit program. After she leaves, Joe feels confident that his audit is in good hands.

On another job Joe is heading up, he is assigned another accountant who does not have a reputation for completing work on time. This senior accountant comes to his office and has a negative attitude, looks unsure, and is in a bad mood. He is having a difficult time and asks if he can come into the office to talk. Joe responds that he is busy and that the senior accountant should make an appointment with him some other day. Joe immediately shuts the door and tries to forget that he was there.

Later that day, Joe is walking across the office, hoping to see the rising senior accountant, but unfortunately, the negative person bumps into him in the hall. Slightly irritated, Joe tells him he can't talk right now. Paradoxically, it doesn't matter how much Joe would like this person to go away; he continues to see him around the office. He never gave the senior accountant a chance for them to get to know each other and discuss his background and work experiences. In Joe's mind, he isn't good enough to staff the job. Joe complains to human resources and exhausts a lot of energy before the audit even starts.

We develop a different relationship with the debits and credits of our experiences, even without meaning to do so. The people in this example represent positive and negative experiences. Just as we don't allow negative people to come into our office, we also push away negative emotions and thoughts by trying to suppress them or wishing they would go away. We don't get to know them. We avoid and resist them just like Joe did.

Of course, we want to keep negative experiences to a minimum. First, they are simply not pleasant. By avoiding them, we think we can get rid of them at least temporarily. Second, our culture teaches us to keep negative experiences out of our lives. A managing partner who tells one of his employees that they won't "make it" in the accounting business is effectively telling his employee to block any emotion that causes pain. The partner is showing his lack of empathy, and there is likely much going on inside him that has not been faced with awareness. This is one of the tragedies of our culture: the inability to confront one's own shadow.

This shows up in many different ways. For example, there is still very little compassion in business settings, primarily due to our conditioning and childhood wounds that have not been faced in mindful awareness. The old school way of approaching this business dilemma is to "write-off" this dark cloud through employee benefit plans, human resource chats, social gatherings, and happy hours to "lift morale." Thankfully, in some businesses, that is starting to change. In *The 15 Commitments of Conscious Leadership*, the authors point out a new paradigm for sustainable success, which looks at leading "above the line" where leaders are mindfully aware and compassionate human beings (34).

Sometimes, we notice that great things happen when we get angry, provided we are able to channel that emotion to our soul's longing. When we mindfully accept the anger in our body, very often we respond with virtuous acts of courage, generosity, and compassion. We feel our passions in the body. What would it be like if we learned early on in our professional training or before to stay in touch and listen to our bodies? In my experience, when I am in touch with my body, I focus less on myself and more on the common good. In the modern world, we believe that the intellect is all there is. Not so; while the intellect and left brain thinking are powerful tools, accounting today is in greater need of the passions and right brain functioning. Can this be done in your role as an accountant? Yes, but it may require a rewiring and a re-direction of attention from exclusively thinking to more conscious awareness.

Mindfulness helps us extract valuable information about our negative experiences through conscious acceptance of them. These experiences tell us something valuable about ourselves. Anxiety, for example, can tell us when our workload has crossed the line. A conscious firm would have meditation rooms and mindfulness workshops to help their staff manage stress and discover what is really important to each of them. They would begin meetings with a one-minute breath meditation. Too many firms still believe having ice cream on Friday afternoons, breakfast on Saturday mornings in tax season, April 15 celebrations, softball games, and annual reviews are enough to keep the team healthy and happy. Conscious firms would take a different approach; they would go *beyond balancing the books.*

We should be mindfully aware of our emotions rather than trying to push them down. For example, when you feel overworked consistently, it may imply that an essential core value of yours, such as inner peace and well-being, has been impeded. Now, peace is a powerful word and has a different meaning for everyone. But true peace passes all conceptual knowing and has its roots in being present for the fullness of life now.

Furthermore, if we don't face our difficult emotions, we will not be able to build up the confidence necessary to handle them when they arise unexpectedly. Seeking a professional counselor is thankfully no longer a taboo and should be encouraged at all levels in a business environment. Mindfulness helps you do that by building up the muscle holding the lantern.

Questions

- *Let's return to Joe. Do you think it will be a good thing for him, as the audit partner on the engagement, to invite the "negative accountant" into his office to discuss the audit? Remember the goal of acceptance is not to create positive emotions or to make the negative ones go away. The goal is to cultivate a different relationship with them.*
- *How do you ordinarily deal with difficult emotions at work?*
- *What would it be like to keep an open door for every kind of emotional debit or credit?*
- *What would it be like to give every debit or credit a hug?*

- *Take a moment and imagine you are the line right down the center of a T account. Now imagine a clear light starting from the crown of your head that runs all the way down to your feet. In this clear light, you notice all your beliefs about time and money. You ask the questions: Are they true? Are my beliefs reality or just beliefs? Are my beliefs a subjective viewpoint of my environment and security? Then ask: Who am I in relation to those beliefs? Can you invite an acceptance stance around the fleeting and subjective nature of your underlying beliefs that are mostly limiting you in one way or another?*

I invite you to journal your thoughts as you reflect on these questions.

Inner and Outer Self

This poem can help integrate your soul nature with the work you do in the world, so you can live in alignment with your true purpose and have meaning in your work and personal life. This poem takes you on a journey from the beginning and returns to a place of pure potential within you.

A Spring has Sprung

Spring has sprung, the bush is blooming,
In the inner most part of the soul.
Fertile and ever so new Now,
Naturally made in the One Image.
Breaking out and called to action,
You Hear the words "God Is."
If you wait for this birth,
All good, consolation and bliss are yours.
If you miss it, then you will miss all goodness.
What you then seek outside falls away,
Like thoughts and emotions do.
Whatever comes forth in this birth,

Brings enduring substance and pure Being.
Then light spills over into the faculties,
And the outer self is new moment to moment.
You ask, how do I know if this has happened in me?
Something touches your heart with tenderness,
Turning away from transient things more and more.
It happens with such delight,
Past and future reign small compared to this.
The more you are free of yourself,
More truth, understanding and light reigns.
In the very ground of your soul,
You have gained more than you were ever taught.

True Nature

You have unlimited capacity and potential to live your true purpose, and you don't necessarily have to leave the accounting profession to do that! What is it that holds you back, and how can mindfulness help you live that life now? I would suggest that any limitation is due to your limiting belief system—the imbedded underlying subconscious beliefs that are at the root of inner and outer conflicts. These beliefs do not want you to notice them or shine the light of conscious awareness on them. If you did, they would simply fade away and die. These beliefs are mostly negative and relish so-called problems.

Shakespeare addresses this when he writes: "Our doubts are traitors, and make us lose the good we oft might win, by fearing to attempt." Our doubts often come from fear. You may have enough doubt that you will not even attempt to do something, but then you risk missing out on the good that comes from it. Mindfulness helps you see your doubts so that you know them well. Doubts can help you avoid something bad or keep you from something good. You can first mindfully accept your doubts and feel where they lurk in your body. Then, with awareness and keen discernment, discover if those doubts are holding you back or not.

In mindfulness, you cultivate an inner acceptance in the only moment that counts: the present moment. You are not accepting your circumstances in an hour from now, tomorrow, or next year. Just this moment. This acceptance brings forth an opening for you to look at your circumstances through the lens of the present moment in awareness, your true nature. As you gain a foothold in the *Now*, you can then examine your situation along the following pathway:

- Ask yourself: What is the problem? It is more powerful to do this practice when you are experiencing some turmoil, either at work or in your personal life situations.
- Focus and locate where in your body you feel physical discomfort as a result of the situation. You can do a body scan meditation, or you can simply do the three-minute breathing meditation we addressed in Chapter 1.
- Ask yourself: Are my thoughts surrounding this situation familiar to me? In other words, do you notice a pattern of thinking surrounding your current situation that is recurring by nature?
- How are you feeling? Try to name the emotion such as "this is irritation," "this is anger," "I notice anxiety," and so forth.
- Ask yourself: What is the worst possible outcome in the circumstances? What is even worse than that? You may begin to notice in your conscious awareness that these worst-case scenarios are not real. They are just thoughts about a situation, often future-based. Recall a situation from the past in which your worries and concerns were later proved to be far worse than the reality of the actual circumstances. With this

perspective shedding ease and light within you, move on to the next step.

- What is the best possible outcome that could happen under these conditions? If you're like me, there will be a period of silence, then maybe something like "Well, I don't know" will come up. You'll start to realize that your thoughts are dominated by negative outcomes. The potential positive outcomes have taken a back seat; they may not even be in the same car.

- Now, with a grasp of your best possible outcome, ask yourself: Why isn't this happening already? If you are honest, you're likely to notice the same negative underlying belief structure that has prevented you from moving forward.

- At this point in the process, take your time and come up with a statement that contradicts your underlying negative belief system. Continue to repeat this affirmation so that it sinks into your subconscious mind and is with you from now on. Bring the light of *presence* to your new affirmation. Offer thanks to the universe for allowing you to work through this process in its own time and place. As Oliver Wendell Holmes, former Supreme Court justice, famously stated: "A mind that is stretched to a new idea never returns to its original dimension." In other words, once you start living your positive affirmation in daily life, you won't return to your previous negative belief systems.

Conflicts Reveals Character: Vulnerability Strength

Getting along is easy when we are conflict-free. I agree with you; you agree with me. We have similar preferences, and we roll along in our relationship until some conflict or misunderstanding arises. In these moments, we can really know the mark of a person based on how they respond to conflict. In a healthy relationship, both people know conflict is inevitable, and they display a healthy character when a conflicting situation arises.

155

In my coaching, accounting practice, and even in my personal life, I often meet with a person outside the usual setting over a cup of coffee to share thoughts and feelings about a conflict or misunderstanding with mutual dignity, respect, and calmness. This informal meeting is usually very meaningful for me and the other person in the conversation. The research behind Christopher Bergland's *Psychology Today* article, "Face-to-Face Social Contact Reduces Risk of Depression," supports such meetings contributing to the overall health and well-being for both people in the conversation.

What is most important to me in this personal meeting is a sense of felt embodiment. When I am in touch with what is going on internally, I am much better equipped to express myself to someone who may have a different perspective and who is sitting right in front of me, even if it's through an online platform such as Zoom. Staying in touch with the inner body helps me connect to the present moment, where I am able to communicate with my whole body, mind, soul, and spirit. The primary purpose of the meeting is to lift both people up who may have, in their own respective ways, experienced some hurt or pain. The sending of a text or e-mail when there is a conflict or misunderstanding simply does not communicate the full extent of feelings and meaning surrounding many situations.

However, I have noticed that in certain settings, people are not always willing or ready to meet face-to-face to talk about a conflict. So, it is vital to understand an unhealthy way to respond to conflict. Rather than allowing themselves to be vulnerable, some resort to control. This is when a state of alert acceptance is required on your part to notice how the other person is responding to the conflict. In this mindfully accepting stance, you maintain boundaries and a sense of dignity. Here are some of the key markers of an unhealthy response to conflict:

- Wanting to make the conflict all about the other, or what is often called "projecting." However, if we look closely, there is much more going on inside the person unwilling to meet in person, or on a platform like Zoom, than they are typically willing to acknowledge.

- Tightening up and a contraction in the body while showing no particular regard for the other or how they might feel about the situation. There is a lack of true empathy.

- Displaying anger that has been covertly hidden while trying to hide this discontent at all costs. It is very important in the unhealthy response for this person to maintain a false image of a kind and grateful person.

- Projecting blame and fault on the other for the conflict. There could be mocking, lies, excuses, delays, and silence amidst attempts to reconcile, reach closure, and talk in person.

- Avoiding the topic or nature of the conflict by keeping a distance from any real and meaningful discussion of what happened in the first place. The inability to handle the slightest criticism from anyone.

- Identifying very strongly as the "victim." This could surround family, career, and health, just to name a few.

- Having a relentless sense of entitlement. This could center on an inheritance, career, material possessions, or physical appearance.

- Showing an inability to cope when someone may have a different perspective on something, including what happened to cause the conflict. Feeling extremely threatened and a lack of any real coping skills to sensibly discuss face-to-face what happened in the first place. People like this find no meaning in such discussions. If there was an image that portrays the underlying discontent in a person like this, it would be with both hands covering their face and crying. They are a wounded child with nowhere to turn, or so it seems to them.

The good news is that these challenging situations often lead us to new awareness of our own strengths and mindful acceptance of how we feel with compassion. This is a healthy way to respond to conflict.

We are here to grow as human beings, and without challenges, we are stagnant. We discover new skills and perspectives in these times when conflict arises.

Acceptance is the key, leading to a state of ease and lightness where we are no longer dependent upon things being a certain way such as good or bad. This acceptance is inseparable from the present moment. The conflict becomes part of the whole, and we start to realize that when it rains, so to speak, the cloud containing the conflict includes pennies from heaven. So, we turn the umbrella upside down and as good accountants, we start to count all the pennies!

Nurturing Your Wholeness

Informal Practice

To cultivate a mindset of acceptance rather than opposition to your experiences, thoughts, emotions, and your own true nature, write a love letter to the universal mystery. If you need something to focus on as a metaphor for mystery, try a particular mountain, lake, forest, star, or the Earth itself. Write this letter over a period of days as you consider the vast mystery that informs and expresses itself to you as this image in your mind. The poet Rainer Maria Rilke, for example, wrote more than 150 such letters, in verse. You too, might want to acknowledge your relationship with mystery from the consciousness of acceptance. You will recognize the limitlessness of the mystery on the one hand, and the very unique characteristics of your object of attention on the other. Our true nature knows this to be real.

In order to stay on the mindfulness path, we need a well-developed capacity to take care of ourselves in the face of sometimes overwhelming emotions and memories, interpersonal ridicule, and discord. We could also discover our own sub-personalities begging for their needs to be met or their addictions to be fed. We require a mature sense of self rooted in acceptance to care for ourselves, our families, and our environment in order to sustain health and well-being. I like to write poems to express an internal state. Here is another one of them, this poem to universal mystery.

Marvel of Marvels

In the *Now*, waiting for spring to arrive,
Opening up to the great wellspring of Being.
You speak, Life, Heart, Love,
Diving deep into the well and the ocean of Truth.
Lingering now in the moist Earth,
Noticing rough patches here and there.
Yet, Acceptance shines within,
Filling the room with a light from a mountaintop.
A melody of song and gentle sounds,
Returning home to a place I've been before.
Marveling at the image in an image,
A glimpse of the deep well.
It touches and moves you,
To connect to the present moment, now and now and now.

Self-Love Meditation

If we do not allow the natural love for ourselves to be expressed, love does not reveal its beauty very often throughout the day. How do you express your love each day as an accountant?

Get in a comfortable position in a chair, perhaps seated toward the edge with your spine straight. Take the very first action of self-love right now: namely, your ability to breathe at will, in all different kinds of ways. Our breath has been there literally our entire lives, changing as needed to the demands and circumstances, flowing effortlessly when we are resting. Taking multiple full and deep breaths every day has been proven to change our bodies and minds for the better.

Take in five full and deep breaths as follows, holding them for a moment at the top, and naturally exhaling:

- Inhale a nice deep breath, expanding your belly and lungs as much as you can. Hold it, and exhale gently with relief.
- Inhale fresh oxygen that will be supplied to your blood stream, holding it to soak it in, and exhale without any effort.
- Inhale feeling rejuvenated and invigorated by this breathing, hold it, and exhale easily.
- Inhale noticing how breathing fully comes naturally to you, pausing to soak it in, and exhale any tension or worry.
- Inhaling fully is an act of self-love, pausing to feel this love, and exhale into complete relaxation.

Let your breath flow at a pace without any effort from you. By doing so, you are providing yourself with self-love and acceptance as deep breathing supplies oxygen to your brain and stimulates the "rest and digest" system. By breathing deeply and often, you are commanding your body to rest, which relaxes and rejuvenates you. This is self-love in its simplest form that you can do at any time.

Now, honor yourself by relaxing your mind even further. Notice how your thoughts are rising in your mind, one after the other. See them come, and see them go, completely accepting them as they are. Some thoughts linger for some time, and some thoughts only come for a split second. If you can really focus, you will notice even smaller thoughts, such as describing the world around you, or labeling the things in your surroundings.

Let your hearing become super alert now, and try to focus on some sounds around you. I invite you to pause in your reading and just listen. Maybe you can hear the sounds of your breath or raindrops falling against the window. Perhaps, you can listen to a sound arising from nature such as a trees blowing in the wind, or perhaps passing cars or people talking to each other. Just go from sound to sound, focusing only on one at a time accepting all types of sounds. Now, stop focusing on any sound in particular and just allow all of the noises around you to come in equally. When you hear them, they almost act as waves of relaxation, calming your mind, which will ease as you tap into awareness of your senses. Let's use the power of visualization to induce self-love.

Begin to imagine yourself full of an abundance of self-love. Picture yourself now, choosing healthy foods, and vividly see yourself eating well. When you eat well, see yourself enjoying these moments, and feel the nutrition that these choices bring you. Imagine now that you have a strong will to avoid junk foods and unhealthy drinks (all too common in busy season). See yourself in great detail confidently saying no to all these things. You feel very proud now, when you avoid eating something unhealthy. Eating healthy is an essential component of self-love

Another form of self-love is observing your mental chatter. In order to have great self-love, you must expand the good things you feel about yourself and challenge any negative thoughts as soon as they arise, fully present and accepting things as they are right now. So, hear yourself saying:

- When I fully love myself, I am able to fully love others.
- Deciding to love myself is a wonderful agreement.
- Each day, I allow my love for myself to grow more and more.
- I am worthy of love, and I honor the joy that comes with it.
- Deciding to love myself unconditionally, no matter what happens, feels wonderful.
- I feel love and respect.
- My sense of who I am deepens as I love, especially when I do so in conflicts.

- I love and accept everything about myself.
- I completely and always love myself.
- Today, I love myself more than yesterday.
- Truly loving myself is easy for me.
- The more I love myself, the better my entire well-being is.
- I love every moment of my existence.
- Every part of me that makes me who I am is encompassed with life, heart, and love.

Now, as we come to a close of this meditation, take a deep breath and know that whenever you love yourself, you will find love.

The Acceptance of Soul

In modern society, and especially in business settings, there is a quiet refusal to openly discuss and understand the working of the soul in us. This is a good example in which you can both accept this quiet refusal and at the same time lead by example in how you do your work as an accountant by expressing your soul. For me, "soul" means the aspect of life that reflects the deep meaning by which one lives, including the interconnection of people and the more-than-human world. There is a tendency to step away from true nature and the "wild" aspects of our individuality and also the very oneness we share with each other and all creatures. The first step as accountants is to become more at ease with the wild nature of our unique capabilities and to accept where we are right now. (By "wild," I am referring to our creative impulses and also the letting go of control-based strategies.)

This acceptance, augmented with a yearning for where you want to go, allows for the possibility of soul to open up for you. One of the most overlooked areas to launch the power of soul in us is in our own sacred wounds. Acknowledging and accepting the power underlying those traumatic events in our lives can lift us into new terrains and further our well-being. Did you leave your job unexpectedly for some reason? Were you denied partnership for some reason? These and other circumstances can leave emotional wounds. When this happens, it can be the very opportunity for personal and professional growth into new ventures and vistas that were not planned. Acceptance is the key for a transformation. As you move over rugged terrain and look out from a mild vista, you'll start to notice your soul at work. Each one of us has come into this world with a seed inside waiting to do the work you were meant to do. It is our job to nurture the soul when things are relatively stable. In doing so, we contact our wild nature and the nurturing, imaginative, and healing capacity within us. You'll unpack the riddle within that points you toward doing your soul's work.

Practicing *presence* and meditation does not mean that you will be called to leave your current job, profession, or personal situation. Very often, you will use your current circumstances to do the deep soul work you were meant to do. As you know, not all our accounting work is exciting and interesting and yet accepting these moments is part of our soul work. That has been the case for me. I bring soul to my work as a CPA. I do this while I prepare a tax return or financial statement, speak with a client, undergo peer review every three years, and in many other areas. I do the same in my professional coaching practice. Mindfulness has been a framework to deepen my soul practice in daily activities. As we addressed earlier, you will have your own unique framework for mindfulness in your work and personal life. That is one of the beauties of the practice. It is not a belief-based practice; rather, it is experiential.

Psychologist Bill Plotkin writes, "Soul leads not upwards toward God but downward toward the dark center of our individual selves and into the fruitful experience of nature. . . . It shows us where and how to make our stand. On this half of the spiritual journey, we do not rise towards heaven but fall toward the center of our longing."

The soul is a person's unique identity, much deeper than the personality and yet infused with it. Meister Eckhart writes on the soul this way: "O noble soul, consider your nobility!" In other words, you are so much more than your personality and mental and emotional conditioning. He further points out: "My soul is younger today as when she was first created. I shall be ashamed if she is not younger tomorrow than she is today." When the soul takes leave of the mental, emotional, and cultural conditioning it has endured, it travels in a sort of free nothingness. The soul is then able to endure an unknown knowing. Meister Eckhart writes: "Now as the soul loses herself in all ways, as we have said here, she finds that she is herself that same thing which she has sought without success." When I read this passage again and again, I am reminded of the saying, "getting out of your own way." How often do we strive and seek our soul when, in fact, it is our very nature here and now in this present moment? Stay awake, present, and alert for this nobility in you.

The soul is invited, so to speak, with such delight and light to be non-mental and non-emotional, so that love can then shine through. For as long as the soul is mental and/or emotional, she will hold onto perceptions and images of the other. As long as she holds onto these preconceived notions, she will be blocked and not enjoy unity or simplicity. It is sort of like a sunflower opening up to stillness as the ray of the sun encapsulates it. Lacking simplicity, the soul does not truly love the other, for the essence of love depends on simplicity as a cornerstone of acceptance. The soul is continuously invited to let go of any mental and emotional activities and be left in simple awareness, stillness, and *presence*. For if you "think" you love someone as "other," "co-worker," "husband," "wife," "partner," "child," "image," all this is let go. You are invited to love as a "non-other," "non-co-worker," "non-husband," "non-wife," "non-partner," "non-child," or "non-image" (in other words, all mental labels). Yes, you love the other as simply "One," removing any kind of duality and drop into this oneness now, and now, and now. It is a strange land, but one that is here for you over and over again as you move *beyond balancing the books*.

This poem points to reflecting on applying the essence of love at work and in daily life:

How Is It

Every now and then,
I hear the song of an eagle
Being
And trusting the open
Sky
And contemplating.
How is it that I
Can possibly refuse
Being mindful
At work and
At Play?

For most of us, spirituality is a great mystery beyond intellectual understanding. For some of us, it is a right given at birth. For almost everybody, spirituality is related to the notion that there is more to life than meets the eye. Creation and creativity go together, making each one of us a unique being with dignity, value, and worthy of deep respect, which far transcends our worth to the economy, our country, our families, and our professions.

For some, spirituality implies religion, while for others, it is a relationship with purpose that doesn't involve a transcendent dimension of who you are. In my opinion, the number one marker for spirituality is courage, and that courage comes from a big heart. We begin with wholeness: recognition of something much greater than our individual senses of self. We can refer to our ancestors as living proof of that. What does spirituality mean to you? How do you live that spirit in your daily work as an accountant and in your business relationships? Here might be some examples:

- Recognizing within yourself a *presence* in which thoughts, emotions, and sense perceptions come and go.
- An abiding peace that is always with you no matter the circumstances.
- An interconnectedness of life between self, the Divine, others, nature, the Earth, and the universe.
- A bonding with silence.
- A quest for meaning in everyday life and especially at work. A sense that life has value, meaning, and purpose.
- A commitment to values and a dedication to live in accordance with them.
- An intimate, transcendent knowing and a comfort with not knowing.
- Living the essence of love, both within and with whoever you come in contact with.
- Knowing where you came from, where you're going, and where you will return.
- Recognizing the ultimate illusion of your separate sense of self and living within that framework.
- Seeing pain and suffering as an opportunity to go deeper within and connecting to Oneness, while shedding light on the pain.
- Feeling Joy as your noblest act.

- Recognizing that you are part of humanity, and humans are not here to become happy; rather, humans are here to be more conscious.
- Recognizing that the present moment is all you ever have and intentionally make that your home.
- Allowing yourself to be vulnerable at times, fully acknowledging a need to set proper boundaries.
- Coming home to an "Original Goodness."
- Getting in touch with your body and giving it attention throughout the day.
- Recognizing that there are more stars in the universe than there are grains of sand on all the beaches of the Earth. Living with a sense of awe.
- Seeing that your body is in the soul, and not your soul in the body. From this vantage point, knowing your soul can become as big as the universe (two trillion galaxies big).
- Knowing if you wake up Now, you don't have to do it after death. The Eternal Now is Eternal Life.
- Love is surrender—a giving of yourself for the other—and love is recognition of yourself as other. That surrender and recognition is awareness of awareness—Conscious *Presence.*
- Expressing compassion as your fullest extent of being. Compassion is where peace and justice meet.
- Expressing eros (physical desire) as a passion for living and sensing its author as wisdom, meaning to love life.
- Learn to love your anger, anxiety, depression, and lust. Just find ways to steer them and give creative outlet for them.
- Discovery what really, really matters: Beauty and Joy.
- Finding that life is about conscious living and not birthday cakes.
- Realizing nature holds a clue for the Divine—everything is a miracle.
- Sensing love leads to forgiveness, forgiveness leads to peace, and peace leads to a fullness of life.

What the accounting profession needs most are mystical (right brain) people; more specialization is a distant second. Meister Eckhart was himself an administrator. He would preach to the offering box if no one was there to listen. As CPAs, we have been bombarded with training and tools to navigate the technology, tax codes, FASBs, and various other rules, regulations, and standards. What is needed now is a new consciousness, one that is embedded with not just the thinking mind, but the whole mind, body, soul, and spirit. How does each individual accountant go about doing this? Of course, everyone will have their own unique approach. I would suggest to start using the practice of mindful acceptance and bringing present moment awareness to your activities.

Question

> I am a CPA who has worked for a small firm for many years. I am not spiritual and feel that my work life is separate from my personal life. How can I be mindful in only certain parts of my life?

When do you feel more connected to something beyond yourself? "I can't say it happens in certain situations or when I am with certain people like my family. It usually comes as a surprise, out of the blue." I hear you say "out of the blue." Is there a metaphor or an image that reminds you of the color blue? "Yes, the sky is blue." Okay and what is in the sky? "The sky is mostly empty space with some things we call planets and stars." Yes, and can you sense that there is something in you that resembles the sky? "Well yes, usually when I come up with a solution to a problem at work, I feel a rush of energy and lightness about me." Exactly.

That energy comes from the space within you and the thoughts that make up your solution are a little bit like the planets and stars in the universe. You are the space for your thoughts to arise. You made room within yourself to come up with a creative solution to one of your client's problems. You have been doing this all along in both your personal and business life. Mindfulness is about letting go of control. We can, however, set up the conditions in which creative solutions and original thoughts can come up for us. You are a mindful professional.

What you call it doesn't matter: spiritual or not spiritual. As Meister Eckhart reminds us, "If the only prayer you say in your entire life is thank you, it will be enough."

Mindful acceptance is a way of being in the world that can be cultivated and nurtured in times of ease as well in moments of struggle. With equanimity, we begin to see that both are two sides of the same coin as we do our soul-based work as accountants and professionals. How do you know if your work is soul-based? You'll know when your work is not driven by the outcome you hope to achieve. You'll know when you do your work without a "why." You'll know from the peaceful energy emanating from within, and you'll know by the people you come in contact with, who are reflections of you in their essence and who have their own struggles and yearnings for soul. That is true acceptance.

As we come to a mindful acceptance of the end of this chapter, we now turn to mindfulness and goals and how setting and moving toward your goals is totally compatible with *presence*.

Chapter 6

Setting Goals While Tending the Garden of Your Inner Life

The key to realizing a dream is to focus not on success but significance, and then even the small steps and little victories along the path will take on greater meaning.

—Oprah Winfrey

Yes, when we focus on "significance" the universe opens up, for what is in the universe is in us. Meister Eckhart writes: "The eye with which you see God is the eye with which God sees you." When we are connected, there is an energetic frequency that leads us into the flow.

171

Take Tina, for example. She is a controller for a busy medical group. Since starting out with this position, she has been in the flow. Tina handles all the typical controllership functions and inquiries from the group's physicians, and she does so with lightness, ease, and care. She has a learning mindset that fuels her growth both externally and internally. Tina's dream is to start her own online women's self-care business to help mid-career women shift their perspective and find their center. She wants to share her own experience and help others cultivate a sense of being in everyday life amidst the "busyness." Tina has two teenaged boys who she gently guides through all the challenges that teenage boys typically experience. Together with her husband's help, she lovingly makes a difference in their lives. For Tina, goals are a part of her life, and she is quietly living them out.

The Obstacle

One of the most common obstacles to the cultivation of mindful awareness is an excess focus on the future. In a future-oriented mindset, there is a constant struggle to keep "doing" (what's next) and little room for "being" (just now). Mindfulness practice helps to strike a balance between doing and being wherein the present moment is your primary focus while knowing full well where you want to go. However, it is important to set goals. Research has consistently shown that having goals improves performance, motivation, confidence, and overall well-being (35). On the other hand, research has also found that an excessive focus on goals can negatively impact well-being.

The Four Dimensions of Goals

Embracing the Positive

The first and most vital aspect of setting goals and following through on them is being positive. The nature of positivity in goal setting goes beyond what you might ordinarily think. Rather, in mindful *presence*, positivity refers to a sense of awe, wonder, joy, and love in setting out to do what you want to accomplish. These qualities are virtues that reside within your body and have energy that has no hidden agenda. This energy is waiting to be born in you again and again. For many, this is sometimes challenging as our culture teaches us to keep doing and thinking. As a result, we learn early on, often unconsciously, not to give enough attention and praise for simple things.

Discovering a sense of awe allows the creative energy of the universe to link with the creative energy of the individual. As the poet Mary Oliver writes: "Every day I see or hear something that more or less kills me with delight." Or as missionary Richard Wilhelm writes on work in the Chinese concept of *Tao*: "Humanity participates by nature in all cosmic events, and is inwardly as well as outwardly interwoven with them." This infinite energy is the fundamental source of creation, which in many traditions is God.

To set out and establish a goal, no matter how small, is an act of creation. There is interconnectedness between you and universal intelligence. When this is done with mindful awareness, you consciously participate in that interconnectedness. You are prepared with a clear understanding of yourself and your inner nature. You'll be vigilant and alert, sensing a deeper meaning in the step you are taking in the present moment as Oprah points out. The small things you do on your path toward a goal are of equal value when you fix attention within moment to moment, uniting your intentions, thoughts, and desires so that no one can take them from you.

Goals are an aspect of an "original blessing." Contemporary theologian and mystic Matthew Fox writes: "We burst into the world as 'original blessings.'" Mindfulness of goals helps us to remember that blessing when we connect to present moment awareness and thus strike a balance between being and doing. The Indian poet Kabir writes about this very process of work and goals this way: "Do you have a body? Don't sit on the porch! Go out and walk in the rain!" When you walk in the rain, you'll get wet, and sometimes that is just what is needed along the way to help you navigate the peaks and valleys as you proceed in reaching your goals.

For me, sometimes the rain could be the emotion of anger. However, I have noticed when anger is channeled into meaningful work, it serves a higher purpose, and the fruit of such work is the forgiveness that liberates. Carl Jung writes about this rain in the following way:

> *Life itself flows from the springs both clear and muddy. Hence all excessive "purity" lacks vitality. A constant striving for clarity and differentiation means a proportionate loss of vital intensity precisely because the muddy elements are excluded. Every renewal of life needs the muddy as well as the clear.*

As accountants, when we are working on a project and our time exceeds budget due to some rain (unforeseen circumstance), that very rain is necessary for us to grow and develop as human beings. Even with the "Larry-like" accountant we addressed in the introduction, who counts wins and losses, the rain is needed to wake us up from inner and outer turmoil.

A key component in your positive relationship to goals is tracking your feedback in relation to your work progress; indeed, an important element in achieving your goals is to monitor your progress. You can ask yourself at any point: "Am I proceeding according to the goal established?" On a consistent basis, research has demonstrated that providing regular feedback on progress increases persistence and enhances performance (36).

Meditation on Goals: Letting Go

Meditation is about choosing to let go. Letting go is an aspect of being positive. As we perform our accounting services, how often do we let go? How do you go about letting go? Letting go is a habit that can be developed; it is an aspect of mindfulness. Letting go is not a mental activity but rather being present at a higher energy vibration. What are some reasons you may want to let go in connection to your goals at a certain juncture? First, you don't want to feel the pain, and you certainly don't want unnecessary suffering. The challenging moments are a sign to pause, look within, feel into your body, and quietly discern your next steps.

Let's take a simple example of cleaning up your e-mail inbox. You start to feel frustrated and want to get this work over as quickly as possible. You feel it is meaningless. Your intention is to get more organized; however, you start to dismiss the project as fruitless. Feeling some anger, you pause and go within as you sense and recognize your deep value for freedom of expression. With discernment, you realize that your task of cleaning up your e-mail inbox is another form of your expression for freedom: freedom from clutter. You have let go of the inner critic for the moment and focus on your needs and values.

When you are mindful, suffering is not part of your vocabulary. Of course, painful things will still happen, but there is a tendency to experience much less psychological suffering. How so? We let go of internally complaining when things don't go our way as we work toward our goals. We do not bewail our losses. As an example, one of your largest clients is taken over in a merger that results in the loss of a relationship as well as your fee. You knew this was coming for well over a year. What is your state of consciousness during this period? Were you worried? Were you able to maintain your objectivity when consulted on the merger? How does it feel to "lose" the client? Can you let go? If your mental and emotional activity includes some form of bitterness, discouragement, or resentment, you probably have not let go.

Mindfulness can help you look at your thoughts and emotions as you take a step back and become aware of your internal state. You may find an unexpected feeling of gratitude for the good that this client has brought you, which has helped you reach your goal in some way. You may also find that your schedule has new openings to do some creative pursuits that perhaps you may have postponed while you were busy handling this large client. Whatever the case, you are staying positive by letting go. That is true meditation.

Embracing the Negative

The second aspect of goal setting and following through is the negative pathway. We addressed the challenges that come up in the positive pathway and how to let go. Here in the negative path, rather than let go, we embrace the shadow side of our sub-personalities that often comes up and attempts to discourage us or hinder us in proceeding with our goals. This shadow is a hidden part of our personality. Carl Jung writes: "There is no coming to consciousness without pain." Getting to know these shadow parts of the personality in an intimate way allows for an understanding, acceptance, and possibly a pathway to transform these parts into something more productive.

In this negative pathway of goal setting and processing, we address the sorrow, grief, and brokenness within us rather than repressing, reframing, and ruminating about it. Ken Wilber, author and founder of Integral Institute and a scholar on human development, writes: "The process of addressing the shadow is what I call 'Cleaning Up.' It is taking something that is psychologically broken and fixing it—a process called shadow work. Virtually no one can escape it, and if not fully faced in awareness, it affects your human growth and spiritual development."

Our shadows will affect our goals. Interestingly, Wilber points out that shadow material is almost always, to some degree, generated by any major growth process. So, as you embark on establishing goals and moving into new territory, it is essential that you become aware of your shadow parts as they are likely to come up at the very moment when you start to see light at the end of the tunnel! What can you do? You can talk with a trusted licensed professional or coach to help you embrace the shadow. I find holding my shadow with loving kindness and acceptance to be soothing. As you grow and proceed with your goals, you will notice that you have new viewpoints at work, in the world, and in your relationships. You'll be moving toward your goals, but more importantly, you'll be at a higher stage of conscious awareness.

Sometimes, you may look back and become fixated on prior emotional and reactive tendencies with your work and relationships, causing some kind of shadow element to come up. For example, you join a new audit team and head out to your client, and as the audit continues, you notice that you are progressing much more quickly than your peers on the audit team. You start to develop a new viewpoint: one that is very positive as it builds your confidence.

However, in doing so, your judgmental mind creates stories about your peers who are not as proficient. So a "wall of separation" between you and your peers kicks in. You start to believe that you are a far superior accountant; in fact, you believe you are the best in the firm. This sub-personality aims to maintain your new found sense of superiority and will protect it in unforeseen ways. Gone unnoticed, this could build and amplify into a superiority complex, sense of entitlement, lack of empathy, manipulation schemes, and much havoc. This can make it very difficult for you to bare attention, be mindful, and step into awareness in the face of these elements as you grasp after them or even try to avoid them. The tendency to feel superior then becomes an aspect of your personality, causing distress to yourself and to others, and you don't even know it. That is why it so important to "clean up your act" by doing the work.

This process of shadow work in the negative pathway and related goal processing and human development can be depicted in the great Ancient Egyptian buildings with stick figures on the side: humans depicted in only two dimensions and lacking any real depth at all. However, as humans grew and developed with the arrival of the Renaissance and then the Enlightenment, a third-person perspective is added, and all of a sudden paintings pop out at you with depth and perspective; the human face becomes a real face. In the mind, "what if" and "as if" conditioned worlds become possible to conceive. "We can send a human into space in a rocket ship." This goal-oriented mindset self-transcended the conformist mode and conventional rules. And yet, as we know, shadow elements emerged wreaking havoc on people, populations, and nature. This might be called the collective shadow, imposing on the collective goals of society.

The scientific revolution brought further development, collectively and individually. Yet again, as goals were advanced, the shadow was not fully embraced collectively or individually to any significant degree. We see similar shadows in religions, education, and politics. Otto Rank, who was one of Sigmund Freud's closest colleagues, writes: "When religion lost the cosmos, society became neurotic. And we needed to invent psychology to deal with this neurosis."

Our shadow elements take up residence in the body on all levels: mental, emotional, physical, and spiritual. The body serves as a file for the soul. You may have forgotten the client you worked on last week, or the negotiation with the IRS, but your body remembers it all. For this reason, having access to your body through mindful awareness greatly helps you tap into your more subtle emotional field. As accountants, we are very often in our heads, missing opportunities to reach into the living storehouse of wisdom that is our bodies. Did you ever notice when someone raises their voice, your body moves ever so slightly in reaction? You soon forget it, but your body doesn't.

Each year, many accountants set their individual goals. Let's say you set a goal to increase your billable hours this year by 20%, a realistic projection and goal to set as you want to generate more income for the firm, increase your visibility with clients, and help their businesses to prosper. As you set out to achieve your goal within a mindfulness stance, you embrace your shadow tendencies as they come up in the moment. Ken Wilber writes:

> *The shadow itself is most basically composed simply of the opposite tendencies that are presently held in awareness. The easiest way to contact the shadow feelings toward any object, person or event (your goal) is simply to assume the exact opposite of what you consciously think about it. If your conscious attitude is negative, your unconscious attitude is positive: if your conscious attitude is positive, your unconscious attitude is negative (for example, if you consciously love your spouse, your unconscious loathes them; that's the whole shocking point about the shadow). Keeping that opposite in mind—whatever it is—is the simplest way to prevent the creation of a repressed and disowned shadow concerning any issue or person.*

So, getting back to our example, as you set your positive goal of increasing your billable hours by 20% this year, be aware of the opposite—that there may be an unconscious belief that you really don't want to increase your billable hours. You may not want to really put in the extra time, increase your visibility at the firm, and help your client increase their profits. Why would you want to be aware of this? In my view, it is so that you will be more sensitive to your circumstances and people as you proceed along the path of your goal. You will be more aware and compassionate to people around you when you are fully aware of your "dark" tendencies. Even more important, you'll be conscious and aware, which bring about in you a choice. A choice of how to show up.

Embracing the shadow elements while working toward your goals means new elements—uniquely transpersonal ones—begin to emerge.

The unconscious shadow material remains a focus, albeit at a higher level of conscious awareness, creating a new view of the world and you in it. So as you embark on fully embracing all aspects of yourself moving within your goals, you'll discover new vistas, vantage points, and viewpoints to look, listen, and embrace every step of the way.

Your Future Self and the *Now*

In this segment on the future self, I'll share how mindfulness can help you become aware of how you want to show up in the world, rather than simply reacting to the stressors of work, current events, and responsibilities. For example, what would it be like if you weren't worried about work or about your mortgage and college funding payments, or perhaps feeling overwhelmed during tax season? Or even feeling tired from your daily commute to the office and traveling to clients? What if, instead of feeling overwhelmed, bored, and stressed, you were able to step back and say: "Oh, okay. I'm just overwhelmed," or "Oh, that's worry," or "Okay, that's just stress. I got this."

Rather than saying, "I am stressed," and feeling you are in the middle of it all, instead just recognize that it is okay; "It's just a thought," or "That's just a feeling." For some of you, this may sound weird or crazy, and you may well think, "Yeah, but you don't know the situation at my firm." And you're right; I don't. It's really important to remember that for most, mindfulness practice paradoxically takes time for change to happen, but change does happen. For accountants who are successful at what they do, and even for those who feel in some way that success has escaped them for now, mindfulness is a way of being in this world. Mindfulness is a habit that fosters overall well-being. We're not just referring to becoming better accountants, although that is definitely a byproduct, just as feeling less stressed is a byproduct of mindfulness practice.

Moreover, mindfulness is about living on your own terms with inner freedom moment to moment. Your thinking mind won't understand this, nor does it need to. This is about intentionally choosing how awake and present you want to be for the life you're living right now. Mindfulness is about bringing forth your wholeness, your *presence*, your wisdom, and your compassion. To find your future self and live it now, we must not only have the energy but also a quality of passion that is sustainable. Our thinking mind can't do that alone. We need our full body, soul, and spirit. We require a sense of interconnectedness with all humans and the more-than-human world. How do you want to be now, five, ten, or twenty years from now? The state of your consciousness now will determine where you are at any point in the future.

Every time you realize you're distracted and take a moment to acknowledge it, something is changing, not only in your thoughts and consciousness but also in the brain itself. Dan Siegel MD writes in *Aware: The Science and Practice of Presence*: "Various ways of measuring brain activity have been used to demonstrate that wide regions of the brain become coordinated and balanced with the generation of such inner states of compassion. The brain seems to thrive on this state of care and concern, what I simply call kind intention." These findings suggest that when we intentionally and meaningfully, with authenticity and honesty, generate kind thoughts, we create integration with our bodies and brains.

If you experience stress, feel overwhelmed, or become anxious a lot, these emotions are really uncomfortable. You'll probably want to get as far away from them as you can, and that's understandable. But it is also really important to acknowledge that you can't stop anxiety. As we know, it has been tried many times, and it doesn't work. What can you do? You can develop a different kind of relationship with it, in which you eventually feel at ease with it and potentially can even start to embrace your anxiety as a way of further understanding your mind.

So as you move through your day as a busy accountant, remember to simply be aware, being present for the sensations in your body.

Whenever you remember this, it's a wonderful thing because all of sudden you're actually present. Again, it's as though you cut through the negative feedback loop between thinking and emotions. You step out of the loop of thinking, which fuels the emotions of stress and anxiety. Instead, you're actually present with your body and what you're doing. Then see what happens.

Embracing Creativity

The third aspect of goal setting and following through is the creative path. We have looked at the positive and negative paths and their links to goals. Now, we turn to creation itself and discover how to tap into this gift not just once, but as a continuous path and process in our accounting functions and in our personal lives.

The nature of creation is a birthing of something where previously there was nothing. Isn't that what your underlying intent is when you establish a goal? We can call that embracing the unknown or darkness. The stars in our galaxy and beyond are born out of the darkness of space, our concepts and analytical minds are born out of the darkness in our brains, children are born from the darkness of their mother's womb, and movements of liberation are born out of the darkness of pain and suffering. Miraculously, creativity is also born out of keen awareness of joy and delight.

Yet, even on this path of creation, we have to be aware of the collective and individual shadow. A study done in America found that 80% of six-year-olds were creative, but only 10% of forty-year-olds! Thus, something dies between ages of six and forty. How can this be re-kindled? A good starting point is a present moment focus and acute awareness of your internal state and your sense perceptions. Albert Einstein writes: "The greatest formal talent is worthless if it does not serve a creativity which is capable of shaping a cosmos." That is how important your accounting career is—shaping the cosmos—to a higher purpose through *presence*.

Similar to a tornado that swirls ferocious winds from its interior dimension, we have interior powers of birthing that are as destructive as they are awesome. Creativity is not just for the artists and poets; creativity is for all professions, especially accountants, (I am not referring to the proverbial joke about creative accounting—not at all) from the junior accountant performing a cash audit and a simple tax return to the managing partner. It's not about billable hours, completing a job within budget, making partner, passing peer review— all of which are relatively important but certainly not absolutely important. What is absolutely important is your state of consciousness at any moment in time, and compassion is the fullest expression of Being. Mindfulness and meditation are preparations for the movement of your heart to compassion and is, as Meister Eckhart put it, where "peace and justice kiss." In the Christian tradition, Christmas is about giving birth. God is waiting for us to be born! Noticing this birth in you is a sign that you are having a breakthrough. When a bolt of lightning strikes a tree, all the leaves turn in unison and notice. It's a little bit like that with the human body in awareness.

Poet Mary Oliver makes it clear in *A Poetry Handbook* when she writes: "Creativity is not about waiting for inspiration to strike. It's about hard work and a commitment to the process of any creative activity." You show up each day, patiently and diligently. You show up not with worry but with attentiveness and trust. Through her attentiveness, Mary Oliver used poetry as a life-cherishing force, a vision, and a trust. She writes: "Poems are not words, after all, but fires for the cold, ropes let down to the lost, something as necessary as bread in the pockets are to the hungry." In turn, accounting is not about numbers, after all, but water for the heat, something as vital as *beyond balancing the books*. All of life is an art. How you balance the books in your career and personal life is an art.

Art is also a deep meditation, a process that changes us and moves us to create. Matthew Fox writes in *Original Blessing*:

> *It is true, as Paul says, that "we are God's work of art," then everything we have said about art as meditation applies to the delight, wonder, admiration, surprise that God takes at our birth and continued unfolding as a painting is related to a painter, as a clay pot to a potter, as a book to its author. This bespeaks no mildly intimate relationship.*

Embracing Transformation

The fourth aspect of goal setting and the follow-through process is the transformation path. Firmly rooted and aware of the prior three paths and their elements, we now turn to the transformation itself, a shift from being based in thought, emotions, and sense perceptions to making your home in the true nature of mindfulness: conscious awake *presence*. Any real goal worth pursuing in business will have this feature—one that is enduring and has roots in the cosmos. Thomas Berry, a cultural historian, believes that the history of creativity has led the cosmos, through its most recent creators, the human species, to the place of transformation where we now find ourselves. It is not easy work, but then again, nothing worthwhile ever is. There will be plenty of shadow work as transformation happens in you, but we have each other to offer support and guidance in one way or another.

The thirteenth-century Sufi mystic and poet, Rumi, audaciously expresses one type of transformation, one of the sacred fool who doesn't play by the rules or standards of everyday culture, when he writes:

> Conventional Knowledge is death
> To our souls, and it is not really ours,
> We must become ignorant
> Of what we've been taught,
> And be, instead, bewildered...
> Forget safety.
> Live where you fear to live.
> Destroy your reputation.
> Be notorious.
> I have tried prudent planning
> Long enough. From now
> On, I'll be mad.

Rumi has tried the traditional methods of goal setting and follow through and realized it is a kind of death to the soul. He points us to think "out of the box" when he says to "destroy your reputation," for only then can you truly nourish your soul.

Power of Manifesting

One of the practices that I have found to be transformational is to employ the power of visualization. This can be done anywhere and at any time. The foundation for this practice is to be fully present in the *Now*. As you begin this practice, it may be helpful to be alone or out in nature. Then, gradually practice wherever you may be.

Connecting to the *Now*, you begin to realize that everything you ever wanted or dreamed about has already manifested to you in the *Now* as a full recognition of who you are and of all that is necessary and true in your life. This is not a trick of the mind or some mere fantasy as mainstream culture might want to portray. Deep down in this moment is the fullness of being—who you are in your essence. This is the first step in the creative process and manifesting what you desire.

The great ancient teachers have pointed toward this same practice but were misunderstood. Jesus said "Ask and you shall receive." In the asking you receive, as it all happens in the eternal *Now*. It only appears to us to happen in time. Of course, providing your desire is aligned with universal intelligence. The good news is that this is a continuous practice in the present moment. It is also important that you do this at times when there really isn't anything you desire or want. Do this practice in a state of gratitude. The *Now* and authentic thankfulness, kindness, and gratitude are the same here as you rest in the deep *Now* as your natural state. It is very helpful to remember that your life is always now! So, you are returning to your true nature with this practice naturally—again and again.

Then, once you are firmly rooted in the *Now*, call to mind your heartfelt yearnings. Merge these desires with the *Now* state, where everything you ever wanted has already been manifested for you. Feel deeply into the *presence*. Then see what happens. This mystical creative process has its roots in love. It works because you trust in life, which is always now. It works because whatever you desire in this state of *presence* will only be what you truly need and yearn for. This is so because deep down you know that you are already whole and complete.

Pairing the Opposites

Informal Practice

Sometimes, we notice a different dichotomy when setting and pursuing goals, different aspects of ourselves with their respective talents vying for prominence at different stages of the process. For accountants, this may be a familiar one in which our rational, ordered, calm, self-disciplined, or even chaotic tendency competes against the aesthetic, fluent, eloquent, and flamboyant parts of our personality. This could happen when you start a new project or land a new client, with all the potential to influence and guide businesses in creative and interesting ways.

Bill Plotkin writes in *Wild Mind*: "In western culture, perhaps the most common means of symbolizing this distinction is by the way of the Greek gods Apollo and Dionysus and the differences between them." Apollo is said to be rational and logical, whereas Dionysus is spontaneous, flexible, and courageous. Have you experienced this distinction in your accounting work simultaneously? If so, what do you do? I invite you to journal your experience.

Mindfulness helps us to embrace paired opposites and step away from a dualistic stance (debits vs. credits), which is an either-or mindset, to an allowing of the opposites to play out. How do you do this? First, notice the different feelings and emotions inherent in each pair and also some dynamic tension between them. Second, name the feeling and emotion as close as possible. Try to locate where this emotion shows up in your body and attend to it there. The emotions stemming from Apollo might be your sense of independence, competence, clarity, and integrity. The emotions relating to your Dionysus tendencies may be compassionate, loving, and spontaneous.

As you embrace the opposites coming up in a situation, gently hold them both in your awareness, one at a time. If possible, hold both emotions simultaneously and see what happens. Give yourself some space and turn attention away for a period of time. Then gently return to the emotions when you are ready. This mindfulness practice can be extremely helpful as you work toward your goals, as inevitably you'll experience different and often opposite parts of yourself wanting to take center stage at the same time. You'll be turning an internal conflict into a blending of opposites where the best of both worlds can be fully utilized to reach your goals.

According to Meister Eckhart in his "talks of instruction," he teaches:

> *The most powerful form of prayer, and the one which can virtually gain all things and which is the worthiest work of all, is that which flows from a free mind. . . But what is a free mind? A free mind is one which is untroubled and unfettered by anything. . . We should pray with such intensity that we want all members, our body and all its faculties, eyes, ears, mouth, heart and all our senses turn to this end, and we should not cease in this until we feel that we are close to be united to the presence and to whom we are praying: God.*

Mindfulness, prayer, and goals are brought together in an act of loving embrace.

Goals During Periods of Adversity

Anthony De Mello was a Jesuit priest known throughout the world for his spiritual talks. He writes in *Awareness: The Perils and Opportunities of Reality:*

> *There's a story of the disciple who went home to the master and said, "Could you give me a word of wisdom? Could you tell me something that would guide me through my days?" It was the master's day of*

silence, so he wrote on a pad. It said, "Awareness."
When the disciple saw it, he said, "This is too brief.
Can you expand on it a bit?" So the master took back
the pad and wrote, "Awareness, awareness, awareness."
The disciple said, "Yes, but what does it mean?" The
master took back the pad and wrote, "Awareness,
awareness, awareness means awareness."

Ultimately, you can't understand awareness, you can only be it.

During periods of adversity, nobody can show you how to take the next step toward your goal. These moments are a period of self-observation. This can be such a delight as well as extraordinary. With mindfulness practice, you begin to know things that cannot be described. It is called happiness. Not the kind of fleeting happiness that is all too common in our culture. True happiness is subtle, non-clinging, intuitive, and curious. Paradoxically, it reveals itself during difficult periods. Most of us have had this experience. Very few of us are able to sustain it as an ongoing realization. What could be the reason for this?

There is a famous story about a lion that came upon a flock of sheep and, to his amazement, found a lion among the sheep. It was a lion who had been brought up by the sheep ever since he was a cub. It would bleat like a sheep and run around like a sheep. The lion went straight for him, and when the sheep-lion stood right in front of the real one, he trembled in every limb. And the lion said to him, "What are you doing among the sheep?" And the sheep-lion said, "I am a sheep." And the lion said, "Oh, no you're not. You're coming with me." So he took the sheep-lion to a pool and said, "Look!" And when the sheep-lion looked at his reflection in the water, he let out a mighty roar. In that moment, he was transformed. He was never the same again. This is what adversity can do for you.

Anthony De Mello puts it this way: "If you are lucky and the gods are gracious or if you are gifted with divine grace, you might suddenly understand who 'I' is and you'll never be the same again, never. Nothing will ever be able to touch you again, and no one will ever be able to hurt you again." If it does happen that you are touched by some hurt and emotional pain in adversity, it will be short lived, and you will deepen from it. Your happiness is sustainable.

There is another story of an elderly lady who wished her therapist "insatiable" happiness as she departed on her way. The therapist thought to himself: "I don't want that. It would mean I can never be satisfied." He thought of the insensitivity of those words from his patient, and let it go. He didn't identify with his irritation. Do you know what a big difference that is? The therapist went on and lived in true happiness, one that cannot be compared, while the lady grew more and more cold-hearted, controlling, and manipulative.

If you allow the irritations, annoyances, and frustrations to come in as you pursue a goal, the amazing paradox is that these emotions are likely to pass by much more quickly. It is important not to have a misconception about happiness, like most do. Most people don't know this, but humans are not here to be happy in the conventional sense; rather, humans are here to be more aware, more conscious. And this applies to your work as an accountant. Did anyone tell you that? Instead of chasing "the pursuit of happiness," pursue awareness now, this moment.

Awareness is an extraordinary phenomenon in consciousness. The sages from different traditions have pointed to this in teachings such as "deny self" or "die to self." Why would anyone tell you to "deny self" if the "self" wasn't ultimately an illusion? The "self" is a historically conditioned entity with all its stories and interpretations, likes and dislikes, including the Larry-like qualities from our tale of two CPAs in the introduction. The sages are pointing you toward awareness. You'll know the "self" is not real as you courageously make your home in awareness. Your goals are much more likely to become a reality if you do, and your actions will be much more pleasant.

The poet Rainer Maria Rilke writes in *Letters to a Young Poet,* "Destiny itself is like a wonderful wide tapestry in which every thread is guided by an unspeakably tender hand, placed beside another thread, and held and carried by a hundred others." He further writes, "We must embrace struggle. Every living thing conforms to it. Everything in nature grows and struggles in its own way, establishing its own identity, insisting on it at all cost, against all resistance."

The Parable of Two Suitors

Recall the tale of Larry and Amy in the introduction for this book. Both are CPAs: Amy is mindful, and Larry is mindless. Now, let's assume both have been promoted to managing partners at their respective firms and are considering you for employment as a tax manager.

In this parable, let us imagine that instead of being a disenchanted, anxious, and frustrated accountant, you have been practicing mindful *presence* and are a deep soul, open to the mysteries of the universe, filled with great spiritual beauty and creative intelligence. And imagine you have been approached by Larry and Amy to join their respective firms. To whom would you open up your authentic self? Would you open up to Larry, who basically sees you as lacking in purpose and having no interior dimension to speak of, no spiritual value or capacity, who sees you as inferior to him, who relates to you as though your existence were valuable primarily to the extent that he could develop and exploit your resources to satisfy the various needs of him and his firm? His motivation for knowing and hiring you is ultimately driven by a desire for efficient control over you for his self-enhancement.

Or would you, the accountant, open yourself up more deeply to Amy, who viewed you as being at least as intelligent and noble, a worthy being permeated with a mind and soul, aspirations and purpose, filled with spiritual depths and mystery as she? Amy wants to know you because she genuinely sees you as her equal, even though she is managing partner. Her goal in bringing you into her firm is not to control, but rather she sees in you a richly responsive and empowered individual participating in the firm's co-creative enfolding of new realties. To whom are you more likely to reveal your deepest truths? Larry or Amy?

If you are reading this, it is likely to be Amy. This is not to say that you wouldn't reveal anything to Larry under the duress of his obnoxious approach. He is slick, so it seems like what he says to you is authentic, at least for now. However, you can sense in his tone of voice and body language the angst underneath his façade. Your mindfulness training is serving you well as you pursue your goals. Just imagine if your only choice was to join Larry's firm, one built on a disenchanted vision. Your loss and that of your young colleagues would be immense. The driving purpose and mind strategies so prevalent in a Larry-like firm have served their time.

On the other hand, Amy's firm is reinventing what it means to be a CPA. She and her firm are employing the three B's. Beyond—be your Authentic Self, Balancing—merging the human and being as one, and Books—accounting for what really counts: living and working with deep meaning and purpose. In Amy's firm, every meeting is started with a one-minute silent meditation. Her staff has on-going training and support from mindfulness coaches. The firm has several meditation rooms reserved for quiet time during the day where accountants can pause to connect more fully with their true nature, the line in the middle of our T account. On top of that, the firm is currently one of the most profitable CPA firms around and mirrors what it means to embody the complete release of human potential from the managing partner to the receptionist.

Mindfulness of Goals Meditation

As pointed out earlier, a strong goal-driven mindset can interfere with the effectiveness of mindfulness practice. You may have decided to embark on a mindfulness journey because you wish to become less stressed or to be more equipped to deal with other circumstances. These are perfectly valid reasons to do so. However, when you practice a particular exercise in terms of success or failure, it could interfere with the ability to be present and may even cause negative emotions to come up. Boredom, for example, is a common emotion that could arise, supported by a belief that you aren't doing the mindfulness exercise properly. When you notice a sense of boredom, you can acknowledge it, knowing this is a common emotion during a meditation.

In the following guided meditation, there is no need to reach a goal such as "doing it right." Just allow yourself to be here and now. You can let go of a "striving" mindset, which will take you away from the present moment. As you do this mediation, pay particular attention to any thoughts that reflect a goal-driven mode (such as "tomorrow I will be at ABC client"). When this happens, gently return attention back to the present moment.

- In this meditation, we'll use our breath as an anchor for attention to *presence*. Gently, let go of any goals you have for this meditation. Allow the idea of correct or incorrect to fall away.
- Come into a posture that is comfortable to you. It will help if you sit straight, shoulders relaxed, with hands comfortably on your leg area. Try to have a posture that signifies dignity. You can close your eyes or gaze downward. Become aware of how your body is connected to the chair and your feet to the floor. Simply notice. You may notice other physical sensations,

maybe a pain in the stomach or shoulders. That's okay. Just simply observe it without attempting to make it go away. Just notice your body as it is present here and now.

- Now, let's move attention to your breathing. Notice how the air moves through the nose and your chest expands when you breathe in. Also, notice how it relaxes as you breathe out. You may also notice how your belly moves as you breathe. No need to control your breath or modify it in anyway; simply witness it as it naturally occurs, breathing in and breathing out.

- Allow yourself to be present in this moment. When distractions come up, such as with a thought or sounds, just acknowledge it and gently return to your breath, breathing in and breathing out.

- Instead of focusing on the breath in a rigid way, let attention rest softly on breathing. There is no need to force it. With an open and gentle attitude, follow your breath.

- Remember distractions are part of any meditations as they are in everyday life. When this happens, turn attention back to your breath in a kind way, perhaps placing a hand on your chest as a gesture of loving kindness. Notice how your body reacts to your breath.

- Even if you find yourself distracted many times, remind yourself that you are holding the lantern of attention and can turn the light back to your breath at any time. By focusing on breathing, you are making your home in the present moment.

- Now, if you want, you can slowly open your eyes or gaze upward. Come back with attention to the room you are in and offer gratitude for this meditation.

Mindfulness in Business

Richard McKnight, an organizational psychologist has worked extensively with stress management and leadership personnel in business, describes his experiences this way:

For most workers, managers and executives I have worked with in the last 10 years, business organizations are seen as cold, impersonal machines that take raw materials, capital and people in on one end, perform some process or service and produce money out the other end—or should. In the prevailing model, the ideal business posture is characterized by words such as "competition," "aggression," and "winner." "Our business is only making money," one executive said to me, "and the only way we can do that in our industry is by keeping everybody uncertain and mean, inside the company and outside it" (37).

The physical and emotional trauma that results from this dominate mindset is harmful to employees, society, and ultimately the bottom line. Mindfulness can foster a transcendent purpose in the daily routine activities of our work and in the "big picture." Mindfulness can help bring back the cosmos in our work as accountants. Having mindful *presence* results in being in love with the world and provides a framework for integration and direction in our lives and in our work. McKnight says, "People have needs in three areas: body, mind and spirit. Yet most companies, if they acknowledge that people have needs at all, act as if there are only two requirements for producing good work: money and job security" (38).

Strategic Thinking and Goals

More organizations have implemented mindfulness at work programs, including Google. The Institute for Mindful Leadership undertook training one hundred and twenty-three General Mills directors and managers using their seven-week Mindful Leadership and Wellness curriculum. General Mills conducted research on the effectiveness of this training. Participants were asked to answer a nineteen-question survey before the course and again after the course. The results of the training are summarized in Exhibit 5. After holding the training for General Mills, it was expanded to include other major organizations.

195

In another survey, eighty leads from twelve organizations who participated in the Cultivating Leadership Presence through Mindfulness program reported the following:

- 93% said the training had a positive impact on their ability to create space for innovation.
- 89% said the program enhanced their ability to listen to themselves and others.
- Nearly 70% reported that the training made a positive difference in their ability to think strategically.

Exhibit 5: Mindful Leadership and Wellness Results

Employee Behavioral Outcomes	% of Employees Indicating "Almost Always" or "Very Frequently"	Pre-course	Post-Course
Increase Employee Engagement	I am able to notice when my attention has been pulled away and redirect it to the present.	29%	77%
	I take time each day to optimize my personal productivity.	22%	42%
	I feel like I am able to be myself in the workplace.	57%	86%
Promotes Sounder Decision Making	I am able to make time on most days to eliminate some task/meeting with limited productivity value.	9%	43%
	I am able to respond with clarity, even under pressure.	32%	68%
Reduces Behavioral Risks	I rush through activities without being really attentive to them.	26%	6%
	I find myself doing things without paying attention.	31%	6%

Source: The Institute for Mindful Leadership

In 2011, the Institute for Mindful Leadership and the Harbin Clinic partnered to study the effects of mindful leadership training on error reduction in radiation oncology. This program combined a full day of training at the Harbin Clinic with four online continuation sessions. Error prevention in radiation oncology became a significant issue after patient morbidity and death from mistakes in radiation delivery was reported in the lay press in 2010. The study's definitive conclusions show that increased mindfulness improved the patient safety culture, which was one of the goals of the training.

Reframing through Mindfulness

As accountants, mindfulness can help us make decisions more quickly by helping us let go of our evaluations. Research has shown that reframing positive as negative and vice versa aids as a way to release the grip our evaluations have on us (39). Seeing as the world continues to be complex and uncertain, mindfulness can help you in your ability to reframe quickly and smoothly after a moment of upheaval. Allow some space to open up around uncertainty, breathe into what's happening, and give yourself the gift of a pause so you can reevaluate the situation and your storyline. There is a relationship to what we addressed earlier around the judgments we bring to situations. We can choose our responses through training our minds.

Interconnectedness and Systems

Einstein wrote about dualistic thinking, which is the antithesis of mindfulness, in this way:

> *A human being is part of the whole . . . he experiences himself, his thoughts and feelings as something separated from the rest—a kind of optical delusion of his consciousness. This delusion is a kind of prison for us. . . Our task must be to free ourselves from this prison by widening our circle of compassion to embrace all living creatures and the whole of nature in its beauty.*

Rather than saying, "I think, therefore I am," go *beyond balancing the books* and sense, "I am, therefore I think."

As we have touched on throughout, mindfulness meditation helps us experience this sense of oneness. We live mindfully so as not to be stuck only in the thinking mode, and to bring emotions in all their glory to center stage. According to Richard Kowalski, in his book *The Mindfulness and Mind Balancing Handbook*, "We have complex processes of production and information exchange linking us together. Our growing interdependence has not yet found its way into our consciousness, which is still mainly dominated by the individualistic thinking of 'me' and 'other.' " The practice of *presence* can evoke a feeling of oneness with the universe, breaking down boundaries between ourselves and others, ourselves and the universe. Did you ever practice contemplating the interconnectedness of things? Here is a practice to try for yourself:

Bring attention to a flower, either one that is nearby or an image of one so that you can see it. As with earlier meditations, get into a comfortable position with your back erect and shoulders relaxed. Take a few deep breaths and set your intention for this practice: to experience the interconnectedness of things.

- Place attention on the flower. Bring to mind how many conditions have come together for the flower to bloom. Earth and minerals, clouds and rain, sunshine, oxygen, farming. Bring all these elements in as you contemplate the flower. They are part of the flower. They are within the flower. The flower does not exist in isolation.

- Now, bring to mind yourself. Contemplate all the conditions and causes that came together for you to exist and to continue to exist. Your parents, the water you drink and food you eat, the rain, the air you breathe, the sunshine, the space around you and within you that you share with every living creature. Just like the flower, you don't exist in isolation.
- Bring to mind all the hard work that goes into producing the many goods you use.
- Think about the impact you have on others with everything you do.
- Consider how others support and nurture you.
- What does this interconnectedness mean to you? How does an awareness of interconnectedness impact how you act?

Leadership: Feelings and Goals

Real leaders are awake, aware, and observant of themselves, others, and the world at large. The keys to this resonance are courage, compassion, and mindfulness. Real leaders are emotionally intelligent, not afraid to open up and discuss their feelings, and seek to live consciously of self, others, nature, and society. You know conscious leaders; they are approachable, curious, kind, non-judgmental, and tolerant. They are transparent to their partners, staff, clients, and other outside parties. You feel their energy as they inspire you, often triggering new ideas and energy so you too can advance within the firm and in your career. Most of them don't reside in the corner office.

On the other hand, dissonant leaders are cliquish. They suck out the energy of their employees, displaying avoidance-oriented feelings and behaviors including aversion, intolerance, irritability, fear, and control. They have a strong sense of entitlement with little or no empathy. Part of the reason this is so prevalent is that these leaders think the bottom line is unaffected by their control tactics as they focus on short-term results. These individuals are deeply broken, and yet they manage businesses, people, and events and are often considered successful in the eyes of the world. They resemble Larry in our introduction. They lack mindfulness.

It takes work to move from dissonance to resonance, and as you notice when you look around, far too many are still unwilling to do the work. Mindfulness can be the intervention that propels such a transformation. In the accounting industry, partners and senior managers emphasizing control in their work and on others is really more of a story of personal control and fear. However, when you practice mindfulness, we come to a realization that we can't control our thoughts or our experiences moment to moment. You start to sense that real leadership is about letting go. I am referring to the art of letting go of our judgments, fears, and frustrations so we can be available in this present moment to what is actually happening in the *Now*. You'll notice that this is a much different perspective on leadership and managing an accounting firm, clients, staff, and life situations than you may have been accustomed to.

Rising up in the accounting industry has been about having certain innate characteristics such as charisma, salesmanship, and a solid grasp of technical knowledge. This focus is shifting to a set of desired behaviors, capabilities, and competencies that can be cultivated so that leaders tap into their interior sensibilities like emotional intelligence, humility, and compassion while including all those positive traits that exist, including technical abilities. In fact, research from the *Clinical Psychology Review* (Keng et al., 2013) has shown that thinking will be more focused and clearer with mindful awareness. *Presence* can be the framework to take you from point A to point B.

This shift is all about a new perspective. The etymology of the word perspective really means to "see through," giving rise to an awareness from a refined vantage point where you can clearly observe. At its core, perspective is not about a new "mental position," although thoughts can come in once you look with awareness to "see and perceive" what is in front of you.

The dissonant leaders will give you an impression that they are self-confident, but they really don't take input well. They are working with an underlying superiority complex. They might even believe that they are the "brightest" accountants in the firm. When you have a perspective on this, you realize that there is something more than meets the eye going on inside such individuals. Mindfulness can inform you and bring up a choice for you to respond to that person or not. Simply put, mindfulness will help you not to be drawn into the same type of mindset as the dissonant leader.

Sometimes, you may be able to ask a question, giving rise to new information about this person that can help you develop a new perspective. For example, you may discover that this person was often shamed by family and friends and often experienced conditioned love in their interactions with close family members. In turn, these individuals have a hard time showing empathy and understanding toward others. The emotion of shame is often misunderstood and not recognized in the moment. Most of us have experienced this at some point in our lives. You'll know it in moments when you feel vulnerable and someone who you have placed trust in doesn't show an understanding or regard for your feelings. In these moments, your body shifts, head turns downward, and you want to escape. If this has happened to you, mindfulness can be a great help in soothing your pain by recognizing it, accepting it, and giving it the attention it wants. In other words, you give yourself the understanding that you were seeking from others. You take back your own power!

You would be amazed how often this happens in business settings. Sadly, it is often responded to with anger and shaming back. Here are some perspectives that can help you recognize the dissonant leader:

- The dissonant leader does not understand the essence of love. I am referring to compassion, affirmation, and acceptance of each other. The dissonant leader does not bring these qualities to the table. To them, love means you have met conditions, just as they were conditionally loved when they

201

grew up and even as they grew and started to develop a career. So, they learned to apply these conditions to others. In a business context, this means you have met their stringent and narrow conditions. The moment you don't meet these conditions, they can't show even the limited view of love that they hold.

- The dissonant leader does not know how to trust. They don't see safeness in relationships. They are defensive, on guard, and cautious, and this is one of the reasons they have a low ability to receive input.

- The dissonant leader only cultivates relationships if there is a quid pro quo. Their relationships are not like what you or I, as mindful accountants, would describe as relationships. Instead, dissonant leaders cultivate assets. They are not interested in knowing you from a wholeness perspective, but instead they are thinking you are available and useful to them. We are referring to a sense of dignity and respect that exceeds whatever your function calls you to do as you engage in your work as an accountant.

- The dissonant leader does not cultivate a sense of gratitude. They may say that they are a grateful person, but that is more talk than action. The dissonant leader has an attitude of entitlement. What have you done for me lately?

- The dissonant leader is driven by shame and devaluation. Shaming is a type of communication that hurts your humanity; there is a lot of guilt. It allows them to have an upper hand in their minds. When you make a mistake, they'll covertly message you that you have no value to them. They don't really believe in equality.

- The dissonant leader has not developed a sense of an inner life. To them, the world is what you perceive through your senses or is measurable. Did you do this correctly or incorrectly? They forget to focus on the why. They forget about understanding the reasons why we do what we do.

- The dissonant leader disdains having their weaknesses, flaws, and emotions exposed—their lack of the essence of love, trust, and compassion for the human side. They keep a façade up as they learn to just look the part.

Now, let's look at how you can respond as an accountant to these types of individuals, either within your firm and organization or with your clients.

- Be alert. Alertness arises from awareness and says, "Let's review the facts."
- Recognize what you can and cannot control through mindful discernment. It's okay not to be in control. Become comfortable with the unknown. Be comfortable with the present moment. You will be in control of how you respond to that dissonant leader.
- Have a sense of boundaries and operate according to your principles and standards.

With perspective, you'll see that this person is operating from a damaged place, and you'll understand why they respond as they do. In turn, you won't let this type of person dictate who you are and impede your well-planned goals filled with meaning and purpose. You can bring in a sense of compassion to this individual, which is the topic we now turn to in the next chapter.

Chapter 7

Compassion: Where Peace and Justice Meet

Your task is not to seek for love, but merely to seek and find all the barriers within yourself that you have built against it.

—Rumi

Recently, I attended a webinar on the Paychex Protection Program (PPP), an SBA-backed financial assistance initiative aimed to help businesses during the COVID-19 pandemic. To my surprise, there was an alligator in the virtual room! Not a real alligator, of course, but an inflated toy alligator one of the presenters introduced at the start of the program. Little did I know that this alligator made his metaphoric presence felt throughout the presentation up until his final goodbye at the closing of the webinar.

You may be wondering, what does this have to do with compassion? We often come across metaphoric alligators in business, whether that is in our own office, with our clients, third party vendors, webinars, and yes, even ourselves if we are honest. When we recognize the teeth biting tendencies in others and in ourselves, or what is referred to as the "flight, fight, and freeze" tendencies, we can take stock and re-position ourselves to uncover insights and practices.

Mindfulness can help do that, allowing us to notice these "teeth biting" emotions in ourselves by stepping back so we can see and feel what is going on inside. These internal and external "alligators" can be clues for knowing ourselves better. As we dive into the swamp of darkness and mud where the alligators reside and greet these feelings with clearer eyes, we develop as human beings. When we dive into this abyss, we are like playful dolphins with mammalian care systems and frameworks infused with compassion for the unknown parts of ourselves—the shadow parts.

Where do you look for the shadow parts if they are unknown? The poet Rumi notes: "Everybody's scandalous flaw is mine." What we tend to see in another is often a good place to start. It's a little bit like a mirror right in front of us. You'll likely know it's your shadow by the intensity of the emotional reaction you have to the alligator, especially when you don't know the person behind the alligator very well, or at all. Ultimately, the alligators are here so that we can bring forth compassion for ourselves and others. We'll unpack more of this process of discovery as we continue.

Compassion Toward Oneself

John is a junior accountant at a thirty-five-person CPA firm. He joined the firm right out of college, where he graduated with honors. He is studying for the CPA exam in between his work responsibilities. John is assigned to both tax and audit jobs, enjoying diversified experiences with a firm that specializes in the healthcare industry. He is becoming increasingly anxious and worried, however, wondering if he will be able to fulfill all his work-related responsibilities. While John attempts to hide his frustrations, he quietly soothes himself by taking long, deep breaths throughout the day and enjoys a healthy lunch while listening to calming music on his iPhone.

John is instinctively compassionate toward himself in moments of struggle. At his very core, he is compassionate when he takes care of himself. Compassion often starts when we are kind to ourselves, like John.

Compassion is innate to humans. However, many of us don't know that yet. Of course, culture and our conditioning place barriers to compassion, as the poet Rumi points out. Compassion is not something you do; rather, compassion is something you are. The essence of compassion is love.

I learned about compassion through my own pain and mental turmoil, much of which was self-created. Some of this pain related to my experiences in business, and some was in my personal life. This helped me to feel compassionate to other people and the more-than-human world. For most, we have experiences of compassion throughout life, starting when we are young. However, it is often not recognized as compassion. It may be something simple, like a mother providing chicken soup to her children when they are sick or like John taking a few deep breaths. We often take these acts of compassion for granted without realizing it and, thereby, miss strengthening the muscle of compassion, so to speak.

Compassion in the Waiting Room

One of the ways in which mindful awareness shows up is when you notice your external environment in ways that were previously covered up by anticipation and rumination. I call it a sense of compassion for others. One example involves two of my accounting clients, both of whom are in the healthcare industry. One client is a medical oncology group treating patients, possibly toward the end of life. The other is an obstetrics group treating patients who are about to birth life. Both of these clients have been long-term accounts, and over the years I have noticed, on many occasions, a different energy vibe in the waiting room for each client.

For the oncology group, patients and their family members who accompany them for their infusion therapy and other care are serene, calm, and present as they wait for treatment. In the obstetrics group, I frequently notice anxiousness. One medical specialty is treating people toward the end of life, while the other is at the beginning of life, with two very different vibrational frequencies. For me, walking through both waiting rooms, I sense a deep compassion for each; it feels a little bit like relating to both their inner states and their struggles. These have been moments of real connection and compassion as I pondered the human dilemma at both spectrums of existence, often connecting to these people in subtle ways.

Letting people in from the metaphorical "waiting room" of your life could also happen when you give up your seat on a crowded bus or train. There are countless numbers of "waiting rooms" each day where we can show compassion for others as well as ourselves. Meister Eckhart writes: "Compassion means justice." When we are kicked in the gut, we get stirred with an emotion like anger, and that emotion fuels our passion for justice. So our actions become compassionate as we are present and in touch with our entire being. For compassion is where peace and justice meet.

The people in both of my clients' waiting rooms have names, families, careers, hobbies, as well as aspirations, fears, and frustrations. Yet I pondered, "What is in a name?" I would suggest that a name establishes a breath connection between humans as well as with plants, animals, and the natural world. The sound and vibration that a name evokes in us when felt and listened to acutely in the body takes us out of our conceptual minds and into something deeper. We remove layers of judgment and preconceived notions about a person or, for that matter, a tree, bird, ethnic group, or even the solar system and beyond. Everything becomes mystery, and we tap into an inner spaciousness and peace that is always there.

Even if you don't know a person's name, like me when I pass through both waiting rooms of my clients, "human being" can take us to this state. The uniting of "human" as the surface dimension—including physical appearance, family origin, and personality—with "being" as the subtle and unshakeable field of timeless conscious *presence.* Your mind will believe this is silly, but do it anyway and see what happens.

The waiting room is a space for compassion to blossom; it doesn't have to be in a doctor's office as in my example. I also find a "waiting room" can be something simple like waiting for an elevator, subway, bus, being stuck in New York City traffic, and the like. These are moments when attention can be directed to the present moment—your own inner "waiting room." It includes not just the surface aspect of the moment, such as your surroundings, people, traffic and so forth, but also the essence of the present moment, which we can call compassion.

How much of our time in accounting work is spent waiting? We may be waiting for a client to provide us information so that we can complete a tax return, or we wait for a meeting to start. Yes, you can, in certain instances, move on to other work-related activities, but sometimes we can't—we have to wait. In Samuel Becket's play *Waiting for Godot,* two men wait by a tree, aimlessly waiting for Godot, who doesn't show up. How much of our work day are we waiting for the next thing to happen? And it never happens. Planning your day is good, but I am referring to a habitual mindset that is constantly seeking fulfillment in "what's next."

Compassionate is Mindful Presence

On March 25, 1858, a young girl named Bernadette was seeking to know the name of a mysterious lady whom she was meeting with for the sixteenth time in a shared space of connection, openness, equanimity, and trust. Filled with life, heart, and love, the young girl made three requests in a row to the lady for her name and received back an amazing smile. Bernadette courageously asked a fourth time to the Lady of Lourdes, "What is your name?" The lady looked up, her hands stretched in a gesture of *presence* and openness, and answered, "I am the Immaculate Conception." In other words, she identifies with the present moment, which is always giving birth to the next and to the next.

In my visits to Lourdes and Nevers, France, compassion is everywhere where Bernadette lived in simplicity. I am struck by the deep personal connection between the two in a shared space. When one has something important to say, it reminds us today that a personal face-to-face meeting is warranted, even if that might be on an internet platform like Zoom when a direct meeting is not feasible. That is an aspect of compassion, and it reflects courage, which is really what spirituality is all about. This face-to-face meeting allows for the full breath connection beyond name and circumstances to take place. Truth can more easily be conveyed and received. However, it may take some out of their comfort zone and call on an inner courage, especially if a relationship is ending or there is some misunderstanding.

We too can go to the same place offered by the Lady of Lourdes on this day and every day—**the present moment**—not the surface level of the present. We can visit the essence of the present moment, our inner waiting room—an underlying spacious field of conscious awareness that is in everyone, also known as compassion.

The Physiology of Self-Compassion

According to Paul Gilbert, the founder of compassion-focused therapy, when we criticize ourselves, we're tapping into the body's threat defense system (sometimes referred to as the reptilian brain). When we are triggered by some perceived danger, like in my webinar alligator metaphor, this system reacts, usually in the form of self-criticism. The amygdala registers this danger in the brain, releasing cortisol and adrenaline as we get ready to fight, flee, or freeze. This system works well when there is some kind of physical danger. Nowadays, however, most of the threats we face are perceived attacks to our self-image and our own conceptualized sense of self—in other words, who we think we are (40).

Fortunately, the body is not just reptilian but also mammalian. This evolutionary advance forms, in part, the basis of compassion. When our care system is activated, oxytocin (the love hormone) and endorphins (natural feel-good opiates) are released, which help reduce stress and increase feelings of safety (41).

When we practice mindful self-compassion, we are deactivating the reptilian brain and activating the care system. Extending compassion to ourselves when we feel over-whelmed in busy season is like getting comfort from a parent, and for John, it was soothing. Here is a table that illustrates self-compassion as the opposite end of the spectrum from the stress response normally associated with our reactions to people, places, and events (42).

Exhibit 6: Transforming Stress into Self-Compassion

Stress Response	Stress Response Turned Inward	Self-Compassion
Fight	Self-Criticism	Self-Kindness
Flight	Isolation	Common Humanity
Freeze	Rumination	Mindfulness

Source: The Mindful Self-Compassion Workbook

Compassion in Accounting

As accountants, we are independent and objective as we follow and meet our professional standards. There is an integrity that has been established in our profession that we build upon day by day. However, we can also sometimes feel isolated within our firms, especially due to the nature and structures of most organizations—the need to generate billable hours, competition, tight budgets, and all with little emotional support. These are moments to make a breath connection with yourself and those around you as an act of compassion toward yourself and others, who are distracted in one way or another from the essence of who they are.

One way of doing this is to create inner space and simply sit with the feeling of what you are missing in the moment. What does it feel like not to have the support you need? Where and how do you experience this yearning in your body? Is there a metaphor that describes this experience? Does it have a color or shape? Can you simply sit in the present, watching yourself in this challenge, and hold yourself with compassion for what you're going through? Be gentle with yourself, especially if you have experienced trauma. Seek help from a professional counselor, as I did, when you need to talk to someone about your work-related stress.

In mainstream business and culture, we've forgotten that the strategic mind does not by itself possess the ability to determine what's worth doing in life. This ability belongs to a partnership between soul and spirit. When you are ready, your soul will reveal to you your unique metaphoric and poetic destiny—your unique truth at the center of who you are and how you fit into the more-than-human world. When this happens, however, we need a clear and focused delivery system to manifest our unique gifts that are meaningful, fulfilling, and life-enhancing. If we miss this merger of soul and spirit, then we will have missed our unique calling to move *beyond balancing the books*. Paradoxically, it is a simple noticing from moment to moment to the still voice within you that can bring this forth. The doors are not locked, for this essence, which we can call love, already exists within you. A regular practice of compassion in accounting can convert a debit to a credit and a state to a trait.

Most of us have built barriers to the practice of bringing forth the essence of love into what we do as accountants. Culture does not help in this regard. It's actually a taboo to show love, especially in business, so it is up to each one of us to bring forth our essence into everyday activities and support each other, affirming one another in who we are as human beings. These barriers have been built up to protect us from the hard realities and pressures within our profession. The barriers are mostly internal, including the inner critic, wounded child, and a storyline we tell ourselves of who and what we are. When we are mindful of our struggles and take care of ourselves with compassion, things begin to change. Learning to embrace yourself and your imperfections can provide resilience for you to thrive. I have found this to be a continuous process that makes each day worthwhile.

Compassion is often directed outward toward others when they are experiencing some difficulty. What is not as well-known is compassion that is directed inward toward oneself or self-compassion.

What is Mindful Self-Compassion?

Self-compassion is about treating yourself the way you would treat a friend who is having a hard time, even if the friend has "gone off," is "feeling disappointed and sad," or is just facing a tough life challenge. Self-compassion is about becoming an inner ally rather than an inner critic (43). Imagine your best friend is also an accountant and calls you one night after you were just let go from your firm, and the conversation goes something like this:

> *"Hi," you say, answering the phone. "How is it going?"*
>
> *"Terrible," she says, holding back tears. "You know the firm I have been working for the last five years, where I was hoping to get a promotion next month to partner after another busy season? Well, I got fired today, and I am shocked."*
>
> *You sigh and say, "To be really honest with you, it's probably because you are not strong in tax and accounting, not to mention you are nerdy and an introvert. I'd just call it a day in public accounting because there is really no hope for you now to make it in accounting. I mean, frankly, you don't deserve it!"*

Would you ever talk this way to someone you cared about? Obviously not! But unfortunately, this is precisely the type of inner dialogue we say to ourselves in such situations. Sometimes it is even worse. With self-compassion, we learn to cultivate a friendly relationship with the inner voice. It may sound a little bit like: "I'm so sorry. Are you okay? You must be devastated. Please know I am here for you, and I deeply appreciate you. Is there anything I can do to help you during this time?"

Self-compassion is not a "poor me" attitude or a type of "pity party." Rather, it is very real and an aspect of our true nature. Mindful self-compassion just needs to be cultivated more fully through self-discovery and acknowledgement.

According to research by Kristen Neff, PhD and Christopher Germer PhD, mindful self-compassion involves three core elements that we can bring to bear when we are in pain: self-kindness, common humanity, and mindfulness (44).

Self-Kindness

When we make a mistake or under perform in some way, we are much more likely to beat ourselves up than lend a helping hand to ourselves. Do you know caring people who, when they slip in some way, berate themselves? Perhaps even you do it sometimes. This tendency is counteracted with simple self-kindness. I like recalling a phrase that has meaning for me when I notice this self-critical voice sounding off. (For some, it is helpful to give the inner critic a name that you find comforting or funny.) Then, with warmth and unconditional acceptance, I actively soothe and comfort myself.

Let's say you made an error in preparing a tax return, and your client receives a notice from the government that they owe additional taxes. It turns out that you inadvertently missed picking up an item of income on the tax return. You could think, "I can't believe I did that! I must have been asleep." Instead, tell yourself, "It's not the end of the world. I am a good accountant, and this is very unusual." That is a big difference in how you treat yourself. Through small acts of self-kindness, we can effectively re-wire our brains so kindness becomes not something we say or do but who we are. Kindness then becomes contagious. With this frame of mind, you are much more likely to discuss this issue with your client in a relaxed and comforting way.

Common Humanity

We are not isolated individuals; we are interconnected beings. Quantum physics tells us that we live in a unified universe. Just like everyone else, you too are an intrinsic part of the universe and the

215

more-than-human world. Central to this notion is the recognition that each one of us is imperfect in the world of form. Humans are a work in progress. We are transitory beings.

A sense of our common humanity came up for me a few years ago when my mother was in the hospital for surgery. Sitting in the waiting room, I became anxious as her time in the operating room far exceeded what was expected. Noticing these feelings, I looked deeply at each of the other people in the room, also waiting for their loved ones, and felt a strong bond. Shortly thereafter, a family came over to me and started to talk with me. I felt deeply comforted. When felt in the body and mind, this sense of common humanity works wonders in unexpected ways.

Has this happened to you? Most likely, it has in some way. Rather than dismissing it as a coincidence or luck, through common humanity we can come to know a synchronicity between our inner state and outer circumstances that fosters well-being. There is a saying: "When neurons fire together, they stay together." Our brains can be rewired for inter-connection and compassion.

Mindfulness

As we have been addressing, mindfulness involves being aware of our moment to moment experiences in a clear and balanced way (our T accounts). This implies being open to the reality of the present moment, as you allow all thoughts, emotions, and sensations to enter awareness without resistance or avoidance. In my case, I had a moment of mindful self-compassion in that hospital waiting room, noticing anxiety in myself, being kind within, and then sensing the interconnectedness of others.

Why is mindfulness such an essential ingredient in self-compassion? For starters, mindfulness takes us out of our thinking mind and into the realm of awareness and a deeper dimension of consciousness. Second, mindful *presence* evokes intuition, enabling us to genuinely respond without the veil of mental and emotional conditioning. Third, mindful presence is the foundation for all virtue and goodness within and without and an entry point to the essence of love. Once you get a taste of what mindfulness is about, you can't go back to your former ways for any sustained period of time. When you taste what is Divine, there truly is no return. Meister Eckhart writes about it in this way:

> *If someone loves something passionately with all their might, so that nothing else pleases them or touches their heart, and they desire that alone and nothing else, then certainly whoever it may be, or whoever they may be with, whatever they are doing or are setting out to do, the object of their love will never be extinguished in them. But they will find its image in all things, and the greater their love becomes, the more present to them it will be. Such a person does not seek peace, for it is already theirs.*

A mindful professional will often see things in a divine way and discover something much more than they are in themselves, others, places, things, and circumstances. Of course, this requires work, consistent practice, and clarity of the inner self beyond name and form—your true nature. The challenges that come up each day are there for you to go deeper into mindful *presence*. You can do this in your accounting work by simply staying connected to the stillness within as you go about your work and meeting with people.

For some, mindfulness happens only in certain aspects of their lives. This could be while taking care of a loved one, baking a cake, or gardening. And this is beautiful when it happens. The tendency is to remember these times as beautiful moments, and then recall them again and again. What would it be like to have these moments in all aspects of your life on a constant basis? It might sound like an insurmountable and unbelievable task, but remember from the outset of this book, I pointed you to the very essence of mindfulness in that it is not something you do, but rather something you *already* are.

However, it is helpful to convert the state of *presence* into your very own traits with consistent practice. Even three minutes a day of conscious *presence* can evoke changes in your brain structure and lessen the negative default mode. So it becomes a question of when you would like to put a brake on the daily upset and turmoil in countless little and sometimes big ways that most of us experience each day. That said, here are a few pointers:

First, I would suggest practicing self-compassion and all three components as you let go of your imperfections with acknowledgment. Second, really want to be present, as if your life depended on it (and as Jon Kabat-Zinn has often said, "It really does in more ways than we know"). Third, love your pain and suffering when it comes up, and then see what happens.

How Do I Treat Co-Workers?

Close your eyes and reflect for a moment on the following questions:

- Think about various times at work when you had a colleague who was struggling in some way—had a misfortune, struggled with a client matter, was under pressure to complete a job— and you were feeling pretty good about yourself. How do you typically respond to these types of situations at work? What do you say? What tone do you use? How is your posture? Nonverbal gestures? Write down what you discover.

Now close your eyes again and reflect on these questions:

- Think about the various times when you were struggling at work in some way—made an error, or felt that you weren't keeping up with all the changes in the accounting field. How do you typically respond to yourself in these situations? What do you say? What tone do you use? Your posture? Nonverbal gestures? Write down what you discover.

- Finally, reflect on the differences between how you treat a colleague at work when they are struggling and how you treat yourself. Do you notice any patterns?

Preliminary data from research suggest that the vast majority of people are more compassionate to others than to themselves. Our culture doesn't encourage us to be kind to ourselves, so we need to intentionally practice changing our relationship with ourselves in order to counter the habits of a lifetime (45).

Compassion Beyond Balancing the Books

We often hear the phrase "team player" to describe someone who places the group or firm above their individual needs or desires. The team player can also be described as someone who doesn't "rock the boat" and cause disruptions. I would take these team player definitions and add onto them by introducing mindful self-compassion into the process and expanding the definition of team to include *beyond balancing the books*. Namely, that there is more to the team then meets your eye. Think big—like the cosmos big! All you need to do to test this hypothesis is look inside yourself. No need to rely on externals, just go within and you may find something quite extraordinary.

When referring to *beyond balancing the books*, I mean that *beyond* refers to noticing and tapping into your true nature. *Balance* refers to integrating both the doing mode of everyday living with the being mode—balancing human being. *Books* refers to an accounting for what really counts and living with deep meaning. Hence, the three B's are our wholeness and original well-being.

Mindful self-compassion and what I refer to as *beyond balancing the books* are one in the same. Just as self-compassion includes the three elements of mindfulness, self-kindness, and common humanity,

219

beyond balancing the books does as well. The three elements are not separate processes or stages but rather interwoven aspects of a single process, informing and relating to each other. The three B's of *beyond balancing the books* are icons for self-emptying love. These three "busy B's" go around and around like buckets on a watermill spilling over into each other. As the three B's operate in your life, the watermill converts the energy of love into real authentic action. It is similar to the yin-yang symbol where there is flow among and in between the components, a knowing that is your very own essence realizing itself in a unified field of all reality.

Beyond

The essence of who you are is *presence* and your true nature. Above all, mindfulness is about *presence*. It is about inhabiting our lives fully and bringing all of our awareness into the present moment. Fundamentally, self-compassion is about a way of being, a way of relating to experience, moment by moment. The actual "practice" of mindfulness is a framework through which you can sharpen and cultivate this state of consciousness. As research points out, we cultivate mindfulness when we practice, and yet mindfulness is already here within us (46).

Balancing

More than anything else, balancing is a felt sense, an integrated experience of one's thoughts, emotions, and feelings. Balance is a deep knowing of an inherit space within as a ground from which all conscious doing arises. In other words, it is a merging of human and being as the simple awareness of our breath, not as an intellectual or conceptual understanding but as a felt sense of knowing. Your whole body breathing in and out can take you there, so to speak. This is vital. A rigorous empirical study of over 650,000 people found that people's minds wander 47% of the time (46). That is almost half of our lives! Balance means so much in our lives.

Books

In the books, you discover for yourself an interconnectedness with others and the more-than-human world, bringing forth your deepest yearning and passion into this world as your true nature. It's about living without a "why" and a willingness to let go, piece by piece, of what is not real in your life. It's a full absorption accounting for what really counts: living with deep meaning and purpose.

Compassionate Coaching

Without mindfulness, there can be no compassion. Adopting a compassionate coaching approach to clients and toward colleagues in your office has been linked to better outcomes in firms. According to research, individuals' neural reactions to "compassionate" and "critical" coaching approaches differ widely and, in turn, affect their performance.

A compassionate coaching style is one in which the leader intentionally encourages a positive future to arouse a positive emotional state, while a critical coaching style focuses on failings and what the person should do. How do you feel when we you receive five pages of review notes from your audit manager? While the review process is necessary, does the reviewer bring compassion to the review, or is it done simply from a compliance perspective? With a compassionate style, people are more likely to learn and make behavioral changes. In those coached by leaders who brought compassion to their work, the parts of the brain associated with visioning, a critical process for motivating learning and behavioral changes, were activated (47).

221

As we discuss bringing compassion to our work as accountants each day, I invite you once again to our T account metaphor to examine where you are at any point of time. You can do this exercise now. Are you tilted more to the critical coaching style (debit) with a focus on shortcomings, both within yourself and others? This is often combined with a "what's next" mindset (our waiting room metaphor), for which the present moment is never good enough. There is a continuous feeling of unease, lack, and boredom in you and, therefore, projected onto others. Research has confirmed that this attitude severely undermines our work and overall well-being (48).

The alternative is a compassionate leadership style, which includes all three elements of mindfulness, self-kindness, and common humanity brought together as you go *beyond balancing the books*. First, as professionals, we need to step out of the storyline of the situation, which is often subjective and judgmental. Second, recognize that our thoughts about a situation are simply representations or symbols that stand for reality but are not reality itself. We can drop the idea of what we think a situation "should be" and make contact with openness to what is happening in the moment.

In many ways, mindfulness goes against the natural tendency of the brain and its default mode network, as science calls it. This default mode network essentially does three things, which make mindfulness challenging at times: first, it creates a sense of self (ego); second, it projects that self into the past or into the future; and third, it looks for problems. Hence, we obtain the negative style by default! Have you ever come to the end of the day and wondered how the day went by so fast as you looked to account for eight hours of billable time? The answer: your day was mostly in the default mode network. Your brain uses its "spare" time to search for problems, most of which are not actual "problems." J. Krishnamurti, one of the twentieth century's most mystical thinkers, writes: "Only in discovery can there be joy— the discovery from moment to moment of the ways of the self." And yet, generally speaking, our brains are hardwired for survival, not for happiness. The implications of these findings are that we are so much more than what our brains can tell us "about" who we are.

The incredibly good news is that this hardwiring is only a tiny fraction of consciousness, whereas mindful *presence* is that tiny fraction and everything else, too!

I invite you to listen to my webinar "Mindful Self-Compassion and the Coaching Process" on my YouTube channel. Here is the link: bit.ly/mindfulselfcompassioncoaching.

The Essence of Love

As accountants, we are familiar with consolidations when two entities are combined into one. In a true mindfulness consolidation, the past and the future are combined into the fullness of the present moment—not the surface level of the present moment but the underlying space of the present moment. And there you are as the essence of love—your true nature. This is a poem about a mindful consolidation.

The Essence of Love

Love is surrender, a giving of yourself for the other.
Love is recognition of yourself as the other.
In that space of surrender and recognition a flower is born,
And it wants a tender hand and water to grow.
You are good—I am good,
You are so much joy—I am joy.
It is Love, We are love, I am Love,
I AM.
Peek in, Peek in, Peek in,
Now and Now and Now...

223

Discovering the Good

Why are you here on planet Earth? Some might say: to be a parent, sibling, doctor, builder, citizen, activist, business owner, accountant, lawyer, or whatever else drives a sense of purpose and meaning in their lives. Such roles are relatively important but not the most vital aspect of a successful life. I am hoping that your main purpose here is for the sake of knowing and experiencing love as you grow in conscious awareness. Life is about having right relationships, and that includes your relationship to your work. Yes, we can have the essence of love in accounting. It's the line right down the center of the T account where you are present, embodied, and awake. When you stand on that line, there is a oneness that is rich in power.

When you are at the end of life, people will talk about your accomplishments, achievements, and some of your unique experiences, which is all well and good. But when we try to summarize a successful life, we want to say how well the person loved and invested in other people without any attachments or expectations of a thank you in return. In other words, engaging with people in a non-transactional way, in a non-merchant mentality, is what really matters.

The one word that can describe a loving person is "goodness." Goodness is a very profound word and has many implications. For example, a good person is kind, patient, reliable, affirming, available, encouraging, sensitive, compassionate, curious, and empathetic. Are you known as being good? If so, you know the essence of love. However, some individuals need to be in control and are manipulative and impulsive, walking around with a sense of entitlement and superiority. Unfortunately, they don't receive input from others very well. It's all about them. They see you and your accounting work as a function to serve them, build them up, and affirm them. They lack the essence of love. Their understanding of love is not going to be the same as yours or mine.

As you practice mindfulness in business and in your personal life, it is important to set your boundaries so that you don't get drawn in by individuals who lack the essence of love. How do you know when someone lacks the essence of love? Sometimes it will be obvious to you, while other times it can be hidden, at least for a while. Typically, you will know the absence of love in someone the first time a real conflict or misunderstanding comes up. The tendency with unhealthy people like this is to run for the hills. In other words, they show cowardice and can't sit down and talk things through with mutual respect and dignity. Vulnerability frightens them.

In practicing the essence of love, first examine yourself. You'll want to honestly notice your own practices. Then, in a non-judgmental way, see the people around you that are not practicing the essence of love, and accordingly establish your boundaries. Here are some of the practices you can bring to your work as an accountant every day and some signs to watch out for in others, so you can set proper boundaries for yourself.

Connecting at the Heart Level

In your accounting work, intend a desire to genuinely know people. You want to know what is going on inside them, the things that are unique about them, having a sense that is keenly aware and knows that others have needs, aspirations, fears, and frustrations. You'll ask about their lives and who they are rather than covertly dominating over them and not deeply listening. You can do this because you do the same for yourself.

This type of listening is connecting at the heart level. We can hear truth, much more so than we can think truth. In addition, you will want to have a mindset that is more accurate in the ways you engage with others at work. In doing so, you are likely to practice the essence of love, wanting to understand the other by asking: What is really important to you? How can I be of assistance to you?

225

On the other hand, unhealthy people will see you and your accounting work as functional and possess a merchant mentality. They can't see your essence, sadly, because they can't see their own. That is where you will need to set boundaries. This type of person will have a mindset of neediness, grasping praiseworthiness and linking you to their own goals and achievements. "If you do this for me, then I will love you" is the mindset. There is much fear going on inside this person that is keenly covered up.

Healthy love is anchored in the concept of freedom. When a loving person engages with you at work or in your personal life, they will want you to feel free and be who you are as you learn and discover yourself in its fullness, rather than conform to what they say you need to be. A loving person will have a healthy attitude when conflict arises and will want to talk to you directly and hear you out concerning any differences. Mindfulness will help you discern these situations with new insights and practical ways to solve them.

The unhealthy person will see that love as anchored in duty. This unhealthy person will want you to meet their conditions to help them get things and give them status. They will want you to comply with their sense of right and wrong. There is an ego attachment to the love. (We'll talk more about the ego in the next chapter.) They don't want you to think for yourself. They want to smother and limit you. It is a very sad way to live—a kind of dream world—but very common.

Loving People Manage Conflicts Cleanly

You know that conflicts will emerge in many different types of relationships, including at work. The healthy loving person says, "Let's use our conflict in a way that we can learn from each other." Loving people will talk about disagreements, frustrations, and pain in a way that allows the other person to walk away from the meeting with dignity. A loving person will want to see you and discuss the conflict and its details directly with you rather than through texts and e-mails or remaining silent.

An unhealthy person will show cowardice and be unable to face you out of fear of being vulnerable, open, and honest. They show coercion, shaming, and blaming. To them, love is transactional. This type of person will operate with the impression that in order to get back into their good graces, you will have to thank them. The healthy person will speak in these settings with a tone of voice that has honor and respect. In other words, loving people manage conflicts cleanly.

Loving People are Anchored in Encouragement and Affirmation

Healthy people like to look at others with a mindset that says, "What is it about you that I can speak into that is right?" I sense that speaking into what is right is what Jesus meant when he said "love your enemies." You look for things that are good. The unhealthy person will see love as evaluative, and therefore, they will keep score. As long as you make the grade: I love you. That makes a big difference.

Loving People are Bound by Realism

A healthy person will come into any relationship knowing that not everything is going to be like a storybook. There will be conflicts and difficulties. In my coaching practice, I set aside time to discuss with my clients how we will be with each other when a difficulty or conflict arises. This is an important element in developing a conscious relationship. Healthy people recognize their own flaws and know that these traits will be exposed at some point when engaging with others. There is an acceptance of this very fact of life. They also hope that you will accept their flaws and acknowledge them in an open and direct way. In other words, engage with them to discuss differences, conflicts, and misunderstanding either face to face over a cup of coffee or on a video platform where facial expressions, voice tone, and body language are essential aspects of compassion and forgiveness.

Paradoxically, we can have an increased sense of connection when we know each other's flaws. There is a sense of authenticity. In contrast, unhealthy people are driven by idealism. They want life to be perfect according to their standards. In the beginning of a relationship with these people, they might show respect and compliment you. But when your humanity shows up, they don't have a mindset that says, "Let's be affirming to each other." Rather, they feel disappointed and show an aloof attitude toward you and a strong sense of rejection because you have failed to make them feel like the ideal person they believe they are supposed to be.

Loving People Endure in Relationships

There is a consistency and an attitude that says, "I am here for the long haul. This relationship is not something that I am just going to ride out because it feels good and then throw away when challenges arise." There is a commitment, and it doesn't have to be in writing. An unhealthy person's love is temporal. As long as you make me feel good, adore me, and pump me up, we will be okay. If not, it will be over and on to the next episode.

Loving People Live from Abundance

You have a sense of who you are based on your own dignity, self-compassion, and worth. Knowing this, you'll treat another in the same way. The unhealthy person's love is based on neediness. They see you solely as an accountant. They are empty people who need others to fill them up. They are hungry to be told that they are wonderful and are filled with a co-dependent drive that is part of their approach toward love.

True healthy love changes people. That is why I feel that these characteristics of the essence of love, when applied to business and your work as an accountant, can change people. I also believe that it is vital to know the differences between healthy and unhealthy love so that you can set up your boundaries.

Meister Eckhart writes about the essence of love in the following way:

For love is just the same as the fisherman's hook: the fisherman cannot lay hold of the fish unless it is attached to the hook. If it swallows the hook, the fisherman can be sure of his fish, whichever way it turns, this way or that, he knows he will get it. I say the same for love: they who are caught by it have the strongest bonds and the sweetest burden. And so it is written: "Love is as strong as death and as hard as hell" (49).

Your work as an accountant can be filled with the essence of love as you hold onto the hook and turn this way and that way, performing your duties such as scheduling your appointments, responding to a text, adjusting the books, completing a tax return, and moving from one client project to the next. The key to holding onto the hook is your state of awareness and mindful attention as you go about your day, noticing and nurturing the sweet bond of love within and without. *Presence* is the virtue of virtues, and mindfulness is the practice to help you be ready when you are called to action or non-action, whatever the case may be. On top of that, it is beneficial to your health and well-being.

In Shakespeare's comedy classic *A Midsummer Night's Dream*, Lysander tells Hermia, "The course of true love never did run smooth." In Hermia's case, love is plagued by indifference. In other words, distractions and the wandering mind have taken hold of her. In Shakespeare's play, even when love is mutual and seemingly based on a clear vision, it is often hampered by external conditions. In these instances, the characters are not practicing the essence of love. They are not mindfully present. They can't distinguish the difference between their life situation and life. They are completely unconscious.

Love and Accounting

As you may guess by now, when blending love and accounting, I am not referring to the fact that you love your work as an accountant. If

229

that is the case for you, it is secondary. Rather, the primary focus is the practice of the essence of love. We will now move into some practices to help you tend to and sustain the essence of love in your accounting work.

Attention is fundamental in the essence of love. Without attention, there can be no true and abiding love. Attention is throughout the body. How can you maintain focus on attention during the work day, at least periodically? In my experience, mindfulness has helped me in four main areas:

- Attention regulation
- Body awareness
- Emotional regulation
- A shift in identity and sense of self

Here are two exercises to help with the practice of attention of attention. The first is a formal meditation that can be done in nature or in the office. The other is an informal practice, which can be done often during the day to help you stay centered and be more grounded in the present moment.

Formal Practice: A Walk in Nature (or in the Office)

A walk in nature is a meditation and an opportunity to discover more about you and continue practicing the essence of love. If you can't get out into nature, you can still do this anywhere when you recognize that the air you are breathing is nature. Therefore, you can walk in nature anywhere. You start by having no expectations for the outcome. Your intention is simply to be present and open to whatever arises in your experience, especially internal feelings and body sensations.

- Become fully present. Look around and become acutely aware of your sense perceptions.

- Inquire within by asking questions like: "What wants to be born in me?" "What is really important for me?" "What does the universe want from me?"

- Then let go of the inquiry and become acutely aware of your surroundings again.

- What is awareness drawing you toward? Internally, what does it feel like? Can you describe the feeling or emotion?

- As you continue to walk, what else is drawing attention? If you become distracted, gently return to your anchor such as the breath or inner body.

- Continue with the walk until you find a place to stop. What is coming up for you now?

- Notice and employ focused attention on what is being offered to you in answer of your question.

- Offer thanks and gratitude at work and in your personal life.

I invite you to journal your experience.

Informal Practice: Invite Loving Kindness

We can invite an attitude of loving kindness throughout the day by directing phrases of goodwill toward ourselves and others in the present moment as situations arise, or as we are called to do something that takes us out of our comfort zones.

The Path of Self-Emptying Compassion

Living Presence

By Rumi

Love is recklessness, not reason.
Reason seeks a profit.
Loves come on strong. Consuming herself, unabashed.
Yet in the midst of suffering,
Love proceeds like a millstone,
Hard surfaced, and straightforward.
Having died to self-interest,
She risks everything and asks for nothing.
Love gambles away every gift God bestows.

Rumi is pointing toward the divine purpose of our lives where we are stripped of our conditioned sense of self with its story and mental and emotional reactive patterns. It is the transformation of consciousness through which mindful *presence* is the basis for your sense of identity. You know this in a moment of awareness. Truly, there is no higher stage in this lifetime, where eternal peace and goodness reign, and you have transcended and included everything that came before. As an old proverb reminds us, "Yet in the midst of suffering, love proceeds like a millstone." This self-emptying compassion is you going *beyond balancing the books*.

Living Deeply

Self-compassion is all about mindfully giving ourselves what we need. To do this, we need to know what we value most. Someone recently told me that what she really wanted to do was to clean up her e-mail inbox and eliminate the "junk." I asked her what was important about that. After exploring this question, she discovered what was really important to her about cleaning out her inbox was a sense of freedom.

For some, simple everyday tasks like reading or eliminating e-mails reflect much more than the task; they reflect a deep value of living in freedom, which is often the hidden value underneath all our distractions. Freedom from what, you might ask. Ultimately, it is our mind and related difficult emotional patterns. The value of freedom and other things—like integrity, community, contribution, connection, play, well-being, and meaning—reflect something essential about human nature. These values also reflect choice, which is one of five core elements of mindfulness.

Paradoxically, our difficult moments in life very much depend on our core values. For example, when connection is one of your core values, an abrupt ending of a relationship without adequate closure can leave you struggling for a while to make sense of what happened. Or if you value vacation and weekends, like many of us do, getting a promotion requiring you to be on call and work over the weekend can be troublesome. If you don't know your core values, your unconscious mind will remind you from time to time. Our feelings of frustration and anxiety often arise out of the awareness that we are not living in accordance with our values.

Informal Practice: Living with Purpose and Core Values

When we realize that we're not all that "together" or perhaps landed on the metaphorical "wrong street" at the "wrong time," these are moments to recall our core values. A core value can be made into a commitment to help us remember. What is a commitment in this context?

- A commitment is an aspiration to which we can continually return ourselves whenever we've gone astray in our lives.

233

- A commitment anchors our life in what matters most. It is not a binding contract.
- A commitment functions like the breath in breath meditation—a safe place we can return to when we're lost and adrift in our daily lives.

We want to be compassionate to ourselves when we realize we've strayed—no shame or self-bickering—and then focus on your core values.

Select a core value you have discovered recently in yourself that you would like to manifest for the rest of your life. It could be freedom of expression, inner harmony, autonomy, integrity, connection, social, meaning, or well-being to name a few. Now try writing it down in the form of a commitment. Close your eyes and repeat your commitment silently several times and continue to do so each day until you sense it has become more fully activated in your consciousness.

Kindness: Thankfulness and Gratitude

Ninety-eight percent of our lives consist of little things. I would suggest that same percentage also applies to our work as accountants. From the most complicated tax matter to the accounting for a consolidated group of corporations, each step is a little thing requiring attention. Giving your full attention without labeling is a very satisfying thing to do. You can start by looking around at your office environment and the people you work with each day. You are the awareness rather than the interpreting person, and with practice this aware *presence* becomes your new normal.

Of course, there is a place at work for evaluations, analysis, and feedback. When you do this, attention remains, but now you'll use the analytical mind to address what is in front of you. But when we look more closely, it raises the question: how much of our day is interrupted with unnecessary interpretations of people, places, and events? Sometimes, we overanalyze even our clients' finances.

As *presence* arises in you, the little things become more important and satisfying in your life and work. The true source of this satisfaction is your awareness coupled with an appreciation of the little things. That appreciation is gratitude and thankfulness. It doesn't necessarily mean you have to "think" in your head that you are thankful. Yes, there can be kindness, thankfulness, and gratitude without any mental functions. A simple outflow of attention from the recesses of your being is the key. If your gratitude involves another person, they may even pick this vibration up subliminally.

You become aware of the attention and the object it is directed toward. When you do this internally or externally, that becomes a deeper practice of gratitude.

When someone has helped you, and perhaps they are leaving the firm, giving your full attention directly to that person is what real kindness, thankfulness, and gratitude are all about. There is an acknowledgment and an underlying trust in life, coupled with a positive energy, that supersede any words that might be exchanged. There is mindful compassion. Yes, taking the time to go meet someone who has helped you in a state of aware attention is a little thing.

Self-Compassion and Forgiveness

Forgiveness is about being fully present and opening up to the hurt caused, whether to us or by us. We humans are works in progress, so there is no reason to be unforgiving toward ourselves. There are six steps to compassionate forgiveness:

1. Enter the present moment with our full attention.
2. Open up to what we are feeling and the distress of what happened.
3. Connect to our hearts through self-compassion, and allow it to melt with loving kindness and common humanity.
4. Recognize that the situation wasn't entirely personal but was the result of many interdependent causes and conditions.

235

5. Set intention to forgive. "May I begin to forgive myself/another for what I/he/she did, knowingly or unknowingly, to have caused me/him/her pain?"

6. Establish boundaries by committing ourselves to not repeat the same mistake, to the best of our ability.

Bill Plotkin writes in *Wild Mind*: "In healthy cultures and families, we learn in childhood how to embrace our emotions in ways that serve ourselves and others. In contemporary western cultures, most people must learn this later in life. Many never do."

Here is an outline for emotional consolidation, which is another approach toward compassionate forgiveness:

*   Be mindful through loving connected *presence*. To embrace your experience as best you can and the raw emotion itself, beginning with how it feels in your body, allowing the emotion to express and embody itself through us, using sound, movement, gesture, or posture. In this step, there's no interpretation, censoring, or chatter about the emotion itself, only the full visceral experience of it.

*   Try to discern what the emotion in that particular situation tells us about yourself (not about others), about your fears, frustrations, values, needs, desires, attitudes, and so on. This is intended not to be a harsh self-criticism but rather a compassionate self-examination.

*   "Own" your emotions, in words or action, in a non-violent, kindhearted way that makes your social world right again or that celebrates what's already right. Genuinely let others know what is going on inside you.

- Circle back, the flow of the emotional process now being completed, seeing how it fits within the big picture of your individual self, and hopefully have a wholehearted laugh with yourself and perhaps others about the adventure of being human.

What is our noblest act as we live our personal and professional lives? According to one of western culture's great minds, Thomas Aquinas, who wrote: "Joy is the human's noblest act." That is pretty amazing, given that most of us have come to believe that fighting for a cause is the noblest thing we can do. However, in *presence* we come to understand that even justice exists for the sake of joy. Not as a means to an end, but rather an intrinsic aspect of it. Furthermore, joy is part of compassion, as Meister Eckhart points out when he writes: "What happens to another, whether it is joy or sorrow, happens to me." That pretty much sums it all up.

Chapter 8

The Ego and Awakening at Work

*I long, as does every other human, to be at home
wherever I find myself.*

—Maya Angelou

According to Steve Taylor, a psychologist and author of *The Fall*,
the ego "refers to the part of our psyche which thinks, the 'I'
inside our heads which makes decisions and plans, deliberates,
worries and imagines, and which—most frequently—chatters away
randomly to itself, sending endless stream of memories, images and
thoughts through our minds" (50). It is the "I" inside our heads that
talks to itself carefully and deliberately, and that we identify with as
our sense of self.

The ego has its noble purpose in our lives. Ultimately, the ego as we know it is meant to be transcended as our true nature unfolds in time and yet timelessly. In other words, you always are your true nature. With this unfolding, the ego is included in our psyche in a more mature and fully developed sense. The ego can then serve us rather than rule us.

In this chapter, I will be using this basic framework of the ego structure as we clarify the relationship between mindfulness and the self (ego). In my view and sensing, the physical brain is a channel for consciousness to manifest form in the sense perceived world rather than being the producer of consciousness. The physical brain is a tiny aspect of consciousness.

Consciousness

While traveling in Spain a few years ago, I visited the home of the sixteenth-century mystics Teresa of Avila and John of the Cross. Tucked away inside a glass enclosure is an empty chair in which John gave his sublime teachings to his students. The empty chair for me was a symbol of consciousness. His teachings include the notion that consciousness is not derived by the physical brain. Here is an excerpt:

> The soul (consciousness) lives by that which it loves
> (presence of presence), rather than in the body which
> it animates. For it has not its life in the body, but rather
> gives it to the body and lives in that which it loves
> (presence).

For the reader who would like to explore the topic of consciousness further, I have included in the appendix my top ten suggested reading list. Ultimately, it is your own inner guidance and the related interconnectedness to inner spaciousness that is the guiding force. I see it as a self-emptying fullness.

In my view, there are two main causes for the basic dysfunction we see in humans and therefore in our professional work. First, there is strong sense of individuality and separation from the world around us. I call it a "split." Second are our automatic patterns, which have desensitized us to perceive the world as so familiar, we thereby lose touch with the reality of everyday experience. These two dysfunctions give rise to subpersonalities where we get lost in our thoughts, emotions, and reactions. We become these patterns.

Hafiz writes about the basic dysfunction this way in his poem titled, "Wanting Our Life To Make Sense:" Here is my translation:

> All day long you do this, and then even in your
> sleep . . . pursue happiness.
> We are looking to find something to celebrate
> with great enthusiasm,
> wanting all our battles and toil and our life to
> make sense.
> "I found it, I found it, I found it!" a hermit once
> began to shout, after having spent years in
> solitude, meditating.
> "Where?" a young shepherd boy nearby asked.
> "Where?"
> And the hermit replied, "It may take a while,
> but I will show you. For now, just stay near me."
> All day long we do this with our movements
> And our thoughts . . . pursue happiness.

Egoic Parts

The inner critic is an inner voice that can take hold of the accountant in some of the most amusing of circumstances. (Yes, it is important to bring a sense of humor as you mindfully observe the functioning of the egoic mind structure.) Take Anna, for example. She is a tax manager who works at a local accounting firm. She has always dreamt of starting her own holistic spa where women can come and rejuvenate themselves while tending to their inner world in a meditation garden draped with poetic musings amidst quiet stillness. She has never managed to take the first step and explore the practical possibilities of implementing her dream. Rather, when she ponders it, an inner voice snarls at her ideas as outrageous and doomed for failure.

Or take Michael, whose inner flatterer brings to bear the notion that he is just about the most important accountant at his firm. Upon closer examination, he struggles with intimacy and opening up to his limitations. In his mind, no other accountant can do things quite like he does. Michael might hear an inner voice tell him: "When the going gets tough, the tough get going."

Another case concerns Robin's husband, a stockbroker with a substance abuse issue who often misses work, has frequent affairs, and regularly gets into arguments with his friends and family. She covers for him a lot, calling his friends to tell them he can't make their weekly gathering due to stress at work. Robin, a busy accountant herself, does her best to be indispensable to him as she secretly fears no one else would want to be with her.

Fred makes a lot of money as managing partner of mid-sized firm. His firm has several offices, and each one operates like a sweatshop where long hours, internal competition, layers of review, and administrative backlog burden just about every accountant in the firm. The wages are average, and the office environment is miserable, although no partner will admit it. Fred has no real friends, except the transaction related type—what he calls his "referral sources." His staffs treat him with great deference, trying to maintain their jobs, or are just afraid of him. Most of his partners secretly dislike him. Fred is a robber extraordinaire.

Joan is a tyrant; she is a partner in a well-established CPA firm. She never felt loved or socially accepted as a child. She learned that the only way to get ahead in the business world was to control others, sometimes overtly and at other times covertly. Now, as a lead partner on various engagements, she has created a false image over this underlying subpersonality in order to get what she wants.

These are just a few examples of how the ego distorts reality in the service of self-protection. This distortion leads one to act small and secure a place in the world one way or another. At a certain point, these subpersonalities and their strategies impede one's growth far more than they prove a genuine service. Poet David Whyte writes in *Fire in The Earth and River Flow* (51) about this shocking image of the ego, whose darkness covers up one's true nature:

Excerpt from "The Fire in The Song"
by David Whyte, from Fire in The Earth and River Flow

you made that pact
    with a dark presence
        in your life.

He said, "If you only
    stop singing
        I'll make you safe."

Moving *beyond balancing the books* does require you to question the very assumptions that have absorbed into your thinking and ways of perception. As we continue to examine some of the ways the egoic mind operates in our lives and in our work as accountants, I encourage you to stay connected to the stillness within you as your true nature. This is vital because as you embark or continue on the path of mindful *presence*, you will be challenged continuously in ways that are quite different from what you may be accustomed to.

For example, you will be ridiculed, often covertly, by people who will dismiss you as an "outsider," or you may be working in a firm that operates in a setting filled with bravado, backstabbing, and unhealthy competition. Or maybe your creative impulse to explore new opportunities in non-traditional ways is frowned upon within the organization as a "cost center," even though it seems that you are being supported. Sometimes, it could simply be that you are just doing your job. You do this by focusing intently on what is in front of you, taking one step at a time, while others are frantically going about their day trying to look busy. This is the ego trying to look busy, so it is also vital to connect to compassion for yourself and others as you witness this type of all too common behavior.

Catching Yourself

Let's consider the situation of Salvatore, an audit partner in a large accounting firm. One of his audit managers is seeking his advice in dealing with a difficult client. Wanting to be of service, Salvatore automatically tells her to "go to the firm checklist" of what managers need to do under these circumstances. Immediately, he notices the audit manager shrink back and cut him off. Salvatore takes notice and realizes that his voice was raised and his tone was stern. His willingness to help came off as cold and condescending, and he apologizes. He then asks the manager more about the experience with the client, and together they brainstorm possible courses of action in a positive way. The manager leaves feeling heard, and for Salvatore it is a revelation. His action to assist came across as negative. He begins to become aware of how these patterns play out in the rest of his life. He begins to take a mindfulness workshop and seeks counseling for his anger as he calmly creates a new path for himself.

Reactive emotions are an aspect of the egoic mind we often take for granted as part of who we are in the course of everyday living. These emotions, like anger, fear, and anxiety, are sometimes hidden and at other times quite obvious. So, it requires an acute awareness to notice this is happening to you, which leads to an understanding and a more productive way to respond to a situation or people.

Take Abagail, for example. She is a CEO at one of your clients in the healthcare industry. She gets word that one of her top physicians is not in compliance with standard legal protocols. She instantly feels a rush of energy in her body, and she can sense her anxiety building. Should she take quick action and call their attorney, or should she wait and get a better handle of the situation? She ponders her options and feels conflicted.

Part of her wants to send out warnings to all her managers to inform them of the circumstances and to tighten up their procedures immediately. However, this would subject the managers to possible scrutiny and potential legal issues. Another part of her wants to get a sense of the entire situation so she can make an informed choice. She practices the three-minute breathing meditation as she closes the door of her office. Her emotions reach their height and then subside. An opening of calmness enters her awareness as she asks herself, "What actually happened? What are the facts?" Are we jumping to a conclusion too quickly?

As it turns out, Abagail spoke to each of her senior managers to get their input; it was determined that the non-compliance claim was false. She then called her attorney to respond to the notice with all the facts at hand and a more productive way to respond to the event. In this situation, Abagail stepped back from her automatic response pattern and let go of the egoic mind. She separated the situation (notice of non-compliance) from herself as the observer of the situation and was able in that open space of awareness to make a choice on how best to respond.

What is often overlooked is that this space of awareness is with us all the time and not just when difficult circumstances come up. Awareness is a deeper state of consciousness than thought. Awareness is where wisdom and peace meet.

Question

> Just because I feel irritated about my workload does not mean that it has to drive my actions. What can I do to create space between the situation at work and my thoughts and interpretations surrounding it?

Creating Space between Thought, Emotions, and Related Actions

As I addressed earlier on about the nature of the judgmental mind, we interpret situations in order for them to make sense and to have a perceived sense of control. This is simply what the egoic mind does—it is searching for solutions to establish control, based on past experiences and associations. When someone reacts to a situation based on past experiences, more often than not some kind of trouble develops. You get an e-mail from a difficult client, and as you brace for an encounter that you see as problematic, your body contracts and your stomach is in knots. When you look closely, no problem is actually happening other than the one you are remembering from your last encounter with this client. If you visit that client the next day, you are likely to bring with you the same irritable tone and may inadvertently cause the very adverse encounter you were attempting to eliminate.

As the old saying goes, the map is not the territory. Everyday life becomes your meditation, for true meditation is alert awareness to both your internal state and external situation moment to moment.

Ego as Story

The ego is essentially a mental construct you take as yourself. It is a mind-made "story of me," a narrative that we define as ourselves and that of others. It is an image we create "about" ourselves. The ego develops throughout our lifetimes. Hopefully, the ego reaches a maturity so that it no longer drives our everyday activities but rather serves a function for practical purposes. When we have an experience that we evaluate as good or bad, and the voice chatter in the head says something like, "I am nuts for responding that way," or "I will never make it," or "I will get fired," or "I am the best accountant," we take this chatter as the "self," which is essentially a personal creation rather than some objective truth. The main driver for building up an ego is our identification. When we identify with something, we take this "something" as "me," and it becomes linked as a part of one's sense of self. Some of the ways the ego is built include the following:

- We create our own life stories based on events that happened to us and our evaluation of those events. Essentially, we build a life "story" describing all the important and relevant events and the steps we took along the way. It includes how these circumstances impacted us. It is a subjective and general re-evaluation of the past.
- We compare ourselves to others through a myriad of traits including intelligence, introversion, physical appearances, being wealthy or poor, etc.
- We evaluate ourselves. For example, you tell someone that you are a kind, thankful, and grateful human being.
- We link circumstances to outcomes and situations to traits. We believe we made partner because of our personality and our ability to generate business along with our technical prowess and connections.
- We use strategy, like when a firm wants to present to their staff their benefit package so that it will provide an impression

that they are sharing profits with their employees, when in fact they are not. There is a hidden agenda.

When you find yourself stuck in one or more of these situations, you individually find your own "conclusion" and therefore strengthen the ego in the process. It is the biggest trap that one can find oneself in. How can mindfulness help us with the tendencies of the ego? How do you get to Carnegie Hall? *Presence, presence, presence*!

Presence as an Antidote for Ego

All day, most of us are in an endless stream of doing. In a *presence* pause, we step away from autopilot and connect to our breath (or another portal into *presence* that resonates with you, such as sense perceptions, inner body awareness, or stillness). You sense into the feeling of your breath in your body. When you do this with attention, you are present. In this simple practice of a *presence* pause, you will find increasing clarity, calmness, and creativity. You are a mindful professional doing the work of your profession.

The state of mindful *presence* is the transformation. Once you are firmly rooted in *presence* as your center of gravity, the ego is no longer problematic. So the key is your present moment awareness as your true nature, no matter where you are, who you are with, or what situations you find yourself in. You don't need to attain it, seek it out, and recall prior experiences to help get you there. All these thoughts are a hindrance to mindful *presence*. The words I am writing are not it either. The words on this page, as well as the exercises and meditations provided throughout this book, are pointers and practices for realizing this state of awareness.

A primary characteristic of the ego operating in us is seeing one's value and worth being contingent upon some external factor such as performance, appearance, or social approval (52). Now, there is nothing wrong with giving and receiving compliments for a job well done, attempting to look your best, or finding the right social settings

248

where you feel comfortable and develop relationships. However, it is the total identification with these situations, wherein you rely on these things to provide you with self-esteem, that may be problematic. This ephemeral self-esteem is responsible for untold misery, unhappiness, defensiveness, and reactivity, not to mention emotional and mental turmoil (53).

The greatest threat to the ego is death. Research has shown that when a person is confronted with their own mortality, they tend to react defensively because this clash is perceived as a threat (54). Unsurprisingly, research has also shown that higher levels of mindfulness may counteract the typical ego-defense mechanisms that are triggered when people are faced with their own mortality.

Awareness Meditation

This meditation will help you observe your true nature beyond the ego self. This observing self (awareness) is the *presence* and the door into something deeper than any experience, a place where wisdom, creativity, and peace meet. Practice this meditation first by reading a few lines at a time and then closing your eyes, sinking into that which the words point to. By doing so, you will notice a space opening up within you, which will help you gain some distance from those things in your life you may have become over-identified with. These identifications are different for everyone and could relate to your status at work, possessions, physical appearance, social role, nationality, family, economic status, victim mentality, and so forth. The meditation will be geared to aspects of your career as a professional.

- As we begin, find a comfortable seat and sit in a position that reflects your dignity.

- Now, turn attention to the room you are in and scan the room for its content.

- Begin to turn attention inward and to the center region of your chest—your heart.

- Notice any body sensations you might feel. With each feeling, allow attention to move toward the feeling; acknowledge it and allow it to move on at its own pace.

- As you notice any thoughts that arise, become aware that you are noticing your own thoughts. A part of you is watching your thoughts—we will call that "awareness." That awareness is "you" behind those eyes and ears who is noticing the thoughts, emotions, and body sensations. This awareness has been there with you all your life. It is your true nature.

- Now, bring forth from your memory a work situation from last year. It could be anything that is not too overwhelming, some ordinary circumstance like working on a budget or a financial projection, for example.

- Good, now recall all the things that were happening then. Remember the client, the personalities, the place you did the work, and your feelings about this work. As you notice these things, see if you can notice the person behind your eyes watching, working, and feeling. You were there then as you are here now.

- The person who is aware of this situation is present here and now in the same way as back then. There is a continuum in awareness—you have been "you" your entire life. Can you sense into that as your current experience?

- Now, I would like you to remember an accounting class in college or when you sat for the CPA exam or any other professional exam.

- Look around and remember the events and circumstances that were happening in your life back then while in this situation. Bring from memory the sights, sounds, and feelings you had. Take your time as you bring this up from memory.

- As these sensations come up, find the person behind the eyes, just for a moment, who was there in the college accounting class or sitting for the professional exam. Remember the person who was reading the questions, studying, or whatever else took place back then.
- You were there then as you are now in the awareness.
- There is no need to bring in your left brain analytical thinking. There is a continuum of awareness that extends as a web behind the circumstances of your life. You have been "you" your entire life.
- Finally, recall something that happened when you were in high school. Now, gaze across the room once again and remember the sounds, sights, and feelings you had back then. Also, try to note the moment you recognize "you" as the awareness behind the hearing, seeing, and feeling. Notice that there was a person behind the eyes of the high school student. You were there then as you are now. You realize this not by talking "about" what happened to yourself or others, but rather as the timeless *presence* in which all sounds, sights, and sensations arise. Again, there is nothing for you to believe in this meditation. Simply focus on your inner knowing.
- From the perspective of awareness, so to speak, let's now look at some other aspects of life. First, we'll look at your body. Sometimes the body feels strong and vibrant, and at other times it is sick or perhaps tired. Your body was once a little child, fragile and in need of continuous care, but then it developed and was able to be more independent. It may even have confronted challenges and had parts of it removed in surgery. The cells in your body also come and go, as do body sensations. Everything changes except the awareness behind this surface level phenomenon.

- This awareness remains with you behind your thoughts, emotions, and feelings. Your body moves with you also, but this "you" simply experiences your body but is not part of it.

- Now, let's move on to your roles, including in your life and profession. How many roles do you play now and have played in the past? Sometimes, you play a role as parent, friend, sibling, or spouse. Sometimes, the role can be a respected worker or the office clown. In this world, there are many roles to be played, even now as the role of the reader of this book. However, beyond these roles, there is an ever-present witness whom we have been calling awareness to, which has not changed or moved. This awareness does not bend or attempt to fit into any role. This meditation is not about creating a new belief for you. I am not asking you to believe anything from the outset. Rather, I am asking you to be open, so that you can distinguish between your experience and the "you" who is listening, observing, and feeling. The alert *presence* is the background of all sense perceptions, thoughts, and emotions.

- We will now look at our emotions that are in a continuous flux from calmness, serenity, happiness, and joy to irritation, anxiety, boredom, and sadness. Take a moment and think of the things that caused you upset and anxiety last year that have been resolved. Where are they now? Emotions give us the fact of impermanence.

- Under the wave of emotions, awareness remains the same. You, as the ever present witness of emotions that come, stay for a while and then go.

- What emotions are you feeling right now? Can you sense your own *presence* behind the emotion? Does the *presence* have an opinion about the emotion? If some opinion does come up like, "I shouldn't be feeling this way," can you sense that this opinion is not awareness? Rather, it is the judgmental mind coming in through the one side of the T account. In other words, it's not awareness. I invite you to enter into the stillness.

252

- Kindly now guide attention to your thoughts. Our thoughts can be challenging because they pull us out of awareness and being the witness. When this happens, gently come back to an anchor, such as your breath, and connect back to awareness. Thoughts in you create a conceptual knowledge and help you perform your work as an accountant. They solve client issues through analysis and computations. Sometimes they are compartmentalized into different buckets of your life, and sometimes they keep you up at night. Thoughts are constantly changing, and some of them have a life of their own.

- As you recognize the nature of thought, can you sense into the awareness behind and underneath the thoughts?

- Although you have thoughts, you are not your thoughts. You may, from time to time, get caught up in them or taken over by them, but there is always awareness as the witness of your thoughts, even while doing your work as an accountant. Can you notice awareness in the background as you read these words?

- As we come to the close of this meditation, offer gratitude for being aware of awareness.

Integrating Mindfulness into Your Work

To me, mindfulness is a way of being in the world. I recall those initial glimpses of a felt sense of joy and the absolute delight I had in those early moments when *presence* took hold of me in unexpected ways. Those early glimpses came during a period of deep anxiety and stress, and all I knew was that I wanted more of that joy without understanding what that really meant. *Presence* became my best friend. One of the main areas in which I started to practice mindfulness was at work in my CPA practice, as I have mentioned. I knew there would be obstacles, mainly from my own egoic mind structure. The ego likes to ruminate and worry, and that certainly was an aspect of my conditioned mind.

So, I made a commitment to myself to intentionally make *presence* the most important priority, no matter what came up. As I wrote in the introduction, I had help with some amazing teachers who pointed the way for me. And yet, I carry out the practice in the midst of a very unconscious business world that knows very little about the practice of *presence*. To remind you, when I use the term unconscious, I am referring to the complete lack of awareness. In unconsciousness, one's thoughts and emotions merge with a personal sense of self wherein they believe that whatever they are doing and saying is absolutely correct and true. Furthermore, and perhaps due to this merging of thoughts with a person, there is a split and a sense of separation from themselves, others, and the natural world. Of course, there are moments of consciousness, but for the majority of the business day, there is a complete lack of awareness in most.

In my opinion, the main challenge we have in the practice of accounting is not keeping up with the competition, technology, specialization, technical knowledge, or growing our business and career, per se, but rather bringing mindful awareness to everything we do day to day. Why is it so challenging? In my view, it is part of the egoic mind that has not been fully faced in awareness, combined with the lurking sub-personality structure (shadow) we addressed in an earlier chapter. Two positions are missing in most professional firms organizational structures: the partner in-charge of mindfulness and the director of compassion. Both positions and their respective work responsibilities represent the next phase of conscious business development and a more fulfilling, resilient and conscious business environment for everyone.

To address this dilemma, firms can devote more resources to independent mentoring and coaching throughout the organization to help create a "coaching culture." When I refer to resources, I am first and foremost pointing toward a shift in mindset from only looking at external results to also seeing internal results. This includes a trait of openness and curiosity in which each person is dedicated to their own conscious human development and *presence* practice in the workplace. We have been trained as accountants to exclusively look at external output, and yet there is an internal input that is longing for attention and wants to be more fully integrated with our external world. Let's call it the "Inner CPA" or ICPA.

Spin-Off

Not too long ago, as Matthew Fox points out, "the soul and cosmos were divided up between organized religion and science," and this amplified a sense of separation. Fox continues: "Religion took the soul, and science took the cosmos." This spin-off has caused untold misery by taking the awe out of spirit and spirit out of the awe. It is the same with soul and business. Still, only a minority of business professionals are connected to the deeper dimension of who they are moment to moment. You see how often people react, make decisions, serve their clients, condescend employees, and are frequently in a hurry or acting with certain angst. There is little or no empathy—or at best, it is a cognitive empathy—combined with a controlling sense of entitlement.

This is a daily trauma for many in these situations, and often they don't even know it. This unconscious pattern is all around you, so without resistance to the unconsciousness in others, you bring compassion to your mindfulness practice. The practice is the reward, as you are intentionally and purposefully aware moment to moment in an open and non-judgmental way to whatever is around you or going on within you. Little by little, you will have breakthroughs like I mentioned with my oncology client, in which you'll notice consciousness, empathy, and connection. You will have breakthroughs when you notice you don't get anxious when your client or manager is letting off steam at you. In other words, breakthroughs become a daily phenomenon. This is not just about acting professional, which is too often just a mask for what is really going on inside individuals, but rather a deep abiding peace in the background that you stay connected too.

When you are mindful, you know what is comfortable can also be profitable as you proceed in accounting aligned with your deep yearnings and core values. A feeling of uncomfortableness can be a sign of the ego and one of its many manifestations. Or it could be a discernment that is pointing you away from a particular situation. This comes up for most of us when considering a new job, client opportunity, or simply handling a certain situation. It is vital to listen to the wisdom of your body during these moments. "What do I need now?" is a very good question to ask yourself. Take a walk in nature or across the office hall, listen to some calming music to connect to the stillness, and then see what happens.

Conscious Business

Google is one of a growing number of companies that has introduced mindfulness for their employees. At Google, mindfulness is a way to develop emotional intelligence (EI), awareness of others, not to mention creativity. In Working with Emotional Intelligence, Daniel Goleman has written that EI skills are compatible with cognitive ones; top performers have both. He writes: "The more complex the job, the more emotional intelligence matters, if only because a deficiency of these skills can hinder the use of technical expertise or intellect a person may have."

According to Mirabai Bush in *Awakening at Work: Introducing Mindfulness into Organizations*, not everyone at Google knew this. They were so successful at so many things that it was hard to appreciate that they could still go from good to great (or from great to awesome). After a talk given by Dan Goleman relating to mindfulness, loving kindness, and compassion toward greater EI, over one hundred people signed up for the in-house training. Here is an outline of the Google curriculum (55) that has now been used in a growing number of organizations, which has since been augmented with new scientific findings on the positive effects of meditation.

- Self-awareness (knowing one's internal states, preferences, resources and intuitions): mindful sitting, standing, walking, journaling, body scan, and scan for emotions;
- Self-regulation (managing one's internal states, impulses and resources): mindful sitting, awareness of emotions, working with anger, letting go, and writing about feelings;
- Motivation (emotional tendencies that guide or facilitate reaching goals): journaling and mindfully listening on values;
- Empathy (awareness of others' feelings, needs, and concerns) and compassion (awareness of others' suffering, with the desire to relieve it): tonglen (giving and receiving practice), Just Like Me, loving kindness;
- Social skills (adeptness at inducing desirable responses in others): mindful listening and speaking from the heart, mindful emailing.

This mindfulness-based emotional intelligence (EI), as it is called, can be developed and applied in all kinds of business settings. With training and experiential practice, individuals can sense a shift in perception. I know that is exactly what happened to me. Here are the four steps involved in developing EI for the accountant and other professionals.

- First, train attention in a way that allows you to be peaceful and clear on demand. At any time, whatever is happening to you—whether you are under stress, you're being shouted at, or anything else—you have the skill to come back to a peace that is calm and clear. If you can do that, it lays the foundation for emotional intelligence.

- Second, create inner space. Once your mind is calm and clear, you can create a quality of wisdom that improves over time and evolves into self-mastery. You know about yourself enough that you can master your emotions.

- The third step is to listen to your creative impulse so original thoughts can emerge. For example, when you look at every human being you encounter, think to yourself, "I want this person to be peaceful." Once that becomes a habit, you don't have to think about it (or tell somebody), it just becomes natural. Then everything in your work life changes because people want to associate with you and they like you. It operates on the subconscious level.

- Fourth, name the emotion as best you can and take a deep breath in and out. This practice can settle the emotion so you can further recognize it for what it is.

Buddhist monk and spiritual teacher Thich Nhat Hanh, when asked about business leaders practicing mindfulness, said that as long as they practice "true" mindfulness, it doesn't matter if "the original intention is triggered by wanting to be more effective at work or make bigger profits . . . the practice will fundamentally change their perspective on life as it naturally opens hearts to greater compassion and develops the desire to end the suffering of others" (56).

In my view, a mindfulness workforce doesn't happen in a collective fashion but rather one person at a time. These individuals will bear witness to some unconventional practices, face some obstacles, and thereby go deeper into the practice of turning justice into joy. Here are my thirteen qualities of an awakened workplace:

1. Focus attention clearly rather than continuously multi-tasking and doing.

2. Speak more calmly and engaging rather than speaking as a means to an end.

3. Listen acutely by placing some attention on the stillness within instead of thinking about what to say next.

4. Recognize that each individual and business is not a stand-alone entity but rather is interconnected with all of life, including the more-than-human world.

5. Practice the "essence of love" rather than seeking to control and project.

6. Diversity and inclusion is primary. Want to learn from others.

7. Be compassionate through mindfulness, kindness, and common humanity instead of ruminating, self-criticizing, and feeling isolated.

8. Tolerate ambiguity, paradox, and not knowing.

9. Handle technology as a necessary tool that enhances connection and well-being rather than a means to increase power over another.

10. Everyone from the janitor to the CEO work with meaning and purpose instead of working in an environment with layers of separation that imply division.

11. Encourage meditation breaks and moments of stillness throughout the day to reconnect to well-being rather than constantly doing and having a "what's next" mindset. There is no such thing as back to back meetings.

12. As the basis for all creativity, celebrate the unified wholeness of each individual that resembles the same wholeness and energy of the cosmos rather than implicitly viewing each individual as flawed and broken.

13. Leaders and their staff have a holistic view of their work, including mind, body, spirit, and soul, rather than maintaining a split between business and spirit/soul.

In *A Course in Miracles*, it says: "I want the Peace of God. To say these words is nothing, but to mean these words is everything. Nobody can mean these words and not be healed." There is another line in this work that I love: "You are never upset for the reason you think." When I am upset, I tend to believe I know the reasons why I am upset, and I tell myself this. There is no end to the reasons why a person could be upset in this world, including in our workplace. I have discovered that the deeper reason why I'm upset is that I lose touch with the peace, stillness, and essence of who I am.

As a professional, you'll be continuously challenged with people, situations, and events that upset you. Paradoxically, I would suggest that one of the most prevalent skills of modern day professionals, especially leaders of business firms, is to cover up their upset. There is too much focus on external factors during the day, leaving very little awareness to the inner dimension of thoughts, emotions, feelings, and beyond—*beyond balancing the books.*

Another way of looking at the ego is in what Ken Wilber calls the *Atman Project.* According to Wilber, the true nature of human beings is pure spirit or atman. At the very core of our beings, we are one with the universe, infinite and eternal, beyond space and time and death. Although we have become alienated from this true nature, we still have an intuition of it, and our deepest drive is to regain the wholeness that we've lost. However, we go about this in the completely wrong way and translate the characteristics of our spiritual natures into the realm of the ego. In our deepest selves, we are one with God. But on the level of ego, this translates into a desire to be all powerful, to control and dominate others—hence the desire for status, success, and power (57).

Wilber explains materialism in the same way. In our deepest selves, we are everything, but on the ego level this translates into wanting to *have* everything, hence the desire to possess things and control the narrative.

Getting Triggered

It is relatively easy to get triggered at work, and for the professional, it is very common. In fact, these are opportunities to get to know yourself better. For many, the opportunity is lost, sometimes due to the fast-paced environment of the workplace and our lack of awareness for the subtle triggers such as an irritating co-worker, constant pressures of deadlines to complete a task, and so on. We addressed this earlier in the mindfulness practice of acceptance and identification, but now we look at these triggers as an awakener to transcend the ego in the moment they arise and step beyond—*beyond balancing the books*. Here are some questions that commonly come up in our work as accountants dealing with triggers.

Questions

> I find myself multi-tasking constantly, especially during busy season. How do I learn not to do so much multi-tasking?

How does it feel when you are multi-tasking? "I am very overwhelmed and feel anxious. I don't know if I am overlooking certain issues, and that makes me nervous." Did you ever think about doing nothing for a moment? "What do you mean by doing nothing?" Multi-tasking is an illusion in most situations. Can you become aware of the space between one task and the next? Try experimenting by doing one specific task at a time, like finishing a tax return up to the point at which you have your open issue list.

Don't look at your e-mails or texts while you do this work. Your ego won't like this, but refrain from checking e-mails and texts anyway while you are working on something else. If you are on a conference call, make it a point not to check your e-mails while on the call. Also, take short breaks throughout the day; a simple breathing exercise is an example of "doing nothing." Then see how you feel. You will learn much more about yourself as you take a step back for short periods throughout the day. You'll start to feel like you are mastering your emotions. You'll be transcending the ego.

> There is a very difficult partner in my firm, and I began to practice and tap into the "essence of love" as you describe it. When I did that, I pondered, "Wouldn't it be nice if the whole firm was better?" When I did that, wasn't I being judgmental?

That thought is not a judgment; rather, it is wisdom. When you notice people around you who lack empathy, have a sense of entitlement, and manipulate others, you know that they are doing so out of their own pain or subtle dissatisfaction with their status and place in the world. As you tap into your own well-being, you will become more tolerant and open to the dysfunction that is all around. You may want to internally offer a gesture of good will toward them.

> I was recently passed over for promotion in my firm, and a colleague of mine was awarded the promotion. I feel disappointed, sad, and humiliated—what can I do?

It is painful to have this happen. The first step is to recognize your common humanity with others who have gone through similar situations, although not exactly as you are experiencing. Feel into this connection. Once you enter into a state of sensing your common humanity, then make the present moment your ally rather than ruminating about why this might have happened. Very often, it is impersonal factors that led to your firm's decision. As you make the present moment your friend, you'll realize that this situation does not determine your future. Try looking at this situation as a small drop in the ocean, and you are the ocean. Be open to people who remind you that you are smart, capable, and important to them.

> Old feelings of self-doubt and anxiety keep coming up at work. Lately, they have been overwhelming. What is the best way to deal with them?

You indicated that your feelings are overwhelming. Have you explored seeking a licensed professional counselor? It does help to see our thoughts and emotions for what they are: thoughts and emotions. They are not absolutely true facts. Rather, they come and go and are conditioned by our past. As you become present, internal space will open up for you from those thoughts and emotions. I suggest you give them a name such as "here comes doubter" and see what happens.

> As I look back at what drove me to success, rising to partner and bringing in new business, I realize now it was all ego. Now that I have discovered the benefits of mindfulness meditation, I see my life as living moment to moment. How can I reconcile the two?

Congratulations! Discovering your status and the work you do in the world as only a temporary function rather than defining who or what you are is a breakthrough. Many people say they are not addicted to their work, but when you look closely in moments of challenge, this is not the case. Your work can fit into the "big picture" of what is important in your life instead of defining you. When we place all our energy on a single will to succeed, it can become destabilizing, compromising our health and more. What we find exhilarating at one point in life can be exhausting during other times. Mindfulness helps us discern what is really important in the only moment there is—the present moment—and with that realization comes a peace that you can't describe. Your work in the firm will be the same for the most part, but how you do your work will change; it will be based in *presence*. That is the reconciliation.

Informal Practice: Awareness at your Desk

As you practice mindfulness in daily life and make awareness your primary focal point every day, you'll attend to your body, thoughts, emotions, and awareness itself. Here is a short exercise to "check in" and connect to yourself in a meaningful way during the day as you practice accounting. This four-stage exercise has helped me put ego aside, nurture *presence*, and be less reactive to circumstances.

- First, connect to the present moment and acknowledge what is around you and how you are feeling right now. You're coming home to yourself.

- Become aware of your physical body as the external level of yourself. You may notice that certain opinions about your body arise. Become aware of any sensations in your body and acknowledge them also. Are there any judgments?

- Become aware of such thoughts as judgments. You'll acknowledge the interpretation you have about the sensations. Sometimes these interpretations can bring up feelings of satisfaction or dissatisfaction. These are more interpretations and/or objections to reality. You might notice some "I should" and "I should not have" statements and many other things the mind creates that you build an entire sense of identity around. This sometimes brings up emotions, such as happiness or sadness, and you believe this is all there is of you. So, it is important to become self-aware as a physical body, thoughts, and emotions. This is a huge gain to become aware of these aspects of yourself rather than to be those things.

- Now, as you connect and become aware of awareness, you notice a deep, abiding mindful *presence* in you with no particular form such as body, thoughts, feelings, or emotions. You can ask yourself, "Who is it that is aware?" And rest in the stillness of the present moment.

These four stages of awareness can be approached one by one. They can also be realized simultaneously as one single phenomenon. You glimpse at awareness throughout the day as an ongoing practice. The practice is a reward in itself. I invite you to try it now.

Detachment

The ego is cunning. The ego will do all it can to take center stage in your life. Even an *attempt* to transcend and set it aside can be another form of ego attachment.

When you want something dearly for the sake of itself (like being grateful), wouldn't you want to prepare yourself first so that when it arrives you can recognize it and welcome it? Sometimes, when we ask for something precious, it arrives in a disguised form. You might ask, "How can I be prepared? I always will that I am a kind, thankful, and grateful human being, and I tell people that is who I am. What else can I will?"

First, recognize what you are doing as you label yourself a kind, thankful, and grateful person or whatever label you may give yourself.

Make sure that such labeling is not your ego sneaking in and wanting to take center stage. I have noticed when we put such labels on ourselves (and there are many), it could mean that a shadow sub-personality is lurking to claim something that it doesn't really have. Know that those beautiful virtues of kindness, thankfulness, and gratefulness authentically arise from a detached attitude. A truly detached mind at a specific point in time does not refer to the past or future, which is implied when you're "telling" someone that you "have" these qualities. So, it is important to take a look at that and do the work necessary to address the shadow. Sometimes, that might mean seeking a qualified therapist or coach.

Why do we label ourselves and others? It is most likely that each of us is so fearful of life because we don't understand the whole process of living. We have not come to a place of knowing what it is not to "live." For most, what we call living is the daily boredom, routines, and related conflicts within and outside ourselves with short-lived moments of connection. It also includes our hidden wants and unknown facets of ourselves—what we call "the shadow." Of course, we have our escapes, and in our daily work we see the Larry-like professionals all around us who have difficulties being with themselves. So, it is in fear of the unknown that the problem lies, in fear of having no beliefs, fear of being isolated, and fear of our freedom to be who we are *beyond balancing the books.*

Mindfulness helps us to practice a detachment that exists both before and after any specific thing you want and hold dearly—in other words, making the present moment your home. Only then can you recognize the gifts, truly be grateful, and know yourself for the first time. The preparation is in the state of *presence* as you free yourself of clinging, seeking, pleasure, or any other kind of reward. Shunryu Suzuki writes: "In the beginner's mind there are many possibilities, but in the expert's mind there are few."

Our daily practice in our professional work is not to exclusively rely on our thoughts and emotions but rather on the vertical line in our T

266

account metaphor, in which we bring conscious awareness to all we do. So, in each moment we practice mindfulness, we let go of our preconceived notions about how things ought to be and step into a transformed knowledge often called intuition. In doing so, we are transcending and including our mature ego, entering the wholeness we already are. That is the meaning and purpose of why we are here.

Chapter 9

Mindfulness, Money, and the Accountant's Work

The opposite of courage in our society is not cowardice, it is conformity.

—Rollo May

Dentists get toothaches, plumbers have leaky faucets, basketball players miss free throws, and an accountant's checkbook doesn't balance. None of these are mistakes, just opportunities to learn, fix, and move on with awareness. And so it is also true regarding our relationships with money and work.

Something has to shake you, deplete you, and exhaust you before your ego reveals its fragility in real time. That is why many of us are questioning what money and work are all about. Mindfulness helps us to become aware of our relationships with money, and nowhere does that become more evident than when our pseudo senses of security, power, and prestige are threatened. In other words, when ego takes over. For this reason, shadow work is vital. You want to be successful and powerful? Your shadow likely wants the opposite! Once we come to terms with this dynamic in the psyche, we can hold both sides with equanimity and compassion and be more fully authentic with ourselves and others. The phrase "work smarter and not harder" does not mean "find solutions quicker." Rather, it points to a transformed work ethic based in mindful awareness that has been mostly kept secret. However, there are some good signs on the horizon to further this transformation.

Some people choose to leave mainline careers in search for work that is more authentic to them. Others have started to join conscious groups to discover more about themselves and find meaning in an open and non-judgmental way. Misaligned work and our relationships to money affect the soul. We are starting to see a shift toward more conscious business. I have given examples of accountants throughout this book that made such a shift from being based totally in their thinking mind to being based in awareness.

Accountants have a unique relationship with money since our professional work is about accounting for money, although we don't often view our work in those terms. You don't have to leave the accounting profession to practice *presence* and make mindfulness your home, as I have illustrated. Business needs mindful accountants infinitely more than most people imagine. Still, you won't see a post for an accounting job that includes "mindful accountant wanted" in its description, at least not yet. Sadly, mainstream business is mostly uncomfortable with mindful employees who are present and awake primarily because the leaders themselves are mostly unconscious. Just walk into most offices or watch most Zoom meetings with a group of business leaders.

Relationship with Money

Do you have a strained relationship with money? Or do you have a sense of ease and lightness about it? Do you worry much about your financial situation? Do you compare yourself to your peers in an obsessive way concerning money? Do you worry about not having enough money? These are all relevant questions as we approach mindfulness and money from the standpoint of awareness.

As CPAs, we are trusted advisors to our clients concerning financial matters, experienced and well-trained in accounting, financial planning, and business. Our professional roles and expertise cover a wide range of financial issues that impact our clients. We get involved in distressed business and personal financial situations where our work is truly multi-dimensional, with plenty of hand-holding and guidance during economic downturns or sudden circumstances like divorce, bankruptcies, or COVID-19. Whether working with a client turning a profit or loss, each day we are dealing with money, and as such, a good question to ask yourself is: "What is my relationship to money?" Do you face money thoughts, emotions, and feelings consciously? How does this, in turn, help you in your work as a CPA?

Mindfulness, and therefore awareness, is not concerned with how much money you make or have in the bank. Awareness does not hold opinions and judgments, and that includes money, profit, loss, and net worth. Just imagine, inside of you is this underlying sense of equilibrium—the invisible vertical line of your T account, where you go *beyond balancing the books*. From this vantage point, we can look at the world around us from a consciousness standpoint and know a little bit more about ourselves and where we are. In other words, we see that true reality does not revolve around money. In his book *The Little Prince*, Antoine de Saint-Exupéry writes: "What is essential is invisible to the eye." This is the invisible line of our own T account.

The striving for a money mindset is one of the causes for health, family, and business meltdowns and more, and we can see that by looking out our own backdoor or in our own homes. Is that security, or is that financial planning?

Mindful Financial Planning

Each one of us will likely have our own unique relationship with money just as we'll have our own way of practicing mindfulness. Having the right skills and knowledge of money management can greatly improve your financial well-being. Of course, there are other variables that can sometimes make it very challenging for the accountant to reach personal financial goals. Perhaps you are a second year accountant with debt and find that your relationship with money causes anxiety and frustration. Or maybe you are mid-career and struggling with a mortgage, college funding, caring for aged parents, and more. Perhaps you are near retirement and wondering if your savings will carry you through the remaining years. Or you may have accumulated substantial wealth and are worried about estate-planning and gifting strategies. These and other similar situations can take a toll on the professional accountant.

Our training helped us more fully understand the financial planning and tax implications of all sorts of financial matters, but it did not address other questions. What is my relationship to money, and how can mindfulness help me in my understanding of that connection? In other words, how do I integrate mind, body, soul, and spirit into my own personal money matters? On top of your current financial situation, you bring a lifetime of experiences to work each day that contribute to your relationship with money. Most of the time, this is unconscious, meaning you are not aware of how these patterns play out day to day. Think back to Larry, a partner in a prestigious accounting firm in the introduction to this book, who is totally unaware of his mind patterns and the suffering it causes himself and others.

The notion that accountants are conservative and therefore able to manage their own finances in a way that is exemplary can bring up certain painful emotions. As accountants, we may believe that we should know better in financial matters, and when we make a decision that doesn't work out according to our expectations, we feel even more shame, anger, and upset. Paradoxically, when confronted with financial challenges, we have an opportunity to wake up and discover other ways to cultivate a new relationship with money. This does take courage. When we wake up and persevere without an ego attachment, we step into meaning and a higher purpose.

Mindfulness can help us better understand our own doubts and fears and, in turn, further aid us in shifting perspectives that help our clients with their challenges. To remind you of the clinical definition of mindfulness from Chapter 1, as set forth by Jon-Kabat Zinn, mindfulness is "paying attention to something (money), in a particular way, on purpose, in the present moment, non-judgmentally." The attention is characterized by curiosity, openness, and acceptance. In other words, *how* we pay attention is vital. In comparison, when we concentrate, a kind of force is required that contributes to harsh reactions when we are interrupted. With mindfulness, there is a sense of ease and lightness as we attend to our financial affairs and many other situations. The challenges that come up each day are met with awareness, and our reactions tend to shift. Slowly at first, but with practice and awareness to your emotional reactions, a sense of ease and lightness will start to make their presence felt even in challenging times.

Let's take a simple example. Suppose you go out to lunch and spend $16.50. You smile at the cashier while paying your bill, feeling a contraction in your body and hearing the thought chatter in your head that says you "spent too much" for lunch. You notice the unpleasant feeling that the lunch purchase gave you. You notice these feelings with awareness and without judgment, instead of reacting with further negative self-talk. The ability to notice and step back allows you to make a conscious choice, face the unpleasantness, and discern what might be a better option next time. Mindfulness does not tell you what to purchase or how much to spend. Rather, by practicing mindfulness around money, you will be equipped to make a conscious choice. The contraction in your body and the negative self-talk when noticed mindfully and with awareness is freedom, which helps you establish control over your money, as illustrated in this basic example. Next time, you will likely catch yourself sooner before you make your way to the cashier. Who knows? You might even bring your own lunch to work.

Research has pointed out that mindfulness leads to a shift in perspective, which generates positive outcomes through self-regulation, value clarification, cognitive and emotional flexibility, and exposure to negative states with acceptance and without fear and avoidance reactions (58). Returning to our example of the lunch purchase, we treat ourselves kindly and shift our perspectives in cash management as we recognize that the purchase does not feel good. We get in touch with our needs and values and how we can more closely live within that context even when it comes to lunch. It all starts with our intention to be present and be kind to ourselves through mindful self-compassion.

Mindfulness and Credit

Mindfulness can help us clarify our needs and values. Research has demonstrated that mindful individuals recognize what is truly meaningful to them and are more likely to adopt financial strategies that are less responsive to cultural conditioning (58). One of the strongest antidotes to excess credit and low credit scores is knowing who you are in your essence and cultivating a self-acceptance mindset anchored in the present moment. One aspect of self-acceptance is the notion of having enough material possessions, which reduces the need for excess consumer spending. Self-acceptance is a characteristic of *presence* that builds confidence and fosters good decision making

(59). Self-responsibility transforms the inner critic (that voice chatter in the head), which means we own our experience. As we become aware of our inner reality and notice thoughts, emotions, feelings, and physical sensations, we tap into the wisdom of the body to help us become present and aware. We step *beyond balancing the books*.

Sometimes, we may have to face our debt straight on, which takes courage. Our inner critic can appear and judge us, coming up with a list of "mistakes" and holding us accountable. That is not the type of self-responsibility called forth with mindfulness. On the contrary, there is an *internal* non-aggressive stance toward the debt situation. The third party creditor may be aggressive, but we don't have to meet their fear tactics with the same tone. We acknowledge that holding this debt does not feel good, we hold the fear with compassion, and we place attention on those feelings even for short periods of time. These practices stretch the muscle holding the lantern of awareness on the uncomfortable feeling of having high debt. We then gently move the light away from the feeling for now, with a sense of gratitude for the meaningful work done. When we are ready, we can take the necessary actions to reduce our debt step by step and adjust our financial tendencies with keen awareness. If necessary, we can seek professional help from a therapist or coach.

Mindfulness and Power and Prestige

Mindfulness helps you transcend and include familial, cultural, and social conditioning around money and truly live your unique values with meaning and purpose. As we addressed in Chapter 3, mindfulness helps us become less reactive to externals, and this includes money and power. As we discover more and more of the riches of our inner world, we take stock of our whole being and derive far more joy and comfort from that than the pseudo power crafted by the egoic mind. Money is no longer a tool to just satisfy impulsive desires and to accumulate wealth but rather a tool to advance the common good with discernment and detachment moment by moment. You'll notice there will be less fear and worry as you make *presence* your home base. As a byproduct, you will likely make more money within that framework.

Our focus on the present moment does not mean we live for the present, which would imply impulsiveness. Quite the contrary, we tap into the deeper dimension of the present moment, which is an open field of awareness where wisdom and peace make their home.

Mindfulness and Money

How we pay attention to our money is paramount, not the amount of times we check the status of our portfolio or bank account balance. There is a place for that regular oversight, of course, but the obsession aspect fades away. What are your thoughts and emotions as you attend to money balances and monthly income? Attention involves a finer awareness of your inner and outer world in balancing the human and being dimensions, facilitating an inherent wisdom surrounding money and choice. Attention allows for a greater awareness of risks and preferences as you are in touch with your entire body.

Sometimes, when we place attention on money, we start to worry, and fear may arise. These emotions affect us. Here is a simple practice that has helped me. Instead of calling it "my money," just simply call it "money" or "money in the bank," not "money in my bank." The use of language can help us detach from what often fluctuates. With mindful attention to our use of language, money is seen for what it is.

Ask yourself what is important to you as you hold money in awareness. What is stopping you from creating what you value?

When you are in alignment with your true nature, it becomes much easier to manifest your deepest yearning, and that includes making money. You'll have a broader perspective, and that means you are conscious.

Attention also includes focused listening with your entire body. I wrote this poem in Central Park with an elm tree by my side. It is my interpretation of a poem by Hafiz, "An Apple Tree Was Concerned," about a different kind of prosperity.

An Elm Tree Was Wondering

An elm tree told me it was wondering about
an early season hurricane and losing its feature
of twisted upper branches that form
an elegant silhouette against the stark summer sky.
When the overcast came, it became stressed
due to its shallow root. The elm told me,
don't worry George; I will go deeper into the rich
invisible soil embedded underneath.
They can talk. Trees can come out with
the most amazing things and can even
tell a joke or two.
But it takes inner ears to listen to them,
ears untouched by the clouds.
Ears that listen to people with great humility and
care.

Questions

- *What is it like to be the elm tree, and what emotions come up when you hear about a "hurricane" (recession, busy season, etc.)?*
- *What kind of branches (your work) do you serve, and what are your expectations?*
- *How do you acknowledge the natural conditions (soil-soul) that help you manifest?*
- *How do you listen with great care (different kind of prosperity)?*
- *How does mindfulness bring out your sense of humor at work to "tell a joke or two?"*

Attitudes about Money

The Money Attitude Scale (MAS) (60) considers four attitudinal dimensions concerning money.

1. **Power-Prestige** represents a viewpoint that money is an instrument to gain power over others and a symbol of status and success.
2. **Retention-Time** relates to a tendency to plan and refrain from spending in order to be prepared for the future.
3. **Distrust** represents attitudes of suspicion, hesitation, and doubt in situations involving money.
4. **Anxiety** refers to an inclination to perceive money as a cause of worry and anxiety and as a tool to protect oneself from experiencing those feelings.

Who hasn't experienced one or more of these attitudinal qualities at some point in life? I certainly have. Part of this is in the collective culture, and a part of this is related to your unique experiences and your relationship with money. Where do you stand right now on this attitude scale, now and each day? When I coach clients, we start in the present moment. Some historical background is helpful, of course, to foster working on the shadow and one's compulsive tendencies. However, the essential point is the intention to bring mindfulness to our relationship with money and also on the journey in mindful awareness setting meaningful goals.

We have money attitudes every day, mostly unconsciously. They come up when we are investing in stock, buying a lottery ticket, hearing news of an economic recession, making a charitable contribution, buying an apartment, dining out, and more. Whether we reach for cash, pay with a credit card, issue a check, obtain bank loans, or use our phones—these too reflect an attitude on some level. Of course, money attitudes show up in all kinds of relationships. Just visit the divorce courts to see this firsthand.

Mindfulness can help us engage with money consciously in an open and non-judgmental way. We apply the very same mindfulness practices that we have been addressing throughout this book to help us be present and aware and truly have the option to choose.

In the MAS study, mindfulness was found to be negatively related to power and prestige (61). In other words, mindful individuals derive their identity from a deeper reservoir than the surface level of power and prestige. In another finding, mindful individuals are authentic, in a sense that they do not devote attentional resources toward impressing others with their rank, technical knowledge, experiences, and material goods (62).

Mindfulness and establishing financial goals are compatible. Financial planning actually becomes more alive when you make your primary focus on the present moment, knowing full well where you want to go. Too often, we worry about the future and whether or not we will have enough resources to cover our needs. This takes up a lot of energy with useless thinking. We buy excess amounts of life insurance to cover up our fears, and many times we don't even acknowledge that the purchase of excess insurance is a tactic that we hope will reduce the fear in us. Instead of making fear-based purchases, we can progress with our financial plan in a mindful way, relishing each step and taking care of our basic needs. How do you do this? Pay more attention to awareness, intuition, and the innate wisdom of your entire body system. Seek professional help when you feel you might need expertise in a certain area, and monitor your financial plan periodically, updating it annually to make any necessary changes.

The next aspect on the MAS study found that mindfulness is positively related to retention time (61). In other words, mindfulness lowers our susceptibility to consumerism and promotes a mindset to financially plan (63). In addition, better decision making leads mindful individuals to manage their funds more carefully. The more you learn about yourself and your own unique combination of attitudes toward money, the more your relationship to money can shift, if you so choose.

In the third aspect of the MAS study, mindfulness has been found to be negatively related to distrust (61). In other words, mindful individuals trust the inherent goodness of the universe and have a trust in life. You'll set your boundaries, of course, but trust will govern your steps.

With trust come self-acceptance, clarity, and a sense of having control over the financial aspects of your life. You view your past experience as a way to improve your financial situation, and that includes your relationship with money. Mindfulness builds a person's confidence in their own capacity to make financial decisions and to view financial matters with a more positive mindset. Why is that so? It's because you are in touch with the invisible line of your T account and going *beyond balancing the books.*

Finally, in the MAS study, mindfulness was found to be negatively related to anxiety (61). I can attest to this, as mentioned in the introduction. I discovered mindfulness after having experienced acute anxiety over many years. Now, research findings report that mindfulness is associated with self-regulated emotion and behavior.

The skill of witnessing one's thoughts, emotions, and feelings without judgment, separating them from one's sense of self, is a huge gain in consciousness. This was a revelation for me.

The process of intentionally being present each moment in an open and non-judgmental way helps us to recognize our emotions and feelings each day as we make choices regarding how to spend and save. Mindfulness will help you perceive money without worry in a healthier way.

Money and Art as Meditation

When you are distressed and feeling sad about your financial situation, it can be helpful to tap into the right brain in some creative pursuit. I like to write poems, which are mostly about the natural world with spiritual themes. I have also participated in workshops where other forms of art such as drawing, painting, and vision boards are used to tap into the creative impulse.

Why not try art as meditation when there is some financial or other issue in your life for which you seek guidance? Diving into art allows you to enter a meditative state where relaxation and creativity can thrive. You will release emotions and thoughts through the creative process and relieve stress that facilitates problem solving using all your skills in financial matters. Here is an outline of the steps you can take in processing money matters in the right brain while enjoying one of your own selected forms of art to do so.

- Select a location conducive to exploration that is meaningful to you. I like outside in nature, sitting in a chair, with a view of a lake and birds. I have done this inside in an empty room and also at my apartment. Have all the tools for your trade at hand. For me, it is a notebook, a pencil, and some colored pens.
- Release any anxiety still lingering, especially the old gramophone record in your head that says you can't do this.

281

- Whatever your craft, don't think about what you have seen professional artists or writers do. There is no need to imitate anyone.

- Follow your own intuition on how best to proceed as well as when to add to your work, take breaks, and stop.

- Leave the analytical thinking mind in your office and avoid overanalyzing your work, especially if it feels forced or is causing you some stress. You are exploring and activating your creative side. You will have some rough patches, and there will be days when you feel tired and want to stop. Be compassionate to yourself and give yourself that space.

- Think about colors. What colors make you think about yourself and your life? Which colors reflect your mood and your emotions? You can even use your body as an outline to sketch feelings and sensations abstractly.

- Don't forget your dreams and their symbols, which can be a rich basket for your creative impulse.

- Just start scribbling, writing, or whatever your craft might be and get started. Then see what happens.

Let your art be your best description of the universe using your right brain. Our right brains have similarities with a child before the conceptual thinking mind took over and started labeling everything, thereby coloring the child's perception. Who then could possibly criticize your work as you yourself become a little bit like that child again? Of course, you still have your thinking mind to navigate this world for practical purposes. Think of all the encouragement coming your way as you delve into your craft. Who knows? Your art might someday land on a star in another galaxy, uniting spheres of influence as an artwork of liberation. So, light the lantern in you, and let the muscles in your arm guide the light and your craft, creating rich deposits in your spirit.

Work and Meaning: A Reinterpretation

What is this activity we call "work?" Where does it come from? What is so important about work? These are questions some of the great minds have pondered over the centuries, and many treatises have been written on the subject. For now, I would like us to look specifically at mindfulness, work, and the accountant in light of these very questions, not as a philosophical exploration but rather directly from your own experience.

As we "reinterpret" our work from mindful *presence*, it is helpful to momentarily set aside our preconceived notions about work. As a reminder, mindfulness does not "do" the interpreting. *Presence* consciousness cultivates a mindset so "you" can make choices on how you perceive work and, therefore, how you relate to your work.

First, let's look at the activity of work itself. Work today is mostly derived from the mindset going back to the Industrial Revolution, including technological, economic, and modern scientific understandings of work activity and its role in our lives. While this period has brought about many achievements, it has left us with a fragmented and dysfunctional work place and world, including the notion that work is about a paycheck, pay increases, power, prestige, and the race to retirement.

However, we are now in a "postmodern" period. In some spheres, careers are already transcending and including the universal lessons learned in the industrial period, discarding what can be left behind, and transforming work into an activity with much deeper meaning and purpose. As we have addressed, transcending implies we don't push away what came before; rather, we step into a new and deeper relationship with ourselves, our work, and the choices available in any new relationship.

Today, postmodern science is discovering a universe that is deeply mysterious and, in doing so, is deriving a new creation story. This story reiterates that there is only one work in the universe and our relationship to it. The basic premise in all of this is that we are all connected in a web of energy and light. In order to make this real in your direct experience, you'll want to make your home in the present moment as we have been practicing. The space in between now and now: *beyond balancing the books.* Otherwise, this story will escape you, and you will miss the new creation as you go about working in the old mindset of the Industrial Revolution and exclusively in the debit and credit plane of existence.

Let's take the atom as a way to look at our work as accountants. After all, accountants like to start with the basics. Modern science claims atoms, which make up all matter, are essentially inert. In contrast, postmodern science teaches that atoms are structures of activity located in fields of energy. Physicist Brian Swimme refers to this as "a self-organizing system" and a "storm of ordered activity." How can we bring the discipline of postmodern science into our work as accountants? Well, first we'll have to ask ourselves if our work is "inert." If so, then we see our work of counting the tax seasons and due dates as boring.

Inertia also implies routines, time-tracking, steady paychecks, and predictability—an Industrial Revolution mindset. On the other hand, if we view our work as postmodern science views the universe, our accounting work starts to move, shake, and bake like those dancing atoms in a field of energy and light. Your work becomes both an art and a science *beyond balancing the books.* Can you make the scientific advance and leap into postmodern accounting? (And that does not mean cloud accounting or any other technological advance, no matter how beneficial they may be.) Remember the principle of transcending and including as you move into the next stage of consciousness.

Let's now look at the origin of our work. If postmodern science is telling us we are all connected in a field of energy, then we ought to have a common origin and, therefore, a common work. In a common work, we discover that the essence of interdependence is compassion. As we addressed in Chapter 7, research informs us that an aspect of mindful self-compassion is our common humanity. So, if our work is an essential aspect of the universe, then compassion is certainly its root.

Meister Eckhart writes that our work "draws all of its being from nowhere else but from and in the heart of God" (63). He also writes: "Every creature is doing its best to express God" (64). In other words, God is at play in our work. In our work, we are never alone; on the contrary, we are connected with all other beings, including the natural world. How do we work from this place of origin? I would suggest it starts with solitude. We can be in Times Square, board meetings, preparing a tax return, or meeting with a client and discussing complex accounting standards and still be in solitude, simply by stepping in and out of thought and listening to the stillness that is always there in the background of the present moment.

You can experiment with this practice. Try it the next time you are in a conversation at work, like Amy did in the introduction when she met with the tax partner. Mindfulness is not about perfection but simply coming back again and again to your anchor. Each time you come back, you will be returning to the origin of work and going *beyond balancing the books.*

The poet Rilke writes: "A work of art is good if it has sprung from necessity." How can we know if our work as accountants is a necessity as the forces of commoditization of core service and our search for relevance in the business world is at hand? Why is there so much stress and anxiety over work and money? According to Meister Eckhart, there could be only one reason, and that is we have settled for outer work and have ignored inner work. How many times as accountants do we respond to outside rewards or external threats? If you want to have a living accounting that is vibrant, alive, and moving like the dancing atoms that postmodern science is telling us about, then we must attend to our inner work daily in mindful awareness and go *beyond balancing the books*. In other words, it is not the pot of gold at the end that gives meaning for the work. Why is it that some accountants are so relieved when the job is done, tax season is over, or the day before vacation or retirement? Their mindset is predominated by the past and future. When this happens, the work takes a toll, and negativity sinks into your bones. It doesn't have to be this way.

Doing the inner work has a feminine quality to it. In many traditions, the wisdom figure is feminine. That is partly why it is so challenging for men. At the very core, *presence* consciousness transcends dualism and the separation of gender: male and female are one. In my opinion, that is part of the reason why there are much fewer men in conscious and mindfulness training groups that I have participated in, although this is gradually changing.

Men still want to hold onto the dual-based system in the profession, as evidenced by a 2019 AICPA survey that indicates only 23% of women hold partnership positions. That statistic reflects an overall low stage of consciousness.

One of the ways to address this key issue is through education, within organizations, academic settings, and in other conscious teaching settings. The other route to practicing mindfulness is through the pain and suffering caused by unconsciousness, which can be avoided. As business students, most of us took a course or two in psychology, and perhaps we read a book or two on the topic, even studied or attend religious services, and were raised by loving parents. In all of this, very little is taught on how to live and work consciously with awareness on purpose in the present moment in an open and non-judgmental way. "Be the change you want to see in the world." In other words, be mindfully present.

In searching for relevance in the world as accountants, we can go back to our origin, the T account, and work at what we need to with our feet planted on the vertical line.

This poem is my interpretation of a Rumi poem called "One-Handed Basket Weaving" (65) and our search for meaningful work.

One-Handed Accounting

I've said before that every professional
searches for what's not there
to practice their skills.
A dentist looks for a beautiful smile
where the tooth caved in. A waiter
picks the empty glass. A doctor
stops and brings your health.
Accountants move toward some semblance
of emptiness, which they then
start to fill. Their hope, though,
is *beyond balancing the books*, so don't think
you must avoid it. It contains
what you need!
Dear accountant, if you were not friends
with the vast nothing inside,
why would you always be casting your net
into it and waiting so mindfully?
This invisible ocean of a T account has given you such abundance,
but still you call it "death,"
that which provides wisdom and work.

287

We call it "death" because it is shocking, uncomfortable, and takes us out of our comfort zones. This is precisely where we need to go. When we step into this unknown, we experience fear and frustration, but gradually—and sometimes suddenly—those emotions will transform into hope and joy.

Finally, our last question is what is so important about work?

I would have to start out by saying work is a "work in progress." That is how important it is as we continuously move toward completing our work in the present moment. I am not referring to progress as completing a job but as a means of growing more and more conscious. Your accounting work or any other work you may be engaged in will then be of real service to others, and you will benefit by becoming deaf to the voice inside you that does not believe in happiness.

Chapter 10

The Meaning of Mindfulness: Beyond Balancing the Books

A day is too great a force to bear without the heart open.

—Hafiz

T he real meaning of mindfulness is beyond anything that can adequately be said "about it." Mindfulness is simply being present in an open and non-judgmental way. Knowing that, I have attempted to convey some basic mindfulness tools as well as the practices and exercises that have helped me the last fifteen years in my work as a CPA and in my personal life. The practice is portable and comes along with me wherever I go. As I have pointed out, formal meditation practice can be very helpful, while daily informal practice is as essential as eating and sleeping.

In our work as accountants, we have ample moments to be either mindful or mindless. When you are mindful, like Amy in this book's introduction, there is a sense of connection to something larger than yourself including your role as an accountant. When you are mindless like Larry, there is a disconnection and identification with some mind or emotional stream. As you begin to shift from total identification with your thoughts and emotions to making your home in awareness, the mindless moments become shorter and shorter. You will cultivate a sense of self-compassion rather than beating yourself up.

Business leaders today are mostly disconnected from the essence of love, as I described in Chapter 7, which essentially means they are not present. That will change "in time." You have most likely been the object of someone's projection and frustration at work. Sometimes this is with a colleague, and at other times it is with a client. It doesn't matter what your rank is or how senior you are in the firm, the tendency for leaders, business owners, and staff to project blame and fault onto even the most skilled accountant is rampant. The accountant, in turn, picks up on this negative energy stream and the related "machine-like" treatment and sometimes passes it on to others and so forth, until one person breaks through, awakens, and begins to practice the art of *presence* in work and life.

This breakthrough is more essential then your breaking into the profession and passing the CPA exam. Awakening to *presence* is even more precious than your birth into this world. For this reason, accountants need tools and practices to help them navigate the often difficult internal and external struggles within their firms so they can work with less stress and be present in the face of relentless pushback and confusion. As CPAs, we cannot go into a cave without a lantern and its light. Therefore, turn and call forth the light of awareness in you to see the inherit dysfunction all around, so you too won't fall into the trap. Of course, mindfulness is so much more than a tool to minimize stress and anxiousness. Mindful *presence* is your true nature as you go *beyond balancing the books*. I have invited you to take a look and observe how being mindful can make a difference in your work and life, with such practices as the three-minute breathing exercise introduced in Chapter 1 and many other practices.

You can also select an activity that you do every day to help you get started in your mindfulness practice. For example, if you are a runner, use that time to be alert and present as you run your route through parks and over hills and valleys. Make running your meditation practice.

The thirteenth-century Sufi poet Hafiz so eloquently writes about the human dysfunction in this way: "The Beloved sometimes wants to do us a favor: hold us upside down and shake all the nonsense out." As you develop your own unique practice of mindfulness, you'll know if it is working or not if your predominant state is a quiet heart in the face of adversity and pain. A quiet heart is a "right brain" meditation and a letting go here and there of the analytical thinking mind and the inherit fear that is likely to come up when you are confronted with challenges. It could happen the moment your manager or client is breathing down your neck for the audit report. How can you remain internally calm as you deal with the all-encompassing stress around you? Or, perhaps it is self-created worry and confusion. Where can you go?

The three-minute breathing exercise is a good place. I would also suggest you go to that place of rest in the one-heart and "play" there as you live without a "why" in your mind. Sometimes, we just need to put our minds to bed even during the busyness of our day. A moment of stillness is the doorway to go *beyond balancing the books.*

The T Account Metaphor and the Three B's

The T account is your accounting metaphor for mindful *presence* and living your whole life with meaning and purpose. These powerful practices embedded in the vertical line help bring your authentic self to the workplace as you embody the three B's: *beyond balancing the books.* The three B's are in relationship with your unique potential to claim the life you love. The three components are summarized as follows:

Beyond: Go beyond the mind into the larger mind. In other words, instead of "I think, therefore I am," you'll shift to "I am, therefore I think" and come to know your true nature. You won't look to your thoughts to define who you are anymore; after all, thoughts and emotions are impermanent.

Balance: An integration of doing and being in a relational exchange embedded with the essence of love wherever you are. There is no effort in balancing, only a sense of ease and lightness in this integration.

Books: An accounting for what really counts—living your whole life with real meaning and purpose, connected to the one-heart in soulful seeing and listening. The one-heart perceives without differentiation and is free of sentimental longings. Our rational thinking minds and emotions are part of the one-heart; in fact, all aspects of our being are part of it as we perceive reality from a place of wholeness.

Through the practice of mindfulness and cultivating your own unique way of integrating these powerful exercises into your daily life, you will be stepping *beyond balancing the books.* In a nutshell, the state of *presence* is your own true nature waiting to unearth and make itself more conscious through you, the accountant, and whatever other life roles you play.

The Vertical Dimension

The vertical line is a pointer to oneness and mindful *presence*, and the debits and credits represent the world of duality: right or wrong, past or future, good or bad, first and last, and so forth, as depicted in Exhibit 7. Mindful *presence* gives life and balance to the debits and credits in your life. At the same time, these debits and credits flow back and are interwoven with the vertical line at the center of your being—your heart, that clear organ of soulful seeing and listening. After all, the vertical line is only an abstraction until the debits and credits voice it's reality in an abiding reciprocal loving connected *presence*. In other words, *beyond balancing the books.*

Exhibit 7: The Accountant's T Account

Mindfulness

Debits	Credits
Right	Wrong
Past	Future
Negative Thoughts	Positive Thoughts
Negative Emotions	Positive Emotions
Negative Physical Sensations	Positive Physical Sensations
Negative Situations	Positive Situations

Presence

We can take the next step and expand the circle of our knowing and start to see our fellow accountants, clients, associates, so-called competitors, and the natural world as extensions of ourselves. Of course, we don't see ourselves in their actions, beliefs, skill levels, labels, and personalities, but rather in their very essence as connected oneness with the very same vertical T account line. In fact, we come to realize that if it wasn't for our differences, we would never realize our oneness. If the whole world was green, we wouldn't even know the color green.

Each one of us is responsible to move beyond the horizontal dimension of our own interior debits and credits and drop into the vertical depth dimension of *presence* consciousness. Ken Wilber writes in *A Brief History of Everything*:

> *Everything in flatland (debits and credits) conspires to prevent that recognition. This culture gap—the massive problem of vertical cultural integration—cannot be solved in flatland terms (debits and credits), because flatland denies the existence of the vertical dimension altogether, denies interior transformation and trans- cendence altogether, denies the nine or so interior stages of consciousness development that is truly part of a culture's human capital, but is not even entered on the ledgers of flatland (66).*

The "cultural integration" that Wilber refers to has to start with each individual taking responsibility for their own development. We humans are works in progress.

This oneness—non-dual reality—is the essence of love and is radically ahead of our time. However, that is no longer an excuse, as there are more and more opportunities to apply oneself to this interior depth development. It is a lifetime learning opportunity. Mindfulness is all about new beginnings and starting fresh each moment, not as a belief system but as recognition of the free-flowing spaciousness that is always there, at least in the background, to be realized. Inner happiness or true happiness is when we experience a flow and "forget" ourselves. That is very much like the state of mindful *presence.*

To embark on a path of *presence* consciousness is a gift, and I urge you to pursue your goal relentlessly while you attend to today and let yesterday be. As you pursue what lies in front of you, fix your love on the present moment, close the doors and windows so that your spirit is unified, letting no pests and foes overtake you. In that state of *presence,* you will utter the only prayer that is necessary—thank you.

Thank You

That which I am and the way that I am
together with all my gifts of nature and grace
you have given me, Divine Source, and you are all this.
I offer it all to you, to praise you
And to help all creatures and myself.

The Integral Map

Ken Wilber teaches that human consciousness exists along a nine-level continuum (67) from archaic (Stone Age people) and infants through clear light or non-dual consciousness. The integral map of human development, according to Wilber, begins to build a unified map or framework by noting that every thing or event in the universe is a holon, a whole that is part of a larger whole, and each holon can be looked at from at least four basic perspectives. It has an exterior and an interior (a within and without), and it has a singular form and a plural form (individual and collective). As you bring these together, you have four dimensions or perspectives: the interior of an individual, the exterior of an individual, the interior of a collective or group, and the exterior of a collective or group.

Each time we look at ourselves through the four quadrants, we will gain an important perspective and a great deal of data. Once we realize all four quadrants are equally important, we take a giant leap in realigning and integrating our worldview. Very few worldviews include all four quadrants. Most are involved in one form of quadrant absolutism or another guaranteeing us a broken and fragmented world. Once we combine the quadrants with other dimensions, such as levels, states of consciousness, and lines of development, we start to see a truly unified big picture of ourselves and our world. This perspective, when mindfully applied through presence, is a leap in our own development and worldview and is indeed life-changing (68).

Upgrading the System

When we make our home and center of gravity in the vertical line of the T account, we upgrade our interior accounting system for what really counts (the three B's), and at the same time, we include all the debits and credits that came before. In other words, we transcend and include all prior levels of consciousness, as pointed out in Wilber's human growth and development model. Of course, we continue to clean up our shadow tendencies by showing up and being present.

The fact that you are reading this suggests that this transformation *beyond balancing the books* is already happening in you and, in turn, in your work as an accountant. It can happen very quickly and instantly, when you pause to look, listen, and bring into being a single non-conceptual knowing through the power of oneness in a vertical T account line.

Little did we know when we entered the accounting profession that we brought with us this T account's functioning operating system, though most of us were exclusively based in the debit and credits of the system, at a particular stage of consciousness, so to speak. Now, we can choose to enhance our functioning from a dual-based-only framework like Larry (either/or, black/white, rain/shine, pass/fail, love/hate, inside/outside, debit/credit) to a higher level of one-heart, seeing and listening much more like Amy. As the poet Rumi writes: "Out beyond ideas of wrongdoing and right doing, there is a field. I'll meet you there."

When we experience ourselves as exclusively debits and credits with specific characteristics and talents and define ourselves by profession, ethnicity, relationships, and so forth, we put on masks that make us unique and special, and we do the same for others. Of course, there is a limited place for that, but is there anything beyond? Well, look within, and sing a resounding "Yes" to the melody of the three B's! The word "beyond" points to a "larger mind" that is all-encompassing and present, not in the sense of having lots of stuff in our minds (thoughts, emotions, memories, etc.) but rather a space of potential that includes what we traditionally consider to be our minds (brain). This "larger mind" also includes the entire inner energy field of our bodies. Underlying mindfulness and the three B's is a call for a radical shift in consciousness away from alienation and polarization of the debits and credits and into a unified field of clear divine abundance that can be recognized through one-heart seeing and listening moment to moment. The one-heart is an organ of soulful connection. You see, your heart and my heart are one, even if we disagree on something, and the truly amazing thing is there is nothing you can do about it except realize it now. For this reason, attention to the inner energy field of our bodies is vital in our work as accountants and in our personal lives.

How do you go about lifting your consciousness? I would suggest conscious development has its beginnings in our passions—the virtue of peace and humility in ourselves. It helps to laugh at our human folly. It is one thing to talk and write about it and quite another to make it your reality day to day and moment to moment. I would also suggest it hinges upon right intentions and a yearning through love for your primary inner state to be of mindful presence in all aspects of your life. It seems fair to me to say that all paths and spiritual traditions lead toward this same center and the emergence of a oneness and a non-dual stage of consciousness. Of course, each path has different routes. Thank goodness for that, because it makes it abundantly clear that there is a *center*, for without different routes, we wouldn't truly know our one destination. Paradoxically, the step you are taking now is the destination. Yes, we continue to set goals, as we addressed in Chapter 6, and experience the related practical implications for implementing goals, which include having a keen eye on the step you are taking in the present moment.

Mindful *presence* is deep wisdom and, up to this point, has been a "road less taken" in our world. Thankfully, this is not so anymore as more and more people are recognizing their inherit capacity to be present even under the most difficult of circumstances. The business world has so far lagged behind in consciousness, but even there we are starting to see more and more consciously attuned business leaders and employees who make it a practice to be aware, present, and mindful each day at work. I have shared some with you in this book. People like Amy, who has dedicated her life to being fully present and awake as she steadily performs her role in a large public accounting firm. Or Joe in Chapter 3, who after much suffering and despair had the courage to look internally and discover for himself his core needs and values and took steps to build a life he loves while continuing to practice accounting in a fast-paced firm. Sandra, the CFO of a hospital, also started to take responsibility for her internal turmoil and began a mindful meditation practice through which she cultivated awareness of her breath and inner body, which fueled her ability to reclaim her power. These are just some of the examples highlighted in this book of conscious accountants helping to build a more inclusive and compassionate business environment.

We are being asked to change our hearts from a dualistic framework to oneness. Scientist Rupert Sheldrake says as much when he writes: "The recognition that we need to change the way we live is now very common. It is like waking up from a dream. It brings with it a spirit of repentance, seeing in a new way, a change of heart. This conversion is intensified by the sense that the end of an age is at hand" (69).

Integration

Integration really means a love affair when it comes to mindfulness in daily life. Once you get a taste of *presence*, you'll soon make it your primary way of being in the world. The practice is simply who you are and how you show up moment to moment without thinking about it or making mindfulness part of your "to-do" list. The obstacles and distractions are there for you to more fully integrate your being and responses from awareness rather than through the conditioned mind. As you cultivate open awareness and attention to your relationship with thoughts and emotions, other setbacks will then shift. There will be less and less identification with these mental and emotional formations. There will be a continuous movement and deepening, and perhaps a setback here and there, which will ignite a further deepening, and so forth. So, integration is more about the three B's and their relationship to each other, with each B looking back and rekindling the others into a unified field of *presence* practice and mindful awareness.

Questions

> I joined my father's CPA firm right out of college and have successfully built the firm over the years. Now, as I get closer to retirement, I am finding it difficult to transition out, and I am full of judgments, of both myself and others. I understand that mindfulness helps us not to judge ourselves or others. What steps can I take to relieve myself of this feeling of discontent?

First, understand that mindfulness is not about stopping our judgments. That would be quite difficult as our rational strategic thinking mind is constantly weighing in, which, as you know, can be productive or not. With mindfulness, our aim is to become aware of our judgment, which is a very different process from ridding ourselves of judgments. Trying to remove judgments usually involves some sort of contraction or resistance, and you might even judge yourself for judging. Instead, mindfulness is about increasing freedom and clarity through awareness of judgments.

This awareness is vital, as most of us have been conditioned through many years of judgments and opinions that may be biased, distorted, ego-based, and hindrances to overall well-being. Now, consider the judgments you might have around retirement, the accounting profession, your successes, family, business, and so forth. Rather than blindly believing that your judgments represent truth and reality, mindfulness helps you recognize that these thoughts simply represent your own viewpoints and beliefs. This is both humbling and powerful as you step into your own true nature and realize you are not your thoughts. This was a huge revelation for me.

Many of us derive self-worth through the distorted lens of judgments (thoughts), which is subjective by nature. One day you're on top of the world, so to speak, and the next day you are retired. So, I would suggest that this awareness frees you from whatever situation or circumstance you may be in and the judgments you may have around your transition into retirement. You hold the power to interpret reality, and it always begins with the here and now. It is also very helpful to practice mindful self-compassion as we addressed in Chapter 7.

I find it difficult to accept the current work environment at
my firm. I am an experienced CPA and under continuous
oversight in my firm, most of which far exceeds the necessary
review process that is typically needed to deliver a quality
work product to our clients. I feel resentment and anger
toward some of the partners and managers I work with. I
tried meditation and some of the practices you suggest, but
they have not really helped. Is there anything else I can do?

Can you accept the fact that you can't accept the situation at your firm? The emotions you are feeling, like resentment and anger, are symptoms of something else. Can you accept that right now you are experiencing these strong emotions, not as an intellectual acceptance but rather a sensing that right now this is how I feel? If you can do this, you will be more focused on your inner body and how your body is reacting to your thoughts about the situation. You may forget about these circumstances two years from now, but your body won't.

When you place attention on the feeling in your body of an emotion like resentment and anger, you shine the light of awareness on it, which helps choices arise. You may also notice that these emotions will gradually have less of an impact on you.

You may want to try a body practice to release your anger through voicing the anger like the roar of a bear. To do this, make a connection with the earth with seven body parts, including your feet, hands, and forehead. As you connect to the earth, allow yourself to voice your anger like a roaring bear. Do this in an easy and relaxed manner, coming from your center and not from your own self-will. Our suffering and grief is stored in our bodies, and sometimes we need more than just talk.

What is important to you right now in your accounting career? What promise does this need hold for you? There is something you feel that is missing at this moment. Your thinking mind believes that this fulfillment lies in some future state, whatever that might be. Perhaps it is more contentment, independence, or creativity. What can you do now to meet that need? Do you want to make a lot of money? What might be driving you to become rich? My questions are based in the present moment and the small step you can take now so that any lingering resentment and anger might be transmuted into the light of your conscious *presence*.

In their book *Immunity to Change*, Robert Keegan and Lisa Laskow Lahey write:

> *Courage involves the ability to take action and carry on even when we are afraid. You may say "I'm not afraid." And you are right. You do not feel your fear. The reason you do not is because you are dealing with it through a very effective anxiety-management system, and that system is what we call immunity to change (70).*

We addressed our shadow "protectors" in this book and how their loving purpose is to "save our lives." By allowing this, we miss opportunities for sustained and meaningful change and personal development. These protectors can be transformed in the light of mindful awareness as we do our inner work.

I am a college student majoring in accounting and want to be a CPA. I am struggling with anxiety and sometimes feel depressed. I worry about my future. I have a very busy schedule, including working part-time in a firm where I am learning more about taxation. How can mindfulness benefit me?

Mindfulness is a way of being in the world that is quite different from what you may have been taught. It is important to note that mindfulness is not a quick fix or some temporary solution to current circumstances. Rather, cultivating *presence* in your life will help you reclaim your own power that has been neglected through external and internal distractions and obstacles. You have taken the first step already, which is to recognize that you are struggling and are seeking help. I want to acknowledge your courage for that. I would suggest that we start with where you are right now. Take a moment, and let's take a few deep breaths together. As we do this, place attention on the movement of air through your nostrils and into the lungs. Feel your chest expand and the slight pause at the transition point between your inhale and exhale. Now, keep attention on your breath as you let go.

What did you notice as you were focusing on your breath? "It felt different; I'm not used to that." What was so unusual about it for you? "I felt I was missing out on something." What might that be? "I have so many things to catch up with, and it feels like I am stuck." Tell me more about feeling stuck. "It is strange. I feel I am stuck here and now and not going anywhere." Has anyone told you that your life is never not now? "Not really." Where might your life be? "I am worrying about the future and thinking about what I need to accomplish next. It seems my life is constantly a catching-up and a 'to-do' list. I guess my life then is in the future."

So, let's get back to feeling stuck. I would invite you to sense what it is like for you to be always "stuck" in the present moment. Do you sense anything when you do that? "I feel sad." Ok, sadness might be there for you, but sadness is partial. What else might be there? "Funny, but I also feel a kind of joy." And what might that joy mean for you? "Well, I feel hopeful." What else? "There is an energy to build and a life to love" Yes, that's it—there is a beauty in that energy that is awe and wonder. It is your very own essence and power. Thank you for being honest and open and sharing your struggles. Be well.

Diversity and Inclusion

I have learned much about micro aggressions living with my life partner. As an Asian woman, she sometimes feels subtle and unintentional acts or statements that reflect inherit biases delivered by people who consider themselves free of bias but unknowingly stimulate pain for her. This can lead to people feeling unwelcome, isolated, alienated, and unsafe. One example is asking an Asian person to help with math or sciences, implying all Asian people are intelligent and good in such subjects. When we first met over twenty years ago, I wasn't even aware that she might sometimes be the only Asian person in a room. Thankfully, I have changed and become much more aware. I consider this to be one of my greatest achievements.

There are countless other examples of micro aggressions that are hurtful to people, some of which I learned about through my professional coaching certification program. I have since had the privilege to coach numerous immigrants from all over the world and have come to more fully understand their very difficult circumstances. I would ask the person: "Can you tell me more about your experience? Tell me in such a way that would help me walk with you so I can see it from your perspective."

Micro aggressions are felt by marginalized groups, such as racial and ethnic minorities. Marianne Williamson, the spiritual teacher, writes about it in this way:

> *Love is what we are born with. Fear is what we learn. The spiritual journey is the unlearning of fear and prejudices and the acceptance of love back into our hearts. Love is the essential reality and our purpose on Earth. To be consciously aware of it, to experience love in ourselves and others, is the meaning of life. Meaning does not lie in things. Meaning lies in us."*

Mindfulness can help us become aware of our own patterns of thoughts and emotions in our day to day interactions with others and also with ourselves. Within each individual, a diversity of voices clamors for attention. Can you be kind to your internal diversity and include even those parts of yourself that you try to hide? More so, have you done your own shadow work? The practice of *presence* puts us in touch with the deeper dimension of ourselves so that we can see our own blindness more clearly. As accountants, we can grow by becoming mindfully aware of micro aggression situations and the impact they have on others. Our intent or thoughts about a particular situation notwithstanding, we can learn to acknowledge the feelings of others. Furthermore, we can mindfully educate those who might be unaware of their micro aggressions and the effect they have on others. Poet Maya Angelou writes: "We all should know that diversity makes for a rich tapestry, and we must understand that all the threads of the tapestry are equal in value no matter what their color."

> *"It really boils down to this: that all life is interrelated. We are all caught in an inescapable network of mutuality, tied into a single garment of destiny. Whatever affects one destiny, affects all indirectly."*
>
> —Martin Luther King Jr.

Mindfully Working Remotely

These days, working remotely has become very popular and, in many cases, mandatory as a result of COVID-19. For many firms, the transition into working remotely can be difficult under normal conditions. Now, that difficulty has been amplified as a result of the pandemic. Like in many transitions, it can often be a wake-up call for firms and staff. Think about it: if you are in a relationship and have some real dysfunction before the marriage, it typically doesn't go away once you get married. The same may be the case for some firms transitioning to remote work. Having the technology is basic, but there are mindfulness practices that can help people manage tasks and their flexible work environment. Here are five mindfulness practices for remote work.

1. **Minute without thought:** Begin each video conference meeting with a check-in beyond the normal "how are you doing" chat by engaging in a one-minute breathing exercise to help ground participants in the present moment. One person in the group can suggest this at the very start as a way for the group to connect and implicitly recognize each other in a mindful way. This can really settle people into their core as many people are feeling distressed underneath the surface. It will set the tone for the meeting. In addition, hold firm three-minute breathing moments each day as described in Chapter 1. This will build connection and well-being. If this is not possible as a group, do it yourself.

2. **Focused and transformational listening:** This is the opposite of critical listening, which dampens the spirit and weakens trust. In focused, transformational listening, each person narrows their focus so that attention is placed on both the speaker as well as the stillness within themselves. We listen to the silence, which is the essence of any conversation. In other words, we listen to what the speaker is not saying and make a connection there as well. We hear not only the points in a conversation but also the underlying needs and values of the individual and the collective group. We listen for the tone of voice and how it might change during the meeting as different topics come up. We also notice facial expressions and subtle body movements without judgments. As the dialogue continues, we listen

internally to the flow and what wants to come forth, finding possible solutions. We hold the other person as resourceful and capable of contributing in their own way even in silence. This is the art of true listening, and it becomes even more important in a remote video conferencing setting.

3. **Creating trust:** Trust comes from within each person. In mindfulness, we cultivate trust in the deeper dimension and potentiality of the present moment, which holds the balance between human and being. Why is the present moment the basis for trust? The answer: it is always reliable—we only have this moment (not the surface level of the present moment, but rather the essence of it). Now that is the real meaning of a "trust fund," and no tax identification number is required! We model radical self-acceptance by being authentic in the present moment. We realize that, as accountants, we cannot solve all problems. We also realize that our most valuable resources are compassion, empathy, clarity of mind, and joy. In a remote work setting, there is a tendency to overwork or be even more distracted than normal. Therefore, we want to call forth more balance. How can we do this under such intense pressures? I would suggest that the pressure itself, if channeled properly, can be the cornerstone of mindful awareness. Ask yourself throughout the day as a pointer into mindful awareness, "How am I doing now?" Set reminders on your phone to check your inner operating system. Then, notice the thoughts, emotions, and physical sensations in your body as you sit in your home office, at the kitchen table, or wherever you are. With mindfulness practice, you start to realize that it doesn't matter where you work. The situation has less sway on you in terms of physical locations, thoughts, emotions, and feelings. Yes, you may be more or less productive at home, but that is secondary to your state of mind moment to moment. This is a leap in consciousness that can be brought about from the pain of external conditions. You will have built

emotional resilience, enhanced your well-being, and become a more productive CPA to boot.

4. **Mindful movement:** In mindfulness-based stress reduction training, mindful movement plays a central part in cultivating a full body awareness stance to life. Spiritual teacher Kim Eng teaches "presence through movement" in a full body way to help build the capacity to bring a state of *presence* to our ordinary daily movements. In a remote work environment, some basic mindful movement practices can increase our awareness of the entire body organism rather than just our heads. The most basic practice is to notice your hands as you sit at your desk and tap your keyboard. This can be a very pleasurable practice. You can listen to the sounds of the keyboard as well. The next step is to feel into the hands periodically. You can close your eyes for a minute and ask yourself, "How do I know that I have hands?" Then experience the feeling of hands from the inside of your hands. As often as possible, take short mindful walks. Pay attention to each step while feeling your feet touching the floor, and even deeper, sensing the earth below that supports you. This is a great way to spend your breaks when working remotely.

5. **Non-resistance:** Sometimes, we get triggered and overwhelmed and we run on autopilot. Instead of judging ourselves, we can welcome the anxiety, irritation, and anger, taking a moment to remind ourselves of our commitment to be present. From *presence*, we can then reconnect to our power. When we tap into our needs and values underneath the surface layer of circumstances, we change. Mindfulness helps us get the inner reality right and, with discernment, guides us through the externals (things we need to do for work).

These simple yet profound practices are some of the quality indicators of a successful remote working environment.

The Unknown as Power

While visiting Greece, I was inspired as I looked over the lands where the Greek philosopher Socrates lived and died. Socrates was famous for asking empowering questions of his students. Centuries later, the "Socratic method" became the basis for western legal education in teaching law students how to ask questions in a legal matter. However, Socrates was able to enter the state of *presence* and be in touch with the deeper dimension of consciousness before he would ask his empowering questions. That deeper dimension is the inherit stillness and true nature of every human being. It can also be called an "unknown knowing" through which an individual has let go of conceptualized understanding or any expectations of an outcome. From this place, Socrates was able to guide his students to a keen knowledge of themselves and their own inner strengths. Unfortunately, his teaching was misunderstood.

Becoming comfortable with not knowing is a skill that can be cultivated in accounting. I am not referring to a situation when the accountant is asked a question from a client and informs them that he doesn't know but will get back to them after some research. Rather, in the state of not knowing, you break the web and predominant fear-based mindset that you "should" or "need" to know and rest in simple *presence*, where all creative solutions arise. This was the secret of Albert Einstein when he humbly said to his close friends that he could not understand why so many people thought so highly of him. Einstein knew this state of unknown knowing, and we now know what happened thereafter.

As you use your analytical mind in your accounting work, which is a sort of doing, bring in your natural capacity for being. Frequently "step in and out" of being and doing throughout the day. As I wrote in Chapter 1, mindfulness is not something you do but rather something you are. What a relief, that you don't have to "do" all day. Just remember to cultivate the still *presence* within you as true nature and make that your unknown knowing, and without a technique, go *beyond balancing the books* and rejoice in the good work you do.

Reflection

- *What have you learned about yourself from reading this book and practicing mindfulness?*

Take your time; you may want to further ask yourself this question:

- *What did I really, really learn about myself from reading this book and practicing mindfulness?*

Imagine a pebble is thrown into the lake, and as the pebble sinks ever so deeper, repeat the question once again adding what did I really, really, really learn about myself? I invite you to journal your responses.

- *What do you want to take away and remember most from reading this book?*

Take a moment, and connect to your home base, whether that be your breath, sense perceptions, inner body, stillness, or some combination, and let whatever comes up for you be your response. The response could very well be silence.

Now, gently reflect on what might be an obstacle to practicing mindfulness in daily life. Remember, there is no problem to solve here as you set aside any judgments that come up. I invite you to just kindly notice what might hinder you to move forward with the practice.

Take a moment and reflect on all three questions and give yourself the gift of gratitude for taking good care of yourself in your work and life as an accountant. You are a mindful professional. In the state of *presence*, be "Life, Heart, and Love."

311

Jumping Overboard

The CPA in you is the ship,
The poet in you the life preserver.
Every conscious accountant I know has
Jumped overboard!
Beyond balancing the books.
George, your business is flourishing.
Is that right? You bet,
Although I struggle in time
I'm mindfully present. You, too.

Thank You for Reading My Book!

The success of a book is largely influenced by reader reviews. If you enjoyed *Beyond Balancing the Books*, I would be grateful if you could please help me reach other professionals who would benefit from this information by leaving a review on Amazon at https://www.amazon.com/dp/B0932FJX61#customerReviews

About the Author

George Marino is an accomplished CPA, entrepreneur, consultant, and advisor with more than thirty-five years of success across the accounting, financial services, hospital, healthcare, and professional training and coaching industries.

As the founder and Certified Professional Coach for One Heart Coaching, LLC, George helps others as a transformational coach who listens deeply, shares observations by naming what is present, and asks open-ended questions that lead to infinite possibilities for people. He engages with individuals in a conscious partnership that maximizes their personal and professional potential. He is also a Certified Mindfulness Meditation Teacher trained to teach evidence-based mindfulness meditation for enhancing people's well-being and resilience. George also works with businesses as a mindfulness coach, helping to build a more mindful, resilient, and fulfilling work environment. George completed his certificate from the Eckhart Tolle School of Awakening in 2019 and an iMBA in Conscious Leadership from New York University's Mindful NYU in 2021.

George also serves as the founder, principal, and Certified Public Accountant for George V. Marino CPA, PC, where he provides accounting, personal tax services, planning, and consulting services. George earned a Master of Science Taxation (MST) in Taxation from Baruch College—Zicklin School of Business as well as a Bachelor of Business Administration in Public Accounting from Pace University—Lubin School of Business. He is a Certified Financial Planner from the CFP® Board and a Certified Public Accountant from the New York State Education Department.

George is a volunteer and mentor for the New York State Society of CPAs and for Pace University. He is also a volunteer with First Friends of New Jersey-New York.

His website is www.oneheartcoach.com

Appendices

Appendix 1: Questionnaire

Epilogue: Mindfulness at Work Questionnaire for Professionals

The following questions represent a "mindfulness at work" questionnaire that corresponds with the themes discussed in this book. Individuals or groups might look at their attitudes toward mindfulness by answering the questions and sharing their answers. This dialogue can stimulate openness and curiosity, leading to fruitful searching.

1)   How do I experience my authentic self at work as a professional?
- When and under what conditions?
- How frequently?
- How can that be enhanced?
- How does this relate to my thoughts, emotions, feelings, and physical sensations?

2)   How do I create, notice, and nurture inner space before I think?
- When and under what conditions?
- How frequently?
- How can this be enhanced?
- How does this relate to my sense of peace and joy in my work?

3)   How does noticing my automatic, repetitive patterns of reaction simplify my work?
- How does listening shape my interactions? Is there space?

- How am I humble at work?
- What gets in the way from working with ease, lightness, and simplicity?

4) How does my work go *beyond balancing the books*?
   - Is my work a role that the universe is asking of me?
   - What is mysterious about my work?
   - How is my work related to the one-heart work of the universe?
   - How do I integrate the human and being dimensions in my work?
   - How do I account for what really counts—living and working with meaning and purpose?
   - What is most important to me at work?

5) How might I notice a flowing, self-emptying fullness in my work?
   - When and under what conditions?
   - What does it feel like in my body?
   - Is there a metaphor that describes it? Does it have a name?
   - How does this relate to meaning and purpose in my work?

6) How is being a mindful professional aligned with my needs and values?
   - What motivates me? Under what conditions?
   - What emotions do I feel, and how does this relate to my needs?
   - What do my judgments tell me about my underlying needs?

- When do I feel passionate about work?
- What legacy do I want to leave?

7)   How are mind, body, soul, and spirit related to my work?

- How might the dimension of mindfulness be included in the training for the work that I do?
- What are some of the obstacles that prevent such integration?
- How does awe and curiosity show up in my work?
- Is there a mantra or poem that represents this integration?

8)   How do I mindfully embrace the four dimensions of goal-setting and implementation?

- What joy do I experience in setting out to do what I want to accomplish?
- Do I experience interconnectedness with universal intelligence when establishing a goal?
- How do I employ my power of manifesting?
- What shadow elements do I experience as an attempt to discourage or hinder me in proceeding with my goals?
- How do I relate to the unknown or darkness during the process of manifesting my goals?
- What shift in consciousness do I experience at any point during the process?

9)   How do I "show up" as a mindful professional?

- What elements of the "essence of love" do I bring with me in my professional work?
- How do I connect with others?

- What is my predominant internal state when I connect with others? Does it have a temperature? How do I manage changes in internal states?

- How do I perceive with awareness? How do I perceive in thought?

10)   How has my work stimulated me to "clean up" the shadow tendencies?

- How do I experience the shadow? Under what conditions? Do I recognize it?

- How does this affect my energy level?

- What emotions come up? Under what circumstances?

- How does this affect others? My work?

11)   What qualities of Larry do I experience in my work? What qualities of Amy?

- When and under what conditions?

- How frequently?

- What can I do to help me shift to be more like Amy if I so choose?

- What other qualities can help me deepen in mindfulness?

12)   What is really important to me in the practice of mindfulness at work and in life?

- What is my intention?

- How does it help me to transcend and include what family, culture, and institutions say meaning and purpose should look like?

- What is even more important than balancing work and life?

- What do I want my "Book of Life" to say about me?

- What is really important about my moving *beyond balancing the books?*

13) How has my internal operating system (IOS) changed since I became a professional?
   - What characteristics of my identity have shifted from dual-based to unity/oneness consciousness?
   - How do I experience conflicts with others? Are they learning experiences? Do I discuss them directly, openly, and without judgment with the other person?
   - What virtues are most noticeable to me in my daily work?
   - How do peace, humility, and humor impact my IOS?

14) How does my enthusiasm express creativity?
   - How do I want to help without any intent of a reward or reaching the masses?
   - How does my inner sphere mingle with my work in being creative?
   - How does my work touch the world?
   - How does my enthusiastic energy impact the world in a way that "what is essential is invisible to the eye?"

15) What do I and the unknown have in common?
   - What name do I give to the unknown?
   - How are the unknown and I richly personal and intimate?
   - What can you say about this one-heart connection?
   - What does the "essence of love" got to do with it?
   - How are mindfulness and the unknown one?
   - How can I account for the unknown *beyond balancing the books?*

- How do I see more of the unknown in a single audit engagement? What opinion would I render?

16) How does mindfulness help me face death consciously?
- How is death a threat to the ego, igniting an ego-defense mechanism?
- How does the intimacy of the present moment relate to death and the end of time?
- What does "die before I die" mean to me, or "deny thyself?"

17) What am I doing to transform my profession and its work?
- How am I bringing mindful *presence* and compassion for myself and others to my work?
- How am I returning the focus of my professional work from a dual-based industrial revolution mindset to a postmodern scientific unity perspective with mindful *presence*?

18) What habits keep sending invitations that I unconsciously accept, therefore keeping myself stuck?
- What mindfulness tools can I now use to strengthen the muscle holding the lantern?
- What actions in my professional work bring forth in me freedom and the essence of love?
- What actions in my professional duties delight my mind, body, soul, and spirit?
- How can mindful movement help me stay anchored in the present moment and release the negativity that keeps me stuck?

19) How would I describe the peace I feel as I perform my professional work?

- How does peace grow in me as I meet daily challenges?
- What does my peace know about any storms? Is my peace startled in anyway?
- How can the storm stir a thirst in me that I may have forgotten?
- How does the divine rain kindle me to open my heart?
- How do I seek shelter from the storms in my professional work?

20) How does fear and anxiety show up in my professional work?

- What mindfulness tools do I call on?
- Does my fear and anxiety have a name?
- What does it feel like in my body?
- Does it have a color or shape to it?

Appendix 2: Author's Top Ten Suggested Reading List

Aware: The Science and Practice of Presence, by Daniel J. Siegel, M.D.

Cosmos and Psyche: Intimations of a New World View, by Richard Tarnas

Immunity to Change: How to Overcome It and Unlock the Potential in Yourself and Your Organization, by Robert Keegan and Lisa Laskow Lahey

Infinite Potential: What Quantum Physics Reveals About How We Should Live, by Lothar Schafer

Krishnamurti's Notebook, by Krishnamurti Foundation Trust

Meister Eckhart: A Mystic Warrior for Our Time, by Matthew Fox

The Leap: The Psychology of Spiritual Awakening, by Steve Taylor

The Power of Now, by Eckhart Tolle

The Religion of Tomorrow: A Vision for the Future of the Great Traditions (More Inclusive, More Comprehensive, More Complete), by Ken Wilber

Wild Mind: A Field Guide to the Human Psyche, by Bill Plotkin

References

Chapter 1

1. Langer, E. J., and Ableson, R. P. (1974). "A Patient by any Other Name . . . : Clinician Group Difference in Labeling Bias." *Journal of Consulting and Clinical Psychology* 42, 4-9.

2. Elliot, J. E. (1992). "Use of Anthetic Dialogue in Eliciting and Challenging Dysfunctional Beliefs." *Journal of Cognitive Psychotherapy: An International Quarterly* 6, 137-143.

3. Erisman, S. M., and Roemer, L. (2010). "A Preliminary Investigation of the Effects of Experimentally Induced Mindfulness on Emotional Responding to Film Clips." *Emotion* 10, 72-82.

4. Brown, K. W., and Ryan, R. M. (2003). "The Benefits of Being Present: Mindfulness and its Role in Psychological Well-being." *Journal of Personality and Social Psychology* 84, 822-848.

5. American Mindfulness Research Association (2017). goAMRA.org.

6. Carver, C. S. (2004). "Self-regulation of Action and Effect." In *Handbook of Self-regulation: Research, Theory, and Applications*, ed. R.F.Baumeister and K.D. Vohs, 13-39. New York: Guilford Press.

7. Baer, R. A. (2003). "Mindfulness Training as a Clinical Intervention: A Conceptual and Empirical Review." *Clinical Psychology: Science and Practice* 10, 125-143.

8. Delgato, L. C., Guerra, P., Perakakis, P., Vera, M. N., del Paso, G. R., and Vila, J. (2010). "Treating Chronic Worry: Psychological and Physiological Effects of Training Program Based on Mindfulness." *Behavior Research and Therapy* 48, 873-882.

9. Delgato et al. "Treating Chronic Worry," 873-882.

10. Jain, S., Shapiro, S. L., Swanick, S., Roesch, S. C., Mills, P. J., Bell, I., and Schwartz, G. E. (2007). "A Randomized Controlled Trial of Mindfulness Meditation Versus Relaxation Training: Effects on Distress, Positive States of Mind, Rumination and Distraction." *Annals of Behavioral Medicine* 33, 11–21.

11. Langer et al., "A Patient by any Other Name," 4–9.

12. Erisman et al., "A Preliminary Investigation," 72–82.

13. Lillis, J., and Hayes, S. C. (2007). "Applying Acceptance, Mindfulness, and Values to the Reduction of Prejudice: A Pilot Study." *Behavior Modification*, 31, 389–411.

Chapter 2

14. Carver, C. S. (2004). "Self-regulation of Action and Effect." In *Handbook of Self-regulation: Research, Theory, and Applications*, ed. R. F. Baumeister and K. D. Vohs, 13–39. New York: Guilford Press.

15. Baumeister, R. F., Heatherton, T. F., and Tice, D. M. (1994). *Losing Control: How and Why People Fail at Self-regulation.* San Diego, CA: Academic Press.

16. Duckworth, A. L., Seligman, M. E. P. (2005). "Positive Psychology in Clinical Practice." *Annual Review of Clinical Psychology* 1, 629–651.

17. Siegel, D. (2018). *Aware: The Science and Practice of Presence,* p. 6. New York: Penguin Random House.

18. Krishnamurti Foundation Trust Ltd. (2003). *Krishnamurti's Notebook,* p. 15. Victor Gollancz Ltd.

Chapter 3

19. Bargh, J. A., and Chartrand, T. L. (1999). "The Unbearable Automaticity of Being." *American Psychologist*, 54, 462.

20. Langer, E. J., and Ableson, R. P. (1974). "A Patient by any Other Name . . . : Clinician Group Difference in Labeling Bias." *Journal of Consulting and Clinical Psychology* 42, 4–9.

21. Chorpita, B. F., and Barlow, D. H. (1998). "The Development of Anxiety: The Role of Control in the Early Environment." *Psychological Bulletin* 124, 3–21.

22. Cullen, M., and Brito Pons, G. (2015). *The Mindfulness-based Emotional Balance Workbook*. Ekman P., p. 21. New Harbinger Publications

23. Cullen and Gonzalo, *The Mindfulness-based Emotional Balance Workbook*, 22.

24. Chapman, D., Dethmer, J., and Warner Klemp, K. (2014). *The 15 Commitments of Conscious Leadership*, 84–85.

25. Alberts, H. J. E. M., Schneider, F., and Martin, C. (2012). "Dealing Efficiently with Emotions: Acceptance–based Coping with Negative Emotion Requires Fewer Resources than Suppression." *Cognition and Emotion* 26, 863–870.

26. Levy, D. M., Wobbrock, J. O., Kasniak, A. W., and Ostergren, M. (2012). "The Effects of Mindfulness Meditation Training on Multitasking in a High-stress Information Environment." Proceedings of Graphics Interface, Toronto, Ontario (May 28-30, 2012). Toronto: Canadian Information Processing Society, 45–52.

27. Brown, K. W., Ryan, R. M., and Creswell, J. D. (2007). "Mindfulness: Theoretical Foundations and Evidence for its Salutary Effects." *Psychological Inquiry* 18, 211-237.

28. Alberts, H. J. E. M., Thewissen, R., and Raes, L. (2012). "Dealing with Problematic Eating Behavior, Food Cravings, Dichotomous Thinking and Body Image Concern." *Appetite* 58, 847-851.

Chapter 4

29. Siegel, D. J. (2018). *Aware: The Science and Practice of Presence: The Groundbreaking Meditation Practice*, p. 212. New York: Penguin Random House.

30. Boyatzis, R. E. (2015). "Building and Maintaining Better Leadership Relationships through Mindfulness." *Mindfulness in Organizations, Foundations, Research and Applications*, 251-252. Cambridge University Press.

31. Hunter, J. (2015). "Teaching Managers to Manage Themselves: Mindfulness and the Inside Work of Management." *Mindfulness in Organizations, Foundations, Research and Applications*, 356. Cambridge University Press.

32. Hunter, "Teaching Managers to Manage Themselves," 355-356.

Chapter 5

33. Wegner, D. M. (1994). "Ironic Process of Mental Control." *Psychological Review* 101, 34-52.

34. Boyatzis, R. E., and McKee, A. (2005). *Resonant Leadership: Renewing Yourself and Connecting with Others through Mindfulness, Hope, and Compassion.* Boston, MA: Harvard Business School Press.

Chapter 6

35. Boyatzis, R. E., Passarelli, A. M., Koening, K., Lowe, M., Matthew, B., Stoller, J. K., and Phillips, M. (2012). "Examination of the Neural Substrates Activated in Memories of Experiences with Resonant and Dissonant Leaders." *Leadership Quarterly* 23 (2): 259–272.

36. Boyatzis, R. E., and McKee, A. (2005). *Resonant Leadership: Renewing Yourself and Connecting with Others through Mindfulness, Hope, and Compassion.* Boston, MA: Harvard Business School Press.

37. Fox, M. (1994). *The Reinvention of Work: A New Vision of Livelihood for our Times*, p. 237. San Francisco: Harper One.

38. Chapman, D., Dethmer, J., and Warner Klemp, K. (2014). *The 15 Commitments of Conscious Leadership: A New Paradigm for Sustainable Success*, p. 13.

39. Manderlink, G., and Harackiewicz, J. M. (1984). "Proximal Versus Distal Goal Setting and Intrinsic Motivation." *Journal of Personality and Social Psychology* 47, 918–928.

Chapter 7

40. Neff, K., and Germer, C. *The Mindful Self-compassion Workbook: A Proven Way to Accept Yourself, Build Inner Strength, and Thrive,* p. 32. New York: Guilford Press.

41. Neff and Germer, *The Mindful Self-compassion Workbook*, 32.

42. Neff and Germer, *The Mindful Self-compassion Workbook*, 32.

43. Neff and Germer, *The Mindful Self-compassion Workbook*, 9.

44. Neff and Germer, *The Mindful Self-compassion Workbook*, 85–102.

45. Neff and Germer, The *Mindful Self-compassion Workbook*, 14.

46. Shapiro, S. L., Carlson, L. E., Astin, J. A., and Freedman, B. (2006). "Mechanisms of Mindfulness." *Journal of Clinical Psychology* 62 (3): 373–386.

47. Hall, L. *Mindful Coaching: How Mindfulness Can Transform Coaching Practice*, 67–68. Kogan Page Limited.

48. Neff, K. D. (2003). "The Development and Validation of a Scale to Measure Self-compassion." *Self and Identity* 2, 223–250.

49. Song of Solomon. 8:6–7. "Love is as Strong as Death." New International Version.

Chapter 8

50. Taylor. S. (2005) *The Fall: The Evidence for a Golden Age, 6,000 Years of Insanity, and the Dawning of a New Era*, p. 114. Winchester: John Hunt Publishing.

51. Whyte, D. "If Only You Stop Singing I'll Make You Safe." The Self. Printed with permission from Many Rivers Press, PO Box 868, Langley, WA 98260, USA.

52. Crocker, J., and Wolfe, C. T. (2001). "Contingencies of Self-worth." *Psychological Review* 108, 593.

53. Kernis, M. H. (2005). "Measuring Self-esteem in Context: The Importance of Stability of Self-esteem in Psychological Functioning." *Journal of Personality* 73, 1569–1605.

54. Greenberg, J., Solomon, S., and Pyszczynski, T. (1997). "Terror Management Theory of Self-esteem and Cultural Worldviews: Empirical Assessments and Conceptual Refinements." *Advances in Experimental Social Psychology* 29, 69–139.

55. Bush. M. (2015) *Mindfulness in Organizations, Foundations, Research, and Applications,* "Awakening at Work: Introducing Mindfulness into Organizations," p. 346. Cambridge University Press.

56. Confino. J. (2014). "Thich Nhat Hanh: Is Mindfulness Being Corrupted by Business and Finances?" *Guardian.* Retrieved from www.theguardian.com/sustainable-business/thich-nhat-hanh-mindfulness-google-tech.

57. Taylor. S. (2005). *The Fall: The Evidence for a Golden Age, 6,000 Years of Insanity, and the Dawning of a New Era,* p. 157. Winchester: John Hunt Publishing.

Chapter 9

58. Shapiro, S. L., Carlson, L. E., Astin, J. A., and Freedman, B. (2006). "Mechanisms of Mindfulness." *Journal of Clinical Psychology,*62 (3): 373–386.

59. Brown, K. W., Ryan, R. M., Linley, A., and Orzech, K. (2009). "When What One Has is Enough: Mindfulness, Financial Desire Discrepancy, and Subjective Well-being." *Journal of Research in Personality* 43 (5): 727–736.

60. Yamauchi, K. T., and Templer. D. J. (1982). "The Development of a Money Attitude Scale." *Journal of Personality Assessment* 46 (5): 522–528.

61. Pereira, C. M., and Coelho, F. (2019). "Mindfulness, Money Attitudes and Credit." *Journal of Consumer Affairs* 53 (2): 424–454.

62. Carson, S. H., and Langer, E. J. (2006). "Mindfulness and Self-Acceptance." *Journal of Rational-Emotive and Cognitive-Behavior Therapy* 24 (1): 29–43.

63. Quoted in Matthew Fox (1980). *Breakthrough: Meister Eckhart's Creation Spirituality in New Translation,* p. 475. New York: Doubleday.

64. Fox, *Breakthrough,* 59.

65. Rumi, Coleman Barks trans. (1991). *One-handed Basket Weaving: Poems on the Theme of Work,* p. 106. Athens, GA: Matpop.

Chapter 10

66. Wilber, K. (2001). *A Brief History of Everything.* Boston: Shambhala.

67. Bourgeault, C. (2008). *The Wisdom of Jesus,* p. 32. Boston: Shambhala.

68. Wilber. K. *Evolutionary Dynamics.* Levels of Development: Quadrants, 3-4.

69. Sheldrake, R. (1991). *The Rebirth of Nature,* p. 207. New York: Bantam.

70. Keegan, R., and Laskow-Lahey, L. (2009). *Immunity to Change.* 47-48. Harvard Business School Publishing Corporation.

Index

334

335

T

U

W

Made in the USA
Coppell, TX
10 September 2021